Mastering the Techniques
of Teaching

· ·

Joseph Lowman

Mastering the Techniques of Teaching

Second Edition

Jossey-Bass Publishers
San Francisco

The Boyer quotes in Chapter Ten are reprinted by permission of The Carnegie Foundation
for the Advancement of Teaching, 1990.

The two quotes from the introduction from Masters: Portraits of Great Teachers by Joseph
Epstein, Copyright © by the American Scholar, are reprinted by permission of Basic
Books, a division of HarperCollins Publishers, Inc.

▲
TCF Manufactured in the United States of America on Lyons Falls
Turin Book. This paper is acid-free and 100 percent totally
chlorine-free.

Library of Congress Cataloging-in-Publication Data

Lowman, Joseph, date.
    Mastering the techniques of teaching/Joseph Lowman.—2nd ed.
    p.   cm.—(The Jossey-Bass higher and adult education series)
    Includes bibliographical references and index.
    ISBN 0-7879-0127-X
    1. College teaching—United States. I. Title. II. Series
LB2331.L68   1995
378.1'25—dc   95-12476

SECOND EDITION
HB Printing 10 9 8 7 6 5 4 3

The Jossey-Bass
Higher and Adult Education Series

Contents

· ·

Preface to the Second Edition   xi

Preface to the First Edition   xvii

The Author   xxiii

1. What Constitutes Exemplary Teaching?   1

2. Understanding Classroom Dynamics   39

3. Developing Interpersonal Skills and Teaching Style   65

4. Analyzing and Improving Classroom Performance   99

5. Selecting and Organizing Material for Classroom Presentations   129

6. Enhancing Learning Through Classroom Discussion   159

7. Planning Course Content and Teaching Techniques to Maximize Interest   193

8. Integrating Learning In and Out of the Classroom   225

9. Evaluating Student Performance   251

10. The Art, Craft, and Techniques of
    Exemplary Teaching   287

References   313

Name Index   327

Subject Index   333

Preface to the Second Edition

I t was my good fortune to write the first edition of *Mastering the Techniques of Teaching* at a time of renewed national interest in improving the quality of college teaching, especially for undergraduates. Much has been written since 1984 about what an undergraduate education should include—the classic canon of Western Civilization has been expanded to encompass diverse cultures and perspectives—and to whom it should be addressed. Older, more experienced students have taken their places in significant numbers alongside late adolescents and young adults. Ernest Boyer's thoughtful and provocative essay (1990) on the need for an expanded view of scholarship on American campuses gives hope that the narrow research-versus-teaching debate of the past will be unknown in the future. A number of newer techniques that have become commonplace promote active learning by means of groups, focus and modify courses in progress by collecting information from students, and evaluate more accurately what students have learned. Teaching assessments are now routinely included in faculty personnel decisions at most schools, teaching support centers and training programs for graduate instructors have sprung up all over the country, and new journals and ongoing national conferences dedicated to improving college teaching have been established. But many things have not changed.

A high-quality college education is still undeniably dependent on the skill and motivating power of classroom instructors. Neither innovative ways of organizing classes nor gee-whiz technology have obviated the need for faculty who are skilled at communicating with students and at motivating them to work hard outside of class. Over the past decade, I have had many opportunities to visit colleges and universities around the country, to meet with their administrators, and to exchange teaching techniques with their faculties. These encounters have left me more convinced than ever of the truth of my conservative vision of college classrooms as fundamentally dramatic and interpersonal arenas and of the soundness of helping faculty to improve by encouraging them to emulate the exemplars among them. Rather than advocating a wholesale shift from traditional to nontraditional classroom formats, I also remain committed to helping college instructors use their preferred lecture/discussion mode more effectively. The emphasis in this second edition is still on learning to speak well before student groups, to promote motivating relationships with students as persons, and to enrich classes by frequent—but not exclusive—use of alternative formats. I daresay much of the success of the first edition of *Mastering the Techniques of Teaching* resulted from the large numbers of instructors and administrators who found this perspective compelling.

Although this second edition retains the assumptions and vision of exemplary teaching presented before, it has been expanded to reflect the results of additional experience and research (140 new references are cited). For example, the model of effective teaching presented in the first chapter has been expanded—on the basis of my own empirical studies of student ratings and nominations for teaching awards—to place more emphasis on motivational skill and commitment to teaching. Most importantly, a new learning model is presented there that incorporates both traditional structural and contemporary cognitive perspectives to delineate how teaching affects learning. I attempt to explain differences in student learning as resulting from student qualities, the instructor and his or her teaching, and the course organization. I believe this new learning model is consistent with traditional cognitive research, although researchers who de-emphasize the role of individual differences in academic ability among students may object to it. This model is presented here to stimulate empirical research—even if designed primarily to prove the model wrong—as well as to guide instructors attempting to promote learning among their students.

The chapters on the classroom as an interpersonal arena (Chapters Two and Three) are among the least changed in the book. Eison's distinction between grading- and learning-oriented students and newer techniques for making classrooms more personal have been added. In addition, Magolda's elaborated version of William Perry's stages of college students' intellectual development and their implications for teaching are described. Chapter Four on presentational skills has been reorganized and now takes a broader view of communication to include suggestions on improving movement as well as speech. A greatly expanded form for analyzing speech and movement using videotape recordings is also presented. Chapter Five on lecturing reflects new ideas on organizing classes to promote student involvement.

Chapters Six (on discussion), Seven (on course planning), and Eight (on assignments) have been significantly changed. Cooperative learning and classroom assessment techniques, the case method, and active learning are given much more emphasis in these chapters. My participation in several linked psychology-composition courses taught me much about the teaching of writing, which knowledge is now included in the section on ways of using writing assignments. A new section on the problem-solving assignments so fundamental in technical subjects makes the book applicable to teachers of a wider range of subjects.

Finally, Chapter Nine on evaluation reflects the impact on my thinking of the best book I have ever read on the subject: *Making Sense of College Grades*, by Ohmer Milton, Howard Pollio, and

James Eison (1986). Not only has their distinction between grad-ing- and learning-oriented students been included, but their empha-sis on evaluation as an aid to learning has been integrated throughout this second edition. No one book has ever affected how I teach as much as this one.

The final chapter on evaluating teaching effectiveness and instructor motivation presents what I have learned since publish-ing the first edition on how to develop teaching skills in others, especially novice instructors. The opportunity to work with faculty at diverse schools has greatly enriched my offerings to graduate and other instructors at the University of North Carolina. For example, I have included a number of specific techniques for using videotape analysis that were developed in individual and group sessions around the country. I also present for the first time a ten-question teacher evaluation form based on my model of effective teaching. Treatment of the "So what?" question on instructor motivation in Chapter Ten—Why should instructors bother working to become the best they can be?—has been expanded, but the emphasis on per-sonal values and satisfaction remains.

Acknowledgments

I have found many new friends and collaborators during my travels to teaching conferences and campuses since the first edition of *Mastering the Techniques of Teaching* was published, and much of what I have learned from them is included in this second edition. Milton Cox of Miami University in Oxford, Ohio, helped me appreciate the importance of student learning in discussions of exemplary teaching. For more than a decade, his selection of major speakers for the Lilly Conference on College Teaching revealed a prescient sense of higher education's breaking issues and emerging players. My discussions with Phillip Cottel of Miami University, Ohio, and Barbara Millis of the University of Maryland on the use and power

of cooperative learning groups have been warm, enjoyable, and ultimately, persuasive. William Graves, my colleague at the University
of North Carolina (UNC), provided a tremendous learning experience for me via an IBM-sponsored project to help faculty write
teaching software. That overriding passion of five years resulted in
the publication of *SuperShrink* (1990c), my two computer case simulations. Finally, Maryellen Gleason Weimer of the Pennsylvania
State University, editor of *The Teaching Professor,* has been an ongoing source of stimulation and support. Anytime I have needed a reference, or to bounce an idea off a colleague, she has responded with
wisdom and goodwill.

Several individuals contributed directly to this second edition.
William Balthrop, my colleague in the UNC Speech Communications Department, reviewed chapters on communication skills and
lecturing that included several new techniques I learned from him
in a workshop he conducted for our faculty. Ed Neal, faculty devel-
oper at UNC's Center for Teaching and Learning, shared his large
library generously. The graphic representation of the learning model
presented in Chapter One also benefits from Ed's input: the arrow
focusing instructor and course influences on student motivation was
his suggestion.

It is fitting that my young adult children, who were grade school
students off on sabbatical with their parents when the first edition
was written, made significant individual contributions to this volume. My son Campbell drew on his experience with several exemplary engineering instructors to make contributions to the section
on problem-solving assignments. My daughter Abee was a skilled
and creative library assistant who showed both ingenuity and persistence in tracking down references. To each of them and also to
my wife, Betsy, for her continued support, I express my public
thanks.

Finally, I must thank the many classroom instructors I have
observed directly or via videotape since I first became involved in

the training of college teachers over twenty-five years ago. Regard-less of his or her skill level, I truly relish watching another teacher perform. Rarely have I observed an instructor who has not taught me something important about college teaching, whether it be a new technique or simply a reaffirmation of the human creativity and generosity that good teaching at any level represents.

Chapel Hill, North Carolina   Joseph Lowman
July 1995

Preface to the First Edition

F ew college teachers receive instruction in how to present intellectually exciting lectures, to lead engaging discussions, or to
relate to students in ways that promote motivation and independent learning. This book is designed to fill that gap. The systematic
course of instruction outlined here stresses fundamental teaching
skills rather than the use of technological or structural innovations.
While this book is primarily for less-experienced instructors of college undergraduates, such as graduate students and junior faculty,
seasoned professors and the faculties of graduate, professional, and
secondary schools will find much that is useful here. The text deals
with the elements of teaching common to all academic disciplines—from anthropology to zoology—and is designed to help any
college teacher acquire the skills necessary for outstanding classroom instruction. This book is more than a collection of isolated
techniques for good teaching. A model of effective college instruction is proposed in the first chapter that organizes the specific skills
and suggestions presented later on. The model, which includes nine
unique styles of classroom instruction, is based on two assumptions:
the college classroom is a dramatic arena first and a setting for intellectual discourse second; and it is also a human arena, wherein the
interpersonal dealings of students and instructors—many of them
emotional, subtle, and symbolic—strongly affect student morale,
motivation, and learning. Consequently, specific instruction is

offered on how to speak well before groups and how to understand and interpret the interpersonal behavior of college students and teachers. Speaking skills and classroom dynamics are examined before more traditional topics (lecturing, leading discussion, planning, evaluating) are discussed. The dramatic and interpersonal aspects of teaching are themes that reappear throughout the book; they serve both to suggest and to justify recommendations offered on specific matters. Another theme also runs throughout: the college instructor as skilled artist. The aim of this volume is not to promote "adequate" or "competent" instruction but to start college teachers on the road to becoming masters of this long-standing art. Excellent teaching captivates and stimulates students' imaginations with exciting ideas and rational discourse. Student satisfaction and enjoyment are stressed here as important criteria for successful teaching. Outstanding instructors select and organize intellectually challenging content and present it in an involving and memorable way. They are also interpersonally sophisticated and promote student satisfaction and motivation. Though considerable relevant research is cited, teaching and learning are not thought of here as cold and technological but warm, exciting, and personal—decidedly human processes in which emotion and magic abound. This book's perspective on effective college teaching is consistent with published research, but its origins are experiential and observational. It evolved over my thirteen years' experience as a college teacher of psychology and supervisor of graduate instructors. My approach has been sharpened during the past two years by observing and interviewing twenty-five college professors reputed to be masters at schools in the Southeast and New England. Those studied were nominated by faculty or administrators who were asked which faculty members were thought to be "superb classroom instructors." Two or three inquiries usually produced a common list of four or five top instructors at each college or university. All but a few of those I contacted agreed to being observed and interviewed. Almost without exception, I found the teaching they demonstrated to be of the highest quality: it was intellectually stimulating, clear, engaging, at times inspiring. The students of these instructors obviously held them in high regard. Having seen them in action, I would be eager to have my children in their classes and believe them worthy of emulation.

The purpose of observing these instructors was not to recognize teaching excellence but to identify a sample of highly skilled practitioners of the teaching art representing a variety of academic subjects to assess philosophies and collect specific teaching practices. My aim was not to write a generalized essay about the contemporary master teacher (as did Axelrod, 1973) or a position paper on faculty development. My goal was to seek practical information. A number of tricks of the trade and attitudes about students and teaching were generously shared by the men and women I interviewed, and I present them here for the benefit of all teachers who aspire to improve their classroom presentation.

The first four chapters are fundamental. In Chapter One, descriptions of notable college teachers and contemporary empirical research on college teaching are examined to answer the question "What constitutes masterful college teaching?" The two-dimensional model of effective teaching is described here in detail. Chapter Two examines the classroom as an interpersonal arena in which students and instructors attempt to meet basic psychological needs and reveal their underlying personalities in the process. Richard Mann's research on classroom dynamics (1970) receives special emphasis. Specific teaching techniques and suggestions for dealing with students based on these ideas are presented in Chapter Three. Chapter Four discusses speech, movement, and suspense in the classroom—including traditional stage techniques, exercises for analyzing and improving one's speaking skill, and ways of seeing classrooms and teaching through the eyes of a stage director. The next two chapters are of central importance. Chapter Five concerns the lecture and discusses how to select, organize, and present content to promote understanding and retention. Chapter Six describes techniques for leading discussions in ways that involve students and foster independent thinking. Careful attention to the language college teachers use in discussion sessions is examined in light of the interpersonal psychology of classroom groups. Suggestions are offered for using discussion to promote rapport as well as to stimulate thought. Because most college teaching involves a combination of lectures and discussion, these chapters should interest experienced as well as novice instructors.

The next three chapters offer insights into traditional aspects of teaching: planning courses and individual class meetings (Chapter Seven); using reading, writing, and observational assignments (Chapter Eight); and evaluating students (Chapter Nine). The specific suggestions contained in these three chapters reflect this book's premise that the classroom functions as a dramatic and interpersonal arena as well as an intellectual one.

Chapter Ten sums up and extends the discussion in Chapter One by asking what combination of factors (individual talent, motivation, and supportive teaching environment) is associated with superior teaching. Chapter Ten also discusses ways evaluative student ratings can be used to help instructors improve and describes a comprehensive method for training college teachers. The chapter ends by addressing the question of why, given competing demands for scholarship and administrative labor, a college teacher should strive to excel in the classroom, especially teaching undergraduates.

The perspective of this book is fundamentally conservative. My aim is to teach instructors how to excel at traditional college teaching using group meetings in the lecture/discussion format. Instead of heralding technological innovation as the salvation of contemporary higher education, college teachers are encouraged to view teaching as an art and to rediscover and master the ancient skills that pertain to it.

Acknowledgments

I completed this book while on leave from the University of North Carolina at Chapel Hill, and I am thus grateful to the university administrators for being relieved of my duties to devote more time to scholarly activity. I am also indebted to Williams College, where I taught part-time during my leave. Williams stresses teaching excellence. Mark Hopkins "on a log" presided there during the nineteenth century. By coming to Williams to write a book on college teaching, I did not presume to bring coals to Newcastle, though this "Newcastle" proved an ideal place to write a book about "coal." I am especially grateful to the outstanding teachers who allowed me to observe their classes and who shared their ideas freely. Because several asked that I not acknowledge them publicly, and since my search was never intended as a formal identification of the country's best instructors, I thank them here collectively. Meeting and watching these outstanding men and women was truly inspiring, one of the genuine pleasures of writing this book.

My wife, Betsy Caudle Lowman, deserves special thanks. Though I received my share of support and encouragement (the traditional laurels assigned spouses), Betsy's library research and sharp editing contributed much to the finished product. Betsy is an educational psychologist, and though she does not agree with all of the views on teaching and learning presented here, she contributed greatly to their communication. David Galinsky and John Schopler, colleagues at the University of North Carolina, also provided encouragement and specific guidance.

Chapel Hill, North Carolina   Joseph Lowman
February 1984

To my wife,
Betsy Kathryn Caudle Lowman
—companion, colleague, friend

The Author

. . . .

Joseph Lowman is professor of psychology and assistant dean of arts and sciences at the University of North Carolina at Chapel Hill, where he has taught since 1971. He received his A.B. degree in psychology (1966) from Greensboro College and his Ph.D. degree in clinical psychology (1971) from the University of North Carolina at Chapel Hill. He was visiting associate professor at Williams College during the 1982–83 academic year.

Lowman's early research interests were in the areas of personality assessment and family processes applied to the preventive goals of community mental health. Since the first edition of *Mastering the Techniques of Teaching* was published in 1984, he has published numerous articles and chapters on topics related to college teaching. Lowman has also become a frequent speaker at national teaching conferences and campus teaching workshops and a consultant to college and university administrators on the evaluation and promotion of effective teaching. He is author of *SuperShrink* (1990c), two computer-simulated case studies for undergraduate psychology students. Lowman serves on the editorial boards of *Teaching of Psychology*, *Journal on Excellence in College Teaching*, and *College Teaching*.

In January 1984, Lowman received the first Frank Costin Award for Excellence at the Sixth National Institute on the Teaching of Psychology to Undergraduates, held in Clearwater Beach, Florida. The award was given for a presentation based on Chapter One of

Mastering the Techniques of Teaching. Lowman's teaching at the University of North Carolina at Chapel Hill has been recognized by students and colleagues with a Tanner Award in 1989 for inspirational teaching of undergraduates, a Senior Class Favorite Faculty Award in 1994, and a Bowman and Gordon Gray Professorship for Excellence in Undergraduate Teaching in 1995. Lowman is a Fellow of the American Psychological Association, and his work in psychological assessment was recognized in 1994 when he was named a charter member and Diplomate of the American Board of Assessment Psychology.

What Constitutes Exemplary Teaching?

What all the great teachers appear to have in common is love of their subject, an obvious satisfaction in arousing this love in their students, and an ability to convince them that what they are being taught is deadly serious.

—*Epstein*[1]

If I were to ask you to picture an exemplary college teacher, any of a number of images could come to mind. One image might be that of an awe-inspiring scholar lecturing from the stage of an amphitheater to an audience of students who are leaning forward to catch every word. Another might be that of a warm, approachable person seated at a seminar table among a group of students, facilitating an animated discussion, firmly but gently guiding the students to insight, awareness, self-confidence, and a heightened ability to think critically. Still another image might be that of an instructor engaged with one or two students in freewheeling sessions in the professor's study, over a glass of beer in the students' haunt, or in the laboratory, field station, or studio. In such settings, each student has the opportunity to observe at close range how

J. Epstein. *Masters: Portraits of Great Teachers*. New York: Basic Books, 1981, p. xiii.

their professor thinks and approaches problems. They also see how an older person attempts to live a life committed to ideas and knowledge.

When people are asked to describe the two or three best college instructors they have ever had, most use similar adjectives or phrases, regardless of the subjects they were studying. They most often choose words like "enthusiastic," "knowledgeable," "interesting," "concerned about me and my learning," "accessible to students," "motivating," "challenging, yet supportive," or "dedicated." What are we to conclude about exemplary college teaching from the varied images and common descriptors that the phrase evokes?

Beyond a solid mastery of one's subject, college teaching of the highest order appears to be a complex task requiring the ability to communicate well with students, whether in large or small groups or in formal or informal settings, and to relate to them as people in ways they find positive and motivating. Exemplary college teaching should engender active learning not only of basic facts, theories, and methods but also of the relationships between different branches of knowledge. It should foster the thinking, problem-solving, and communication skills characteristic of the educated individual. Above all else, a student receiving the best that college teaching can offer, whether in a liberal arts, technical, or professional curriculum, should be expected to emerge with an enhanced ability to evaluate information critically—to tell the difference between wisdom and poppycock. Such teaching may draw on many different skills and may be offered in a variety of styles and settings, but its unifying characteristic is that it spurs students to an active involvement in their own learning.

The view of outstanding college teaching presented here emphasizes the traditional skills of lecturing and leading discussions and assumes that learning is most powerfully enhanced when an instructor stimulates students to care about their subject and to work hard to master it. In contrast to approaches for improving college teaching that focus on specific tactics or innovative reorganizations (for example, detailed planning based on behavioral objectives, the organization of courses around individualized or cooperative approaches, or technological innovations using computer and multimedia systems), this approach aims to help instructors master the traditional skills of the exemplary college teacher. My formulation rests squarely on the assumptions that college teaching occurs in what are undeniably dramatic and interpersonal arenas, that it is above all an enterprise involving students' human emotions and personalities as well as their cognitive reasoning, and that it cannot be reduced to mechanical cause-and-effect relationships. This book provides detailed, practical instruction that will enable a graduate instructor or professor to fully master the techniques that constitute the art of college teaching.

Although a number of recent innovations are covered, the primary intent is to help instructors improve their ability to use the traditional skills of lecturing and leading discussions, and to do so in ways that are both engaging and reflective of instructors' personal styles. Once these fundamental skills are mastered, instructors will be more able to adapt structural innovations to meet a wider range of class goals. Unless traditional teaching skills are mastered first, structural innovations are unlikely to lead to exemplary instruction or optimal student learning.

This first chapter considers a number of broad theoretical questions that underlie the specific lessons presented in subsequent chapters. First, to what extent does exemplary teaching result in extraordinary learning? Specifically, to what degree is learning a function of qualities brought by students to their classes and to what degree is it a function of what happens to students when they are there? A theoretical model of learning and teaching is proposed that specifies how much of the learning we see in our students is a function of the students themselves, how much is a function of our teaching, and how much is a function of the way the class is organized.

The next question is: what are the necessary and sufficient characteristics of exemplary college teaching? This question is addressed by surveying the published research on student ratings of instruction and by presenting the two-dimensional model of effective college teaching proposed in the first edition of *Mastering the Techniques of Teaching*. An enhanced version of this two-dimensional model, based on my recent study of nominations for university teaching awards, is also presented. The important theoretical question of instructor motivation, or what sustains a college teacher's efforts to acquire the skills of exemplary teaching and to apply them term after term, is taken up later, in Chapter Ten.

Is Knowledge Taught or Learned?

If the members of an academic community are polled on ways to improve the quality of education, the students are sure to suggest hiring and promoting faculty who are better teachers, while the faculty probably will suggest admitting brighter, better-prepared, and more motivated students. Whose opinion is the more valid? How responsible, in fact, are the faculty for the amount that students learn and for the degree of insight they develop? How responsible are faculty members for students' proficiencies in fundamental skills—reading, thinking, problem-solving, writing, and speaking—or for students' attitudes toward learning? Who is most to blame when students attend college merely for grades, anticipated vocational or social status rewards, or social distractions? Conversely, who deserves credit for those rare students who not only actively master basic content and skills but understand a discipline in fresh and original ways and are somehow able to integrate the knowledge they have gleaned from disparate areas into a single, personal vision?

An old anecdote tells the tale of two boys and a dog named Redd who were walking down a sidewalk together. The first boy said, "I taught Redd here how to talk." The second boy exclaimed, "Wow! Pretty neat!" but after a moment's thought, he continued, "But I haven't noticed him talking." The first boy responded, "I didn't say he'd learned how to talk; I said I'd taught him how to talk."

This little exchange highlights the central issues in any discussion of the relationship between teaching and learning: (1) To what extent is learning a function of teaching? (2) To what extent can teaching be evaluated on the basis of how much students learn? These questions may seem trivial or the answers obvious, but the complexities we encounter when we try to answer them underscore the absence of an effective model of these processes in schooling at the college level (Abrami, D'Apollonia, and Cohen, 1990; McKeachie, Pintrich, Lin, and Smith, 1986). Figure 1.1 presents a proposed model for separating out the major sources of influence on student learning.

Learning is understood here to be evidenced by a broad category of measurable student qualities and behaviors. Many commentators have written about the educational objectives relevant to college courses (for example, Bloom, 1956; Bloom, Madaus, and Hastings,

Figure1.1 Sources of Influence on College Student Learning

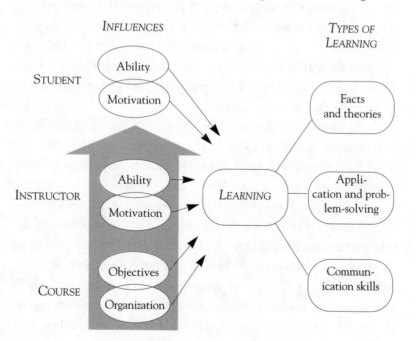

1981). Here, three general categories of learning are addressed: (1) facts and theories; (2) application and problem-solving skills; and (3) communication skills.

As Figure 1.1 illustrates, three independent sources of influence are postulated: the student, the instructor, and the course. Two interrelated influences are identified for each general source, producing six variables, each of which makes a significant direct contribution to differences in learning. Specifically, the student and instructor variables refer to differences in ability and motivation, and the course variables deal with the objectives sought and the method of organization chosen to reach them. The postulated relative strengths of these influences are shown by the order in which they are presented in Figure 1.1, the strongest influence being at the top. Research is needed to test these predictions about order and the relative independence of influences and to discover if the various influences promote the different types of learning equally. If an appropriate data set were assembled, structural equation modelling (a sophisticated type of confirmatory factor analysis) could test this proposed model against alternatives. Although the primary focus of this chapter is exemplary instructors, the parts of the model dealing with student motivation and course qualities are closely related to the techniques for producing exemplary college *teaching* that are presented in subsequent chapters.

Individual differences in students' ability to do academic work constitute the foremost of the six influences proposed here. At every school, students will learn a subject at different rates and at strikingly different levels of complexity and completeness. Even when the predictable patterns of change in reasoning patterns seen in most students during the college years are acknowledged (see King and Kitchener, 1994; Magolda, 1992), individual differences in thinking still account for much of the variation in intellectual quality seen in their work. College teachers are often amazed at the brilliance of some students and the shallowness and concreteness of others. For most courses, students' level of general intelligence, specific academic aptitude, and to a lesser extent, skills or knowledge from previous coursework produce the differences in academic performance seen between them. Students with high talent for mathematics will learn calculus more easily than will students whose strengths are in verbal reasoning. Regardless of the amount of effort some students put into their studies, the complexity of their thinking fails to match that of others. No method of evaluation of student performance is free of the influence of differences in student ability, but as demonstrated in Chapter Nine, tests can be designed that will de-emphasize rather than emphasize fundamental student ability. Our society's populist social ethic tends to deny the importance of differences in fundamental academic ability, but psychological research (Guilford, 1968; Herrnstein and Murray, 1994; Scarr, 1981) and the experience of college teachers continues to confirm the influence of academic ability on the extent and quality of learning.

There can be little doubt that academic motivation, the second student influence proposed here, also contributes a great deal to how much students learn (Lowman, 1990b). (Note that for many students, academic motivation is not necessarily associated with motivation to excel in other settings—for example, campus social life, athletics, leadership, or vocational work. Also keep in mind that students' academic motivation may be heavily influenced by what is valued by their families and peers.) College students are quite free to take or leave what we instructors have to offer, and they vary tremendously in how much they expect to get out of our courses and in how much effort they put into them. Chapter Two on classroom dynamics covers a number of student personality dimensions and group phenomena that influence student motivation. Chapter Nine on the evaluation of student performance makes an important distinction between two major classes of students' academic motivation—their learning orientation and their grading orientation (Milton, Pollio, and Eison, 1986)—and suggests ways to emphasize learning and de-emphasize grading orientations. Student ability and motivation are presented as overlapping in Figure 1.1, to suggest that they affect one another in addition to affecting learning. For example, students with high ability may have learned in the past that they will be more likely to succeed in school and may therefore be more motivated to take their studies seriously. Other patterns also exist: the overachieving student with more modest ability who has learned to work very hard to succeed in school and the underachieving student who is content to coast along on ability alone.

Although their influence on eventual learning is powerful, student academic ability and motivation do not tell the whole story. Enter the instructor.

College instructors also differ—in teaching ability, in their initial level of success, and in their eventual mastery of the skills needed to plan and deliver a course of highest quality. When they first begin teaching, some individuals are better able than others to hold a group's attention, to explain complex concepts clearly, to instill their passion for a subject in others, and to motivate students to become actively involved in learning and to work hard out of class. Fortunately, initial failure or success does not completely predict eventual skill. An instructor can learn and apply techniques such as those presented in this book. With feedback from student ratings and videotape, as outlined in Chapter Ten, the learning process is greatly facilitated.

Being motivated to take one's teaching duties seriously and to strive to become the best instructor one can be surely involves more than simply having good teaching skills. Chapter Ten deals directly with the issue of instructor motivation and how it can be fostered by the teaching environment. The overlapping instructor circles in Figure 1.1 show that ability affects motivation for instructors as well as for students. Just as students' academic motivation often competes with other demands on their time and sources of life satisfaction, so must faculty members weigh their commitment to the classroom against competing pressures and satisfactions, such as those coming from family and friends. This model assumes that college instructors, like college students, vary in how seriously they take their classes.

Course objectives and course organization are the least powerful influences on student learning. The specific content or skills a course aims to cover—whether it is especially difficult, required versus elective, or of high or low intrinsic interest to students—plays some role in how much students eventually learn. Similarly, some systems for organizing college courses are more likely than others to achieve certain objectives. For example, if a course is designed to teach students how to write clear, well-organized prose, and to that end a series of graduated writing exercises is assigned and discussed, students should be more likely to show an improvement in communication skills than if an instructor simply asks students to write a term paper and collects them for grading near the end of the course. In this example, the specific methods used to teach writing will play some part in whether students are able to write well at the end of the course. Lecturing about good writing and discussing examples in class are less likely to improve writing than a format that actively involves students in assignments and gives them much specific feedback on their written work. Similarly, the format used in technical courses to teach problem-solving will also have some effect on how well students learn to solve problems, although it will probably be less than that produced by student and instructor characteristics. Chapter Seven on course planning addresses several organizational options in detail.

Taken as a whole, the model presented in Figure 1.1 shows that we instructors cannot be held responsible for differences in ability and motivation at the time students enter our classes, but we *are* responsible for appropriately motivating all students, from the gifted to the barely adequate and from the overachieving to the underachieving, to do their best work in our class and to appreciate the experience of making that effort. We are also responsible for working to improve our teaching skills, putting forth our best efforts in each course, and seeking ways of organizing our courses to achieve a wide range of learning objectives with diverse students. Even though the rest of this chapter looks mainly at the qualities of exemplary college teachers, remember that in spite of our best instructional and motivational efforts, some students will fail to learn as much of what we have taught them as we would have liked and that others will go far beyond our expectations. The quality of our teaching is best evaluated not simply in terms of what our students learn, but in terms of the probability that all students will be motivated to do their best work in our course and will emerge changed for the better—often in personal ways that go far beyond course content.

Student Memories of Exemplary Instructors

Everyone can remember a few college teachers who stood out from the rest. If we were lucky, we had several who were superb; however, each of us probably had more poor teachers than outstanding ones. We can all remember classes that were boring and frustrating, when we dreaded going to class or meeting the professor in the hallway, when we ritualistically counted off the number of classes remaining in the term. But we also had classes we attended eagerly and finished with regret, classes in which we were motivated to work harder than usual, not as much for the grade as to please the professor and for the personal pleasure of learning. Remembering those men and women who took their teaching responsibilities very seriously, expected a similar level of commitment from their students, and appeared to receive great personal satisfaction from their teaching is useful in choosing models to emulate. Conversely, remembering the negative examples from our past underscores the importance of teaching well.

Although they are rich and suggestive—at times, even inspiring—personal memories lack the objectivity and breadth that the large body of findings from empirical research offers to the question: what makes an exemplary college teacher?

Exemplary Teaching as Portrayed by Contemporary Research

The results of empirical studies of college teaching are highly dependent upon the methods used to generate them.

Methods Used to Sample Student Satisfaction with Teaching

Studying questionnaires that assess students' satisfaction with professors' teaching skills has been a fruitful method of doing educational research for well over half a century (Reemers and Brandenburg, 1927). The last twenty-five years have seen a tremendous increase in the number of published studies using systematic student ratings of college teaching; the total for the years 1974–1993 approached one thousand. These studies reveal that student evaluation forms are being used on every inhabited continent (see Astleitner, 1991; Ikponmwosa-Owie, 1986; Mares, 1988; Perez, 1990; Poonyakanok, Thisayakorn, and Digby, 1986; Romero, Bonilla, Truhillo, and Rodriguez, 1989; Ruston and Murray, 1985). However, the number of publications notwithstanding, research is probably the least common purpose for which students are asked to evaluate their instructors and courses.

Student evaluations have become routine at most U.S. colleges in the past two decades, and their primary purposes have been to aid in faculty personnel decisions and to give instructors personal feedback to stimulate improvement. They are also sometimes used to provide public information for course selection. Seldin (1984) reports that 67 percent of the private liberal arts colleges in the nation "always used" systematic student ratings in personnel decisions in 1983, up from 55 percent reporting such use in 1978 and 29 percent in 1973. Although the routine use of student ratings was once controversial (see Chandler, 1978; Raskin and Plante, 1979; Ryan and others, 1980), the wisdom of collecting systematic student evaluation data now seems self-evident in most circles. Major issues now are:

1. What evaluation procedures are to be used in addition to student ratings?

2. How are various evaluation data to be weighted?

3. How often is teaching to be evaluated prior to the years in which tenure or promotion decisions are to be made?

(Chapter Ten presents a detailed discussion of a number of evaluation techniques for improving teaching.)

In addition to helping individual faculty improve, the best of the contemporary studies of instructor evaluation offer a useful window through which to view the fundamental dimensions of outstanding college teaching.

Before looking at the results of these studies, an overview of the evaluation methods they use will help put the results in perspective. By "methods," I am referring to far more than the typical lists of questions or statements about an instructor's teaching to which students respond on a five- or seven-point scale, usually ranging from "strongly disagree" to "strongly agree." Instructor evaluation, more generally defined, is an attempt to gain knowledge about teaching effectiveness by means of a common and easily quantifiable format that samples the memories of many students and combines them into group ratings. As is true with other kinds of survey research, the idiosyncratic responses of individuals are of little consequence in themselves, as their contribution to the composite ratings is minimal. Furthermore, only group studies provide a basis for attempted replication—and therefore, validation—by other researchers. Group data are fairer than anecdotal reports, as the latter may come from an unrepresentative sample of disgruntled (or enthusiastic) students. Data collected from an entire class can be openly and systematically analyzed.

Research investigations of teacher evaluation questionnaires commonly take one of two forms: (1) studies of student ratings collected from actual classes about actual instructors, which often use factor analysis, or (2) analogue or laboratory studies, in which students evaluate an imagined teacher based on their reading of a short description (or occasionally viewing of a short live or videotaped presentation) and in which specific qualities of the pseudoinstructor are varied systematically for different groups of subjects. Each approach has characteristic advantages and disadvantages.

Most studies of actual classes have used data routinely collected at the end of terms, sometimes with and sometimes without voluntary participation by the instructors being evaluated. Factor analysis is applied to students' ratings to identify the essential qualities of effective college teaching. Traditionally, factor analysis has been *exploratory*, letting a researcher look at the correlations between all possible pairs of questions on a given list and mathematically condensing them into a smaller set of—usually—four or five abstract factors (sometimes called "clusters," depending on the specific mathematical procedures used) that account for as much variation as possible in the answers to the specific questions. The resulting factors are usually relatively independent and their strength can be compared mathematically. They reveal the underlying structure of students' perceptions of their teachers better than scores on any of the original items, some of which may be similar (for example, "My instructor seems approachable" and "My teacher cares about me and my learning").

Unfortunately, exploratory factor studies do not always produce the same results, even when they use the same questions, and the resulting factors are often difficult to interpret and to name accurately. *Confirmatory* factor analysis, on the other hand, is a newer technique that allows one to make a statistical comparison between the factor structure found in a set of ratings and what one has found before or would expect theoretically. This approach has become much more widespread in recent years (see Marsh, 1991), largely due to the availability of the LISREL statistical package (Jöreskog and Sörbom, 1988). Just as no single student's ratings are considered indicative without corroboration by others, the results of no single exploratory or confirmatory factor-analytic study are taken as valid without replication.

Analogue studies allow researchers to isolate a single instructor characteristic (for example, age or gender) and to make inferences about the influence it may have on student ratings. The power to actively manipulate certain instructor qualities with the degree of experimental control available only in the laboratory makes these studies appealing. Because they typically use volunteer research subjects rather than students in actual classes, they are easier to conduct than most studies of actual students and classes. Unfortunately, analogue studies fail to simulate student-instructor relationships sufficiently, and they have the serious disadvantage of producing artificial results that do not hold up when replicated in actual classrooms. As is shown below, in a discussion of gender bias in teacher ratings, experimental effects from analogue studies become weaker and weaker the more information subjects have about the teacher. Analogue studies of a number of psychological phenomena have come under increasingly severe criticism because their results have not been confirmed when tested in the real-life settings they were designed to simulate (Lowman, 1990a).

A newer method of assessing students' satisfaction with their instructors' teaching combines the real-world richness provided by end-of-term ratings of actual classes with the convenience and control of experimental analogues. This is what Herbert Marsh, an Australian professor who has published extensively on student evaluations, refers to as the "applicability paradigm" (1986). Marsh used this technique to test the applicability of student evaluation forms developed in the United States to classes in other countries (for example, Australia, New Guinea, and Spain), but the name he used fails to describe it clearly. Using this approach, a researcher asks a broad sample of students to complete evaluation forms on two actual instructors whom they judge to be the "very best" or "very worst" they have had in the past. This manipulation of the kinds of instructors being evaluated, guaranteeing that college teachers at the extremes of effectiveness are rated, makes the approach similar to that reported by Waters, Kemp, and Pucci (1988). Most importantly, it avoids the problem of poorer instructors being less likely to allow their classes to be studied, which often happens in studies of actual classes. Given the improbability that many students will select the same good or poor instructors to rate, Marsh's paradigm also avoids to some extent the problem of students rating the same instructor, which normally requires averages to be taken over many classes to reduce interdependent data. The expanded model of effective college teaching I present later in this chapter is supported in part by the results of a study I conducted using a recommended adaptation of Marsh's paradigm.

Empirical research using student ratings is amazingly consistent in showing them to be reliable and valid, easily as stable and accurate as other psychological inventories. One recent study of the ratings given 195 instructors over thirteen years showed almost no changes in the patterns of scores (Marsh and Hocevar, 1991). However, recent research has found it useful to distinguish between ratings of teaching effectiveness and ratings of course value (Baird, 1987; Johnson and Christian, 1990). Although researchers continue to debate technical issues related to the theoretical structure underlying the evaluation forms commonly in use on campuses (Abrami and others, 1980; Feldman, 1989; Marsh, 1991), the forms are sufficiently understood to be useful to faculty striving for improvement in their teaching skills; they also provide a satisfactory basis for exploration of the central question addressed in this chapter.

Measurement Bias in Student Ratings

A number of studies have attempted to show that student ratings are biased, "that they are influenced by variables unrelated to teaching effectiveness" (Marsh, 1984, p. 733). In most instances, these studies have been unsuccessful in showing bias, or their results have not held up when the studies were replicated. For example, the overall level of student ratings has been found to have little if any relationship to the time of day courses are taught, the subject under consideration, the extent of the instructor's experience, or the size of the class (see Centra, 1993; Feldman, 1978; Hoffman, 1979; Korth, 1979; Marsh and Overall, 1981; Marsh, 1980; Meredith, 1980).

A common notion among faculty is that ratings merely reflect instructor popularity, attractiveness, or grading stringency and have little to do with competency as a teacher. Arguing against this position are the results of studies showing that students consider the quality of teacher-student relationships to be second in importance to an instructor's ability to present material clearly and in ways that are engaging (Abbott and Perkins, 1978; Reardon and Waters, 1979).

A variation of this misconception is that if students enjoy or are excited by an instructor, the quality of that teacher's material must be second-rate. The source of this puritanical attitude toward learning and teaching is difficult to pin down, but there is nothing compelling about arguments for its validity. Great teachers demonstrate a pleasure in learning and create this love in their students. The best protection against being seen as a modern-day sophist is to aim for substance as well as enjoyment. Stiff, businesslike, or aversive behavior in a teacher is no assurance of quality instruction.

Professors who believe that high student ratings must reflect sweetened or watered-down knowledge often have the covert hope that students who rate them poorly will one day value them more than the instructors they found satisfying at the time. In a number of studies, however, evaluations of faculty made several years after graduation (up to ten years, in one case) have been found to be remarkably consistent with the students' original opinions (Firth, 1979; Marsh and Overall, 1979; Overall and Marsh, 1980). Student ratings thus cannot be dismissed as reflecting merely the poor judgment of youth.

Some will argue that student ratings have no relationship to the way the teachers' peers would evaluate their effectiveness. Available evidence runs contrary to this notion as well (Aleamoni, 1978; Ballard, Rearden, and Nelson, 1976; Kremer, 1990). One study compared student ratings, professors' evaluations of their own teaching, and expert judges' ratings of videotape recordings of the professors' classroom presentations. A similar pattern was found with each of the three measures. The college teachers seen as excellent by their students were also rated highly by the judges and by themselves; weaker instructors also were rated similarly by all three groups. The only notable differences among the ratings was that students tended to rate the faculty members lower than did the instructors or their peers (Marsh, Overall, and Kesler, 1979). Students are remarkably generous judges of faculty—ratings are highly skewed in a positive direction—but they may be tougher judges than faculty members themselves.

Several empirical studies have examined the grade an individual student anticipates receiving as a source of bias. When ratings of teaching effectiveness and grading difficulty have been compared across classes, no consistent relationship has been observed (Gigliotti and Buchtel, 1990). To be sure, some teachers who assign relatively high marks receive high ratings and some teachers who award lower grades receive lower ratings; but instructors also show other patterns—that is, hard graders who receive high ratings and easy graders who receive low ratings—often enough for no overall correlation to exist. A mild relationship has been identified, however, between the grade an individual student anticipates receiving near the end of a course and the evaluation given the instructor (Feldman, 1976), especially when students do poorly. If students perceive their teachers' testing and grading as fair and their own motivation as minimal, however, they are less likely to blame their instructor for poor performance. Recent studies (Baird, 1987; Johnson and Christian, 1990) have shown that student ratings of their instructors' teaching effectiveness are much more highly correlated with ratings of how much they have learned (.57 and .86) than what grade they anticipate receiving (.20 and .28). When asked to evaluate their college teachers, students appear to understand the complex relationships between the quality of teaching they are offered, how hard they work, how much they learn, and the grades they receive.

A final source of bias to be discussed here is the possible role instructors' gender may play in how students evaluate them. Early studies used analogue designs to address the relatively simple question, "Do college students evaluate female instructors as a group less positively than they do their male instructors?" (Harris, 1975). Some studies found that hypothetical female instructors received poorer ratings than males; other studies did not (see Basow and Silberg, 1987; Sidanius and Crane, 1989). Analogue studies were more likely to show gender differences than were studies of actual teachers and classes, which typically showed no gender differences or inconsistent results (Haemmerlie and Highfill, 1991).

The best of recent gender studies have used actual college classes to ask a much more complex question: For male and female instructors, how does overall teaching effectiveness relate to traditionally masculine *instrumental* traits and to traditionally feminine *expressive* traits for different types of students (Basow and Silberg, 1987; Sidanius and Crane, 1989)? Each of these more complex studies has identified the same pattern: male and female students tend to give female instructors slightly lower overall effectiveness ratings than male instructors. This difference is a bit larger for male than for female students, and for male *and* female students in engineering and the natural sciences. Surprisingly, when gender-related dimensions are compared, male instructors are on average judged higher both on the more instrumental aspects of teaching (called Dynamism/Enthusiasm in one of the studies) and on expressive qualities or qualities associated with individual student-instructor interaction, which are traditionally thought to be valued more by women. In general, all students preferred instructors—male or female—who they perceived as dynamic or enthusiastic and as genuinely available for individual interaction. The authors of these two studies emphasize that the significance of the slight group differences they identified is more statistical than practical—many of the female instructors were superior on all measures to the typical male instructor—and that their results do not necessarily reflect gender bias (or measurement error) in the teaching ratings used. A practical implication of these recent gender studies is that all faculty— male and female—should be encouraged to develop and use their masculine *and* feminine traits in their teaching. Masculine and feminine qualities correspond closely to the presentational and interpersonal dimensions (discussed in the following sections) that statistical studies suggest are the most powerful predictors of student ratings.

Dimensions Underlying Student Ratings

The most prominent factors reported in factor-analytic studies concern clarity and impact of presentation. Specific items in this category usually deal with whether an instructor presents material clearly and in an organized way that is easy for students who initially know little about the topic that follows. Some studies suggest that frequent use of concrete examples is associated with the ability to present material understandably. Another strong factor is the instructor's ability to stimulate students' thinking about the material, as opposed to simply encouraging them to absorb it. A factor found prominent in most studies is the instructor's ability to arouse enthusiasm for the subject, a skill strongly related to how much personal enthusiasm the teacher shows.

Secondarily, student ratings have been shown to reflect the quality of interpersonal relationships between instructor and students. Some studies refer to this factor as "expressiveness" and others as "student-teacher rapport"; others discuss the degree to which students perceive an instructor as being concerned about them as individuals. Questionnaire items contributing to this category ask students how warm they perceive an instructor to be and how much the instructor seems to enjoy sharing knowledge with them. Students may learn something important from a class in which the instructor shows a lack of respect or a negative and cynical attitude toward them, but it will be in spite of the teacher's attitude rather than because of it.

Thus, contemporary research presents a consistent picture of outstanding and, conversely, undesirable teaching. Fundamentally, student ratings reflect how well the instructor presents material and fosters positive interpersonal relationships with students. In addition to closely mirroring instrumental and expressive *individual* qualities, these two categories strongly resemble Bales' classic definition of "task" and "maintenance" functions of *group* leadership (Bales, 1950; Bales and Slater, 1955). The two-dimensional model of effective college teaching discussed in the next section has been built around them.

A Two-Dimensional Model of Effective College Teaching

The specific lessons in this book are based on a two-dimensional model of teaching effectiveness in which the quality of instruction results from a college teacher's skill at creating both *intellectual excitement* in and *interpersonal rapport* with students—the kinds of emotions and relationships that motivate them to do their best work. The skill to generate excitement and the skill to establish rapport are relatively independent. Excellence at either can ensure effective teaching with some students and in certain kinds of classes; a teacher who is accomplished at both is most likely to be outstanding in meeting a variety of goals for all students and in any setting. Instructors who can promote each of these desired states boost their students' learning by increasing the degree to which students care about the subject and will work hard to master it.

Background Research

This two-dimensional model of effective college teaching was originally inspired by my observations in the early 1980s of a group of twenty-five or so exemplary instructors of a variety of subjects at several North Carolina and New England colleges and universities. The model is also consistent with the published research on student ratings reviewed in the preceding section. Subsequent observations and research using nominations for teaching awards at the University of North Carolina at Chapel Hill (UNC) has strengthened and sharpened the model.

The chancellor's teaching awards at UNC are driven by undergraduates. Any student and any member of the faculty or staff may nominate teachers for the six awards given each year. A committee equally divided between students and faculty reviews nominations, collects additional information about finalists from departmental chairs and telephone interviews with randomly selected students from previous classes, and makes recommendations to the chancellor, who almost always follows the committee's rankings. Nominations most often come from students (80 percent), who are equally split between males and females.

Over five hundred nominations were submitted for the 1989, 1990, and 1991 awards. Research assistants read each form and independently coded all adjectives or descriptive phrases used at least one time in each nomination. Individual variations on a common word were reduced to a single form (for example, "enthusiasm" was changed to the more commonly appearing "enthusiastic"). Finally, all words were tallied and the thirty-nine appearing at least ten times were selected for analysis. (The adjectives are presented in Table 1.3, which appears later in this chapter.) Most of the adjectives fit closely the dimensions of exemplary college teaching that are seen in published research using student ratings and that are the basis of the model of effective teaching I presented in the 1984 edition of *Mastering the Techniques of Teaching*. The revised model presented here reflects the additional insights suggested by these adjectives.

Dimension I: Intellectual Excitement

Skill at creating intellectual excitement has two components: the clarity of an instructor's presentations and their stimulating emotional impact on students. Clarity is related to *what* one presents, and stimulating emotional impact results from the *way* in which material is presented.

Clarity is nothing without accuracy of content, of course, and it is assumed that most instructors have mastered their content adequately. Knowing material well is quite different from being able to present it clearly, however.

Knowledge is far more than the accumulation of isolated facts and figures. It involves a deeper understanding, an ability to "walk around" facts or theories and see them from different angles. As Bloom argues in his classic taxonomy of educational goals (Bloom, Madaus, and Hastings, 1981), knowledge includes the ability to analyze and integrate facts, to apply them to new situations, and to evaluate them critically within the broad context available to the educated person. (Chapter Seven on course planning discusses Bloom's objectives in greater detail.) For a teacher to do an excellent job, he or she must be able to do far more than simply present the details of a subject—and most students know this. They like to receive an overall perspective and love to compare and contrast concepts in addition to learning individual facts.

To be able to present material clearly, instructors must approach and organize their subject matter as if they too know little about it. They must focus on the early observations, essential milestones, key assumptions, and critical insights in a subject and must not be distracted by the qualifications and limitations that most concern them as scholars. Being able to do this gives them the capacity to explain a complex topic simply.

Exemplary instructors share this facility for clear exposition. Ernest Rutherford, the nineteenth-century British physicist, believed that he had not completed a scientific discovery until he was able to translate it into readily understandable language (Highet, 1950). Similarly, the ancient Greek and Hebrew teachers showed a commanding use of metaphor, making complex points by using simple language and vivid images. It is false snobbery to claim that one's knowledge is too grand to be understandable by a reasonably intelligent outsider. Exemplary college teachers are able to explain ideas and the connections between them in ways that make eminently good sense to the uninitiated.

Most students who receive consistently clear presentations will be able correctly to define, illustrate, and compare and contrast concepts. However, understanding material is not the same thing as being intellectually excited about it—for example, being so highly engaged in a presentation as to be free from distracting thoughts or fantasies, surprised when the class period is over, or compelled to talk about the class to others during the day. To have this kind of impact on students, an instructor must do far more than present material clearly. In other words, for maximum effectiveness on this first dimension, *clarity is necessary but not sufficient*. It must be accompanied by virtuosity at speaking in front of groups. Why is this believed to be the case?

College classrooms are fundamentally dramatic arenas in which the teacher is the focal point, like the actor or orator on a stage. The students are subject to the same influences—both satisfactions and distractions—as any audience. As Epstein's portraits (1981) demonstrate, teaching is undeniably a performing art. To be sure, exemplary instructors organize their lessons to promote clear and complex understanding. But they also use their voices, gestures, and movements to elicit and maintain attention and to stimulate students' emotions. Like other performers, college teachers must above all else convey a strong sense of presence, of highly focused energy. Some instructors do this by being overtly enthusiastic, animated, or witty, while others accomplish the same effect with a quieter, more serious and intense, but equally engaging style. The ability to stimulate strong positive emotions in students separates the competent from the outstanding college teacher.

Table 1.1 describes instructors at the high, middle, and lower ranges of this dimension of intellectual excitement as they might be seen by an outside observer and experienced by students.

A teacher at the upper end of this dimension is an unusually skilled individual. To master college teaching to this degree, an instructor must be able to do more than prepare an accurate,

Table 1.1. Dimension I: Intellectual Excitement.

Student Response	Observer's Description of Teaching	Impact on Students
High: Extremely clear and exciting.	All content is extremely well-organized and presented in clear language.	Students know where the teacher is going and can distinguish important from unimportant material.
	Relationships between specific concepts and applications to new situations are stressed.	Students see connections between concepts and can apply them to new situations.
	Content is presented in an engaging way, with high energy and strong sense of dramatic tension.	Students have little confusion about material or about what the teacher has said.
	Teacher appears to love presenting material.	Students have a good sense of why concepts are defined as they are.
		Ideas seem simple and reasonable, almost obvious, and are easily remembered.
		It is very easy to pay attention to teacher (almost impossible to daydream).
		Class time seems to pass very quickly, and students may get so caught up in the ideas that they forget to take notes.
		Students experience a sense of excitement about the ideas under study and generally hate to miss class.
		Course and teacher are likely to be described as "great" or "fantastic".

Table 1.1. Dimension I: Intellectual Excitement. *Continued*

Student Response	Observers Description of Teaching	Impact on Students
Moderate: Reasonably clear and interesting.	Facts and theories are presented clearly within an organized framework.	Students' understanding of most concepts is accurate and complete; they find it easy to take good notes.
	Material is presented in an interesting manner, with a moderate level of energy.	Students can see connections between most concepts and understand examples offered in class and in the text.
	Teacher seems moderately enthusiastic and involved in teaching the class.	Class is moderately interesting and enjoyable for most students.
		Course and teacher are likely to be described as "good" or "solid".
Low: Vague and dull.	Some material is organized well and presented clearly, but much is vague and confusing.	Students have little idea of where the teacher is going or why material is presented as it is or even at all.
	Most material is presented with little energy or enthusiasm.	Students frequently experience confusion or uncertainty.
	Teacher may seem to hate teaching the class and to be as bored with it as the students.	Most students find taking notes difficult.
		Students see few relationships between concepts and little relevance of content to their own experience.
		Students find it difficult to pay attention, and class time may seem to pass very slowly.
		Students frequently experience a sense of frustration or anger and may dread coming to class, welcoming excuses not to do so.
		Course and teacher are likely to be described as "boring" or "awful".

well-organized synopsis of a content area. He or she must be able to organize and deliver the material with the skill of a seasoned speaker. Such teaching is not simply showmanship or gratuitous attention-getting, as assumed by disparagers who refer to it as "hamming it up," "showing off," or "faking it." As follow-up research on the famous Dr. Fox experiment demonstrated, exciting teaching is not merely acting or entertaining (Perry, Abrami, and Leventhal, 1979; Williams and Ware, 1977). Entertainment involves the stimulation of emotions or the creation of pleasure for its own sake. Exemplary teaching is characterized by the stimulation of emotions associated with intellectual activity: the excitement of considering ideas, understanding abstract concepts and seeing their relevance to one's life, and participating in the process of discovery.

Dimension II: Interpersonal Rapport

In theory, the college classroom is strictly an intellectual and rational setting. In reality, a classroom is an emotionally charged interpersonal arena in which a wide range of psychological phenomena occur. For example, students' motivation to work outside of class will be reduced if they feel that they are disliked by their instructor or controlled in heavy-handed or autocratic ways. All students are vulnerable to such disrupting emotions, and some students are especially sensitive to them. Also, like anyone else, students have a potential to react emotionally when they are being challenged and evaluated in group settings. Even students whose work is superior will become angry if testing and grading practices seem unfair.

Instructors are not immune to what happens in the classroom, either; many events can interfere with their enjoyment of teaching and lessen their motivation to teach well. Most professors have strong needs for achievement and success. The common desire to be at least average makes instructors' professional self-esteem vulnerable to their students' achievement and end-of-term ratings. This is especially true of those teaching for the first few times and for junior faculty facing tenure and promotion decisions. If students are not learning as much as expected, a teacher is only human in feeling threatened and being tempted to show anger by criticizing student efforts. Also, because they are human, instructors want to be liked and respected as individuals, and walking into a room of fifty to one hundred strangers is guaranteed to raise interpersonal anxiety in anyone.

Psychologically, classes of students behave like other groups. The study of group phenomena has demonstrated convincingly that people in almost any kind of group situation, from working on an assembly line to designing a research program, show predictable emotional reactions to their interactions with one another (Cartwright and Zander, 1960; Shaffer and Galinsky, 1989). Issues of *leadership* (or control) and *affection* (or the degree to which individuals feel respected and liked by others) will always be present.

College classrooms are no different. They are complex interpersonal arenas in which a variety of emotional reactions can influence how much is learned and how the participants feel about it. In a classic study, Richard Mann and his colleagues at the University of Michigan (1970) convincingly illustrated these college classroom phenomena by coding and analyzing individual comments of students and teachers in four introductory psychology classes. They offer a rich and insightful portrayal of this emotional substratum of college classrooms, detailing teacher roles, student types, and predictable changes over a semester (see Chapters Two and Three of this book).

Dimension II deals with an instructor's awareness of these interpersonal phenomena and with his or her skill at communicating with students in ways that increase motivation, enjoyment, and independent learning. This is done in essentially two ways. The first is to avoid stimulating negative emotions—notably, excessive anxiety and anger toward the teacher. The second is to promote positive emotions, such as the feeling that the instructor respects the students as individuals and sees them as capable of performing well. These sets of emotions strongly affect students' motivation to complete their assignments and learn material, whether their motivation is a desire for approval from the teacher or an attempt to meet their own personal standards.

Dimension II is especially critical to success in one-to-one teaching situations. For most settings, however, Dimension II is not as essential to outstanding teaching as Dimension I, although it does contribute significantly to class atmosphere and the conditions under which students are motivated to learn. It should also be noted that Dimension I refers almost exclusively to what an instructor does in the classroom, while Dimension II is significantly influenced by teacher-student interactions outside as well as inside class. Table 1.2 contains descriptions of teaching at three levels within this second dimension of teaching effectiveness.

Dimension II is admittedly more controversial than Dimension I. No one is likely to advocate that teachers be vague and dull, though some professors may believe that clarity is all that is required for good teaching and see attempts to be exciting or inspiring as demeaning. However, less consensus would be found among college faculties about the place on Dimension II where an outstanding instructor should fall—whether he or she should be autocratic and aloof or democratic and approachable. Some professors sincerely believe that recognizing students' personal reactions not only is irrelevant to teaching content but also impedes students' growth into mature and responsible adults, because it indulges or coddles them. Other instructors are just as certain that a distant, autocratic style of teaching is a cruel vestige of the past and does not promote independent learning that is likely to continue when the class is over. Faculty holding this more humanistic position emphasize two-way interaction between teachers and students and often use the discussion or cooperative learning techniques discussed in Chapters Six and Seven. Even though Socrates used confrontation as a primary teaching strategy, he is more likely to be their ideal teacher than the irascible "Herr Professor" of the nineteenth-century German lecture hall, whose autocratic behavior toward students had little educational purpose.

Table 1.2. Dimension II: Interpersonal Rapport.

Level of Interpersonal Rapport	Observer's Description of Teaching	Impact on Students
High: Extremely warm and open; highly student-centered; predictable	Teacher appears to have strong interest in the students as individuals and high sensitivity to subtle messages from them about their feelings concerning the material or its presentation.	Students feel that the teacher knows who they are and cares about them and their learning a great deal.
	Teacher acknowledges students' feelings about matters of class assignments or policy and encourages them to express their feelings; may poll their preferences on some matters.	Students have positive, perhaps even affectionate, thoughts about the teacher; some may identify with him or her strongly.
	Teacher encourages students to ask questions and seems eager for them to express personal viewpoints.	Students believe teacher has confidence that they can learn and think independently about the subject.
	Teacher communicates both openly and subtly that each student's understanding of the material is important to him or her.	Students are highly motivated to do their best, in part so as not to disappoint the teacher's high expectation of them.
	Teacher encourages students to be creative and independent in dealing with the material, to formulate their own views.	Students are likely to describe teacher as a "fantastic person".
Moderate: Relatively warm, approachable, and democratic; predictable	Teacher is friendly and personable to students but makes no great effort to get to know most of them.	Students have little fear or anxiety about the teacher or their ability to perform successfully in the class.
	Teacher announces policies and discusses student reactions to them if students complain.	Students know what the teacher expects of them but feel little responsibility to go beyond that level of performance.
	Teacher responds to student questions and personal comments politely and without apparent irritation.	Students are reasonably well-motivated to complete assigned work and to perform well.

Continued

Table 1.2. Dimension II: Interpersonal Rapport. *Continued*

Level of Interpersonal Rapport	Observer's Description of Teaching	Impact on Students
	Teacher is relatively consistent and predictable in behavior toward students; gives ample notice before announcing requirements or changes in schedule.	Students are likely to describe teacher as a "nice person" or a "good guy" or "nice woman".
Low: Cold, distant, highly controlling; may also be unpredictable	Teacher shows little interest in students as persons; knows few of their names and may fail to recognize many of them out of class.	Students feel teacher has no personal interest in them or their learning; some students may believe teacher actively dislikes them or is "out to get them".
	Teacher is occasionally sarcastic or openly disdainful about students, their level of performance in the course, or their nonacademic interests.	Students believe teacher has a low opinion of their ability or motivation to learn course content.
	Teacher seems irritated or rushed when students ask questions or drop by, sometimes even during office hours.	Students generally are afraid to ask questions, and only the boldest will voice a personal opinion.
	Teacher simply announces requirements and policies and seems defensive or angry if they are questioned.	Students are motivated to work primarily by a fear of failure or of ridicule by the teacher and see assignments as something the teacher imposes on them.
	Teacher may be inconsistent and unpredictable— for example, by smiling when saying insulting things about students, by giving backhanded compliments, or by announcing assignments or requirements at the last minute.	Even if students are interested in the content, they may dread studying it or may rethink their previous desire to major in the subject.
		Students feel uneasy in class or around the teacher and may sometimes experience significant anxiety or anger.
		Students are likely to describe teacher as a "bitch" or a "bastard."

In contrast to faculty disagreement about Dimension II, the summary of research on student ratings shows that there is little question about which end of this continuum most students prefer. They prefer more democratic and approachable teachers (Uranowitz and Doyle, 1978)—provided that the teachers are clear and interesting. Factor-analytic studies indicate that students give relatively more weight to Dimension I than to Dimension II (Marques, Lane, and Dorfman, 1979; Marsh, 1991). My study of teaching award nominations confirms this pattern.

Descriptors of Exemplary Instructors

Table 1.3 presents the most common descriptors identified in my study of award nominations, grouped under the teaching dimensions they best fit.

As the list for Dimension I shows, several descriptors reflect *what* the exemplary instructor presents: "knowledgeable," "clear," "organized," and "prepared." Others are more reflective of *how* class is conducted: "enthusiastic," "humorous," "interesting," "exciting," "engaging," "energetic," "fun," and "inspiring." The numbers of adjectives and appearances show that there is much data in Dimension I.

Dimension II has been subdivided here into those adjectives most indicative of *interpersonal concern* and those dealing just with *effective motivation*. The most common interpersonal-concern adjectives ("concerned," "caring," "available," "friendly," "accessible") reveal instructors who genuinely care about students and actively create opportunities to interact with them. In contrast, the effective-motivation descriptors capture the exemplary teacher's ability both to set high goals for students ("challenging," "demanding") and to provide students with the support they need to meet them ("encouraging," "helpful," "fair," and "patient"). These descriptors drawn from award nominations sharpen our understanding of Dimension II by showing that exemplary instructors do more than demonstrate positive concern for students. They are also skillful at

Table 1.3. Descriptors Associated with the Enhanced Two-Dimensional Model of Effective College Teaching.

Dimension I: Intellectual Excitement

Adjective	Appearances	Adjective	Appearances
Enthusiastic	68	Engaging	18
Knowledgeable	45	Prepared	16
Inspiring	43	Energetic	15
Humorous	34	Fun	13
Interesting	31	Stimulating	13
Clear	25	Creative	12
Organized	22	Lectures well	11
Exciting	22	Communicative	10

Dimension II-A: Interpersonal Concern

Adjective	Appearances	Adjective	Appearances
Concerned	45	Approachable	12
Caring	33	Interested	12
Available	27	Respectful	11
Friendly	18	Understanding	11
Accessible	17	Personable	10

Dimension II-B: Effective Motivation

Adjective	Appearances	Adjective	Appearances
Helpful	41	Demanding	14
Encouraging	29	Patient	13
Challenging	28	Motivating	11
Fair	19		

Commitment to Teaching

Adjective	Appearances	Adjective	Appearances
Dedicated	35	Committed	19

General Positive Descriptors

Adjective	Appearances	Adjective	Appearances
Effective	17	Outstanding	14
Excellent	17	Great	10

putting pressure on students in ways students find motivating rather than debilitating. Specific techniques for doing this are presented in Chapter Eight, on making assignments, and in Chapter Nine, on evaluating students.

All of these data are quite consistent with factor-analytic studies in suggesting that both Dimension I and Dimension II skills are necessary for exemplary college teaching while giving a slight edge to those of Dimension I.

Six of the descriptors presented in Table 1.3 do not fit the two-dimensional model. "Dedicated" and "committed" obviously refer to one of the six factors identified in Figure 1.1 as influencing student learning: the instructor's motivation for teaching. The other four adjectives ("effective," "excellent," "outstanding," and "great") are all positive, but so general as to offer little to our understanding of the qualities that constitute exemplary college teaching.

Combining Dimensions I and II

Table 1.4 presents the full model, in which Dimensions I and II are combined to form nine combinations or cells, each representing a unique style of instruction associated with a particular probability that students will learn to their fullest potential. The nine styles are numbered in ascending order of overall effectiveness, with Cell 1 the least effective and Cell 9 the most effective. Given that Dimension I is thought to be slightly more associated with exemplary teaching than Dimension II, low-I/high-II is ranked above moderate-I/low-II, and moderate-I/high-II is ranked above high-I/low-II.

Keep in mind that the nine styles of teaching are generalizations and will not describe every college teacher exactly; individual instructors may show elements of more than one type. Instructors in cells one, two, and three are less than fully competent. The "adequates" will be minimally successful in lecture classes and with relatively compliant students but need increased interpersonal skill to expand the range of students and situations in which they will be effective. Similarly, the "marginals" need to improve their ability to

Table 1.4 Two-Dimensional Model of Effective College Teaching.

Dimension I:	Dimension II: Interpersonal Rapport		
Intellectual Excitement	*Low:* cold, distant, highly controlling, unpredictable	*Moderate:* relatively warm, approachable, and democratic; predictable	*High:* warm, open, predictable, and highly student-centered
High: extremely clear and exciting	*Cell 6: Intellectual Authorities* Outstanding for some students and classes but not for others	*Cell 8: Exemplary Lecturers* Especially skilled in large introductory classes	*Cell 9: Complete Exemplars* Excellent for any student and situation
Moderate: reasonably clear and interesting	*Cell 3: Adequates* Minimally adequate for many students in lecture classes	*Cell 5: Competents* Effective for most students and classes	*Cell 7: Exemplary Facilitators* Especially skilled in smaller, more advanced classes
Low: vague and dull	*Cell 1: Inadequates* Unable to present material or motivate students well	*Cell 2: Marginals* Unable to present material well but liked by some students	*Cell 4: Socratics* Outstanding for some students and situations but not for most

present material. Teachers in cells four and six represent the most unusual combinations of skills. The "Socratics" excel at promoting independent work and will be ideal for students and subjects well-suited to seminars. Their approach will be inadequate in larger classes requiring some lecturing, however. Conversely, the "intellectual authorities" will be able to create intellectual excitement and promote achievement in students who are confident in their own abilities and comfortable with those instructors' distant manner, but younger or less able students are likely to experience anxiety under such instructors. An "intellectual authority" is more likely to be respected than loved by most students.

All instructors in cells seven, eight, and nine are exemplary college teachers. Students are likely to describe the "exemplary lecturers" as those who captivate them by sheer intellectual force and motivate them to learn material because it seems a terribly important and exciting thing to do. Students might also describe these cell-eight instructors as a bit mysterious—persons they would like to know better. Many students do their best work under such a teacher. However, younger students or those with limited academic skills and confidence are less likely to benefit maximally from what this instructor has to offer.

In contrast, students of "exemplary facilitators" are more likely to feel close to their instructors. Such instructors are likely to be able to stimulate independent work of high quality. They are sought out by students after class and are particularly effective in smaller, more advanced classes characterized by considerable discussion. "Exemplary facilitators" are also likely to become important in their students' personal lives; students may come to them for advice or attempt to model their lives or careers after them. Both "exemplary lecturers" and "exemplary facilitators" have their fortes, but each is capable of providing competent instruction in all situations.

The rare "complete exemplars" of cell nine are able to perform superbly in both lecture hall and seminar room and to modify their approach so as to motivate all students, from the brilliant to the mediocre. Few, if any, of Epstein's portraits showed this degree of flexibility; of the teachers I interviewed, I can place in this cell only one or two.

I believe most students will do well under any instructor from cells seven, eight, or nine and are likely to rate all these exemplary types highly, but they may prefer one type or the other. Some will be more comfortable with the impersonality of "exemplary lecturers," preferring to learn someone else's point of view on content. On the other hand, students desiring to express their creativity, to tackle learning more independently, or to have more personal relationships and individualized instruction will prefer "exemplary facilitators." The UNC students who thought enough of their instructors to nominate them for teaching awards showed this range of appreciation in the adjectives they used.

Exemplary instructors, then, are those who excel at one or both of these two dimensions of teaching effectiveness, and who are at least adequate at each. Every competent teacher must have at least moderate skill in each dimension, but there is considerable room for variation. My model is similar to the learning styles perspective (see Bonham, 1989; Grasha, 1990) in assuming that some students may learn more under one style of instruction than another. However, my approach is different in predicting that *all* students will learn more from and prefer college teachers in the exemplary cells. It also assumes that instructor skill on Dimensions I and II is distributed normally; that is, that most experienced teachers are competent, falling at the midrange of each dimension, and that relatively few are above or below the norm. The lessons in the following chapters describe general communication skills as well as specific techniques and innovative classroom formats that are designed to help those with less than adequate skills to improve, those already in the midrange to attain excellence, and those at the top of their profession to expand the kinds of students and settings with which they can excel.

As the learning model presented in Figure 1.1 shows, the motivation of all instructors to apply their skills fully in each course they undertake is critical in determining their level of effectiveness. Chapter Ten addresses this question of instructor motivation—of why, given the other demands on his or her time, any instructor should want to put in the considerable effort required to be better than good enough.

2

Understanding
Classroom Dynamics

*The proper goal of the college classroom is "work,"
and only by understanding the obstacles to work that
flow from the complexity of the teacher's task, the
students' diversity, and the nature of group development can the teacher make his optimal contribution
to the goal.*

—Mann and others[1]

We human beings are more capable of reason and logical, non-emotional thinking than other mammals, but we are also capable of emotional and irrational thinking. Emotions are a pervasive element of our lives. In the process of evolution, the emotional responsiveness so essential in the fight-or-flight situations of prehistory has not entirely disappeared as the conditions of survival have become more stable (Wright, 1994). Nothing from the past is lost as species evolve; new adaptations are selected and added on (Alcock, 1979). It is no surprise, then, that our uniquely human ability to think rationally, with little emotion, coexists with a heritage of strong emotions.

1. R. D. Mann and others, *The College Classroom: Conflict, Change, and Learning.* New York: Wiley, 1970, p. vi. Reprinted by permission of John Wiley & Sons, Inc.

Human emotion in college education is a theme running throughout this book, but two chapters, this one and Chapter Four, give it particular attention. This chapter explores the many ways that emotions influence interpersonal rapport in the classroom. It discusses the positive emotions that encourage maximum effort and confidence and the negative emotions that sap both. The relevance of instructors' and students' emotional needs to teaching and learning, and the strategies teachers and students adopt for handling emotions, are discussed in detail. Chapter Four deals with the role of emotions in creating intellectual excitement and the dramatic techniques available to college teachers for stimulating such excitement.

Even though college classrooms are dramatic arenas with intellectual purposes, faculty members and students have more important relationships than that of performer and spectator. College courses are settings in which myriad interpersonal encounters, some fleeting and others involved, unavoidably occur. As in all human encounters, college teachers and students use strategies to maximize positive and minimize negative feelings about themselves. Though the groups have different interpersonal concerns, largely resulting from the different amounts of power they have in the classroom context, both seek to satisfy basic human needs for affection and control. The ways in which instructors and students meet these needs produce predictable interpersonal phenomena that influence the degree to which, and the conditions under which, students are motivated to master the content placed before them.

Attitudes That Influence Classroom Interpersonal Phenomena

Interpersonal phenomena in classrooms result from student and faculty attitudes and the commingling of these attitudes to produce predictable changes in class morale and motivation.

Student Attitudes

Students vary greatly in the way they approach the work assigned and the degree to which they apply their intellectual talents. Some will do anything asked of them, dutifully reading every assignment on time and memorizing every definition written on the board. Such students may be frustrating to a teacher, however, because of their excessive dependency. Dutiful and compliant students are often unduly anxious about the way their work will be evaluated.

In contrast, some students are contentious and distrustful. This attitude is evident in their tone of voice when they object to instructor comments or in the fatalistic little jokes they make about grades or the value of an education. Such a student might say, for example, "What good is psychology, anyway? What can you really prove about the reasons people behave as they do?" The consistently sharp edge of class comments, openly critical questions about content (often delivered with quick glances that seek support from fellow students), and the avoidance of eye contact and one-to-one encounters with the professor reveal such students as fundamentally angry and distrustful of instructors as authority figures.

Fortunately, most students expect college teachers to be warm and friendly, and they are friendly in return. They smile frequently during class and talk warmly and informally after class. Friendly students are much more likely than their more fearful or angry peers to elicit from a teacher the positive behaviors they seek.

There is an important psychological principle at work here. Both students and instructors generally will be treated by others as they expect to be treated. Research on interpersonal perceptions and behavior has clearly demonstrated an interactive effect: personal attitudes tend to produce reciprocal attitudes in others (Jones and others, 1972; Altman and Taylor, 1973; Pratkanis, Breckler, and Greenwald, 1989). For example, if a clerk in a store believes that customers are rude and inconsiderate, this attitude is likely to be evident, however subtly, and customers can be expected to be less friendly and considerate toward this employee than they might otherwise be. This principle of human interaction has been demonstrated in most interpersonal relationships, and those between college teachers and students are no exception.

Teacher Attitudes

Just as students vary in what they expect from instructors, so instructors vary in what they expect from students. From the beginning of a course, some teachers trust students to be able, motivated, and enthusiastic about course content. On the other hand, some college teachers have little initial faith in most students' intellectual ability, commitment, or honesty. Fortunately, most instructors are not so bound by initial expectations that their attitudes toward particular students cannot change as the term progresses.

Instructors also have quite understandable emotional reactions to the way students behave in and out of class. Anyone is likely to become angry at a student who calls at 11 P.M. to beg off from the next day's exam and then fails to report for a scheduled makeup. It is also the unusual person who is immune to the urge to give a little extra attention or grading consideration to a student whom he or she finds attractive.

Class Morale

As Duffy and Jones describe in their book *Teaching Within the Rhythms of the Semester* (1995), on occasion the class as a group appears to become caught up in common emotional concerns. This is most frequently evident as overall class morale—how eager the students' faces appear on a given day, how responsive they are to questions and discussion. Class meetings just before and after exams are especially likely to demonstrate low morale, even an undercurrent of hostility toward the instructor. Many classes show a gradual decline in student enthusiasm and involvement over the course of the term, often with few clues as to why a good beginning turned sour. Group morale may even deteriorate so much that an overt rebellion occurs, with a few brave leaders petitioning the instructor, dean, or department administrator in protest against some assignment or grading practice that many consider unreasonable or unfair. Fortunately, such occurrences are rare.

College teacher morale may also vary over time. For many, it wanes as the semester progresses, and if an overt rebellion of the kind described above occurs, it may drop painfully low. Some teachers grow increasingly disappointed with student performance and mark time in the hope of a better class next term. But for others, the opposite pattern may emerge: their satisfaction with a class grows steadily, and they find themselves bragging about what fine students they have this term. The last meeting of such classes can bring a genuine sense of loss to the instructor, of sadness that the course is ending. This change in morale, like the others previously described, is both predictable and understandable.

These, then, are some of the attitudes and interpersonal phenomena likely to appear in college classes. Some are a direct result of the individual psychology and social roles of students and teachers. Others result from the interaction of student and instructor concerns—the group dynamics that produce overall class morale or atmosphere.

The remainder of this chapter discusses, in greater detail, the major predictable interpersonal phenomena seen in college classes. The psychology of college teachers is discussed first, then the psychology of students, and finally their collective or group interactions over time. The interpersonal dimension of college classrooms surveyed here will be referred to repeatedly in subsequent chapters. For example, Chapter Three builds on these ideas to suggest specific teacher strategies for creating an engaging and satisfying group atmosphere that is likely to motivate diverse students to work independently.

The Psychology of College Teachers

Some college teachers gain little satisfaction from meeting their classes and welcome the opportunity to spend their time at other academic pursuits, especially the scholarly research on which reputation, promotion, and salary depend. But many—in fact, I suspect, the majority—*do* receive considerable personal satisfaction from classroom teaching, although the culture in many schools and departments does not encourage them to express such satisfaction openly. Other than the mixed blessing of hearing parents brag to their friends about "my child, the college professor," what are the common satisfactions that instructors gain from classroom teaching?

Sources of Satisfaction

Student recognition of an instructor's accumulated knowledge about a subject is certainly important to all teachers. Teaching classes provides an opportunity to display knowledge and to validate implicitly the time and effort spent in acquiring it. Discussing one's area of expertise with colleagues and presenting papers at national meetings offer similar satisfactions, but having a fresh audience, one not yet aware of how much the instructor knows about a subject, offers more certain acknowledgment of subject mastery.

Teaching students what one knows also provides the warm satisfaction that comes whenever one gives away something one values, as when one purchases a present or composes a poem for a special occasion. Teaching is giving knowledge away, and many college teachers are compulsive sharers of what they know, eager to pass on information or insights to willing listeners. Teaching at any level is pleasurable for such individuals. People who find little joy in giving to others are likely to find less personal satisfaction in teaching than those who are intrinsically generous.

For some college teachers, the opportunity to be in charge is attractive. In the classroom, instructors are absolute monarchs with considerable power to reward, punish, and control. Some find it satisfying to give students freedom to direct their own learning; for them, pleasure comes from subtly moving (or motivating) students toward autonomy. Others attempt to satisfy needs for power by controlling students directly. They try to preserve as much power for themselves as possible, lest students slip beyond their influence.

Whereas classroom instruction inevitably requires public performance, being front and center is not universally exhilarating. Many instructors find teaching pleasurable *in spite* of the fact that it must be done standing alone in front of a group. Others, however, clearly relish the chance to captivate, to entertain, to astonish the audience that appears regularly to hear them. A frequently heard adage about college teaching is that "all great teachers are hams at heart." It is not essential for teachers to be "hams" to be outstanding. However, instructors who do enjoy performing are more likely to find their job rewarding.

Many instructors take genuine delight in identifying, recruiting, and guiding talented students. I believe satisfaction from this source usually increases as a teacher matures, but even graduate instructors are pleased when an able student decides to major in their subject. It is not surprising that such gatekeeping activities can be rewarding: who would not be flattered by having a student aspire to follow in his or her footsteps?

Some college teachers derive satisfaction from forming personal relationships with their students as a group. To help create such intimacy, they may make disclosures in class about their careers, their families, or even their pets. No doubt some instructors dwell on themselves to excess, but a judicious number of personal disclosures can make an instructor seem more human and less forbidding to students, as well as contributing to satisfaction for the teacher. Not incidentally, research has shown that instructor self-disclosures make students more willing to participate in discussion (Goldstein and Benassi, in press).

Other instructors encourage individual relationships with particular students by offering them teaching or research assistantships.

Many students will eagerly take advantage of an opportunity to get to know the professor well. Students foster such relationships on occasion by inviting professors to meals, parties, or artistic or athletic events. Developing personal relationships, many of them lasting, with students is one of the most pleasant fringe benefits of an academic career.

College teaching offers many potential satisfactions. However, satisfactions can easily be tainted or even totally destroyed by negative feelings about students and teaching.

Sources of Dissatisfaction

Perhaps the most common way in which students undermine a teacher's satisfaction is by failing to master course content sufficiently. At some time, every instructor is likely to react with anger when reading student work that woefully misses the mark. Setting high standards can motivate students to do their best work, but an instructor who takes these goals too seriously is often doomed to disappointment. As the learning model presented in Chapter One shows, even in the best of schools and classes, the quality of performance will vary from student to student, and the teacher who takes too much responsibility for what his or her students learn is likely to find teaching frustrating. Having high but realistic expectations for student achievement and remembering that the most powerful way an instructor can affect students' learning is by increasing their motivation will help to preserve an instructor's enthusiasm for teaching.

College teachers' needs to control students also are frequently frustrated. They put considerable demands on busy students and are legitimately fearful that the students will not do what they ask. Fears concerning course management nag any instructor, but such fears may be especially strong in teachers who are inexperienced or are planning a new semester after an unsuccessful one: "What if the students do not do the reading? What if their papers are superficial or turned in late (or not at all)? What if administrators or other faculty see me as weak and indulgent?" Questions relating to student classroom behavior also crop up: "What if they do not pay attention in class? What if they do not even come to class? What if they do not respond to my attempts to elicit questions or discussion?" College teachers inescapably are authorities within the school or university organization, and they are responsible for enforcing rules and maintaining order. If the methods of controlling students used by an instructor are ineffective, teaching will not be satisfying.

Dissatisfaction resulting from student failure to learn adequately or submit sufficiently to an instructor's control is related to the formal role of the college teacher, to the duties that teachers are paid for and are clearly expected to perform. Students also have tremendous potential to sour the pleasures of teaching by rejecting an instructor in other ways, both personally and professionally.

Because every college teacher has spent considerable time and energy mastering and promoting a subject, the pleasure of sharing this knowledge is greatly undermined if students state or imply that the subject is boring or irrelevant.

When students reject course content, it is easy to dismiss their scorn as reflecting their superficiality, but it is more difficult for an instructor to protect professional and personal self-esteem when students make negative evaluations of his or her teaching or intellectual competence. Even a successful researcher who acknowledges to trusted colleagues his mediocre teaching skills will find it painful to be rated poorly by students. Though students are much more likely to attack course content or teaching skill than personal academic abilities, teachers are also vulnerable to classroom innuendos, overheard remarks between students, or anonymous direct attacks (such as insulting notes slid under office doors) that denigrate the instructor's content mastery, intelligence, or personality.

Instructor satisfaction and dissatisfaction affect the quality of teaching and learning in several ways. First, satisfaction and dissatisfaction interact with each other. Dissatisfaction obviously reduces a teacher's motivation and morale. The reverse is also true: the more satisfaction instructors gain from students and teaching, the more motivated they will be to teach well and the less vulnerable they will be to occasional negative evaluations.

The kinds of activities that teachers find satisfying also tend to change over time. Initially, joy at having expertise and control confirmed when students respond enthusiastically to a given lecture or discussion is rewarding. These simple pleasures become less satisfying once the novelty and initial challenge of teaching wear off. Individuals who maintain a high level of satisfaction in classroom teaching over many years are those who work at improving their teaching skills and take delight in their expanding capacities. Understanding the individual and group psychology of classrooms also increases a college teacher's resistance to the kinds of perplexing, even troubling, behavior that students sometimes display.

Types of Behavior Toward Students

Educators have long tried to define teaching styles and to measure how much learning each produces. In their excellent study of college classrooms, Richard Mann and his colleagues at the University of Michigan (1970) applied a system created for coding implied emotional and relationship messages of members of psychotherapy and self-analytic groups to four introductory psychology classes, each containing twenty-five students. Each graduate instructor had taught the course only once previously. Data consisted of tape recordings of all class meetings over the semester and questionnaires given to instructors and students. Observers also attended all classes and took notes on nonverbal behavior. Those interested in a technical description of the Mann group's methods and results should consult their book, *The College Classroom: Conflict, Change, and Learning*.

In one of their studies, the Mann group used cluster analysis to concentrate the thousands of ratings of comments from all four instructors into seven independent clusters or dimensions, each of which describes an aspect of behavior toward students. For our purposes, their seven dimensions can be further reduced to three: the amount of control used, the quality of affect shown, and the instructor's degree of satisfaction with the class.

The first of two clusters in the control category describes how actively the teachers directed classroom proceedings (whether they lectured or reacted to student questions or discussion). The second control cluster reflects the interpersonal distance the instructors tried to maintain between themselves and students; some chose to maximize the distance by being formal, while others minimized it by treating students almost as equals. When the size of these clusters in Mann's analyses is considered, it is clear that the way college teachers control students is the most prominent feature of their interpersonal behavior in classrooms.

How instructors felt about students was also of considerable importance, since three of the seven clusters are related to quality of affect. Teacher punitiveness—being openly critical of students or trying to make them feel guilty ("Your exams show that you are not taking this course seriously")—was an important dimension. Positive instructor affect appeared as two independent clusters: teacher warmth and teacher enthusiasm.

The third category of teacher behaviors identified by Mann and his colleagues reflects the way the instructors felt about their teaching. The two specific clusters associated with this category are expressed satisfaction (or dissatisfaction) with teaching ("I am pleased that we are only two classes behind schedule") and apprehension about the future ("I am afraid we will not have time to finish the syllabus if we do not move on").

The Mann group's analyses demonstrate that there is significant variation in the quality of affect that teachers show toward students, the type of control they attempt to use, and the degree of satisfaction they express. How do these teacher behaviors affect students' motivation and learning?

Affective and Control Messages

Studies of human communication demonstrate that all of us communicate far more than we say—or think we say—in words (Watzlawick, Beavin, and Jackson, 1967; Skinner, 1986). The tone of voice, the degree of inflection or emphasis, the expression on our faces, and the gestures we make communicate as much or more than our words. The context of particular statements also can affect, or even change completely, the way those statements are received by others. For example, an instructor who remarks to a class, "I am glad you took the time to read the assignment—this time," offends by adding "this time" to the compliment. If the class had been chided at its last meeting for failing to read the assignment, some students would find today's comment sarcastic even if the qualifier were omitted. As is true of spouses' communications with each other, a college teacher's history of comments influences the way given words or gestures may be taken.

Added to this complexity are the affective and control messages that verbal statements can carry. (Affective messages express how the instructor feels about students.) The following illustration will help to clarify this point. Suppose an instructor wishes to have his or her students review the literature relevant to a topic of their choosing and write a term paper presenting what they have learned. The most emotionally neutral way to announce this requirement would be, "I want you to write a paper covering the major approaches to any topic in the course you wish." No affective attitudes toward the students or their likelihood of success and no controlling messages are conveyed by this statement.

If the instructor adds affective messages such as "I think you will enjoy selecting your own topics and thinking independently about them. I will look forward to reading your papers," he or she conveys the expectation that the students will both enjoy and succeed at writing their term papers. In contrast, if the instructor adds, "I want you to show some independent thinking for a change and not just give me ideas you have copied out of books," students could reasonably surmise that the instructor has little faith in their ability to think independently or conduct themselves honorably and is not looking forward to reading the papers. Though these examples are more obvious than those commonly occurring in college classes, they illustrate how the little addenda to instructor communications can intentionally or unintentionally determine their emotional impact on students.

The same assignment could also have been announced in a much more controlling way. More dominating but emotionally neutral instructions might be, "I expect you to write a paper covering the major approaches to any important topic in the course. Be sure to do a thorough literature search and identify major themes or issues—see the reference desk at the library if you do not know how to do this—and use the last half of your paper to compare and contrast the major points." By giving so many specific instructions on the way to proceed with the assignment, the instructor assumes a more dominant position with the students and consequently makes them more dependent.

This announcement is also more directive than the original one because of two subtle changes in wording. The substitutions of "I expect" for "I want" and "any important topic" for "any topic . . . you wish," though apparently trivial, emphasize the teacher's role as a controlling and evaluative authority. It is more controlling to "expect" than to "want" and to imply that the students should pick a topic that *the instructor* thinks is important.

Teacher messages that are overtly controlling or emphasize the hierarchical power relationship between teacher and student encourage students to be less independent (Lowman, 1990b). Whether a student finds such remarks positive or negative depends on how much the student likes having things structured by someone else; but extensive directions are more likely to be appreciated when associated with affection than when coupled with hostility.

The Psychology of Students

Though college students are not children, some college-age students *are* immature—more adolescent than adult. Some may be acutely sensitive to a teacher's criticism or control. Mature or not, all students want to be regarded positively and controlled democratically and will bristle if these needs are unduly frustrated. This section focuses on the emotional needs of college students, the typical classroom conflicts engendered by these needs, and individual differences in the ways students attempt to meet them. As in the section on the psychology of college teachers, the goal is to increase instructor awareness of the emotional interactions of the classroom so that the task of enhancing motivation and learning is made easier.

Sources of Satisfaction

Every faculty member is aware that students differ in their interest in academics and in their motivation to achieve in school. A few students are so narrowly invested in the world of ideas that they completely disdain nonintellectual activities such as athletic contests and social events. Other students find little pleasure in reading, writing, thinking, solving problems, or attending class, though their academic performance may be adequate. However, most students at any school have at least a modicum of intellectual curiosity and find learning pleasurable for its own sake. They derive satisfaction from discovering answers, excitement at seeing how their minds work, and joy in appreciation of the arts. They also recognize that many of their ideas about life are echoed in the thoughts of the writers they study. This attitude is known as a *learning orientation* (Milton, Pollio, and Eison, 1986).

College study also provides opportunities to meet the need for mastery, for meeting and successfully overcoming challenges. Of course, this need also can be satisfied through nonacademic pursuits such as athletics and student politics, and many students, unfortunately, have never learned to satisfy it through schoolwork.

A related source of satisfaction is bettering one's peers in com-petition. Competition for high grades and academic honors is the form of competition most apparent in the classroom. Experienced teachers appreciate the effort and high achievement that competi-tive needs can produce, but they also know that learning primarily to surpass other students does not lead to lasting satisfaction and can cause selfish or harmful behavior toward others. This undue focus on grades as an end in themselves is called a *grading orienta-tion* (Milton, Pollio, and Eison, 1986). Skillful instructors are able to channel student needs for competition into activities that pro-mote a learning rather than a grading orientation (Lowman, 1990b).

The three kinds of student satisfaction discussed thus far are all associated with the general human need to control events around us (Bandura, 1989; White, 1963). By seeking information, mastering problems, and besting our fellows, we control our environment instrumentally—rather than expressively, through relationships with others. Students also desire to have control in the classroom. Most do not attempt to direct the proceedings overtly, however, although a few are habitual rebels.

It is easier for both compliant and rebellious students to feel in control with a predictable teacher than with a capricious one. Research on parental attitudes (Martin, 1975) and on leadership styles (Cartwright and Zander, 1960; Gibbard, Hartman, and Mann, 1973) has shown that inconsistency creates almost as much anxi-ety as rejection. Most students are likely to find a class satisfying if they believe that they can successfully meet the demands of a chal-lenging but predictable instructor.

Primarily because they are human, but secondarily because they are late adolescents, college students need affection and approval from others, especially authority figures. These needs are potent sources of satisfaction in the classroom, as shown by the importance of items related to such needs in the factor analyses of student eval-uation forms. Foremost among these affectional needs is the desire for a personal relationship with a college teacher. Students' often-expressed preferences for smaller classes may reflect this wish. As Kirkpatrick Sale argues so well in *Human Scale* (1980), largeness in human institutions, whether neighborhoods, businesses, or governments, breeds an impersonality that few people find satisfying. College classrooms are no different.

In addition to a personal relationship, students desire to have their instructor think well of them. Students need affection from college teachers, not as parents or lovers, but as adults who approve of them as learners and persons. Students find learning much more satisfying when they believe that their instructor likes and trusts them.

Students also need the approval of classmates, and not only as friends or dates. Students wish to be seen by their classmates as academically able and also, interestingly, as keeping an appropriate distance from the teacher. Most students fear making comments in class that their classmates may view as foolish or as "sucking up to the teacher." Though most classroom satisfaction of students' affectional needs comes from teachers, a significant portion comes from other students, especially as individuals become emotionally invested in the class over time.

Sources of Dissatisfaction

Like college teachers, students are vulnerable to a number of potential dissatisfactions in their academic lives. The mildest dissatisfaction students are likely to experience in the classroom is the absence of a personal relationship with their instructor. Physical barriers such as size of hall and number of other students can prevent even the most rudimentary relationship from forming. However, smaller classes alone do not guarantee that students will experience a satisfying relationship. Many instructors do not remember students' names, and a few may not recognize students who drop by their office or greet them when coming out of a movie. Most students will allow the teacher several encounters in which to learn to recognize them and be able to recall their names, but almost all will be disappointed if the teacher does not remember them once the school term is well under way.

Frustration of student need for control is more likely to create significant dissatisfaction than is the absence of a personal relationship with the instructor. Poorly organized or unpredictable classes are especially frustrating. When students are unsure what topics will be covered or what the objectives for a teacher's assignments are, they miss the sense of control that comes from knowing why the challenges that await them were selected and what rules will govern the evaluation of their work.

Student needs for mastery can be frustrated in several ways. Uninteresting or confusing presentations can dampen almost any student's curiosity and desire to seek challenges. Although some students relish overcoming obstacles more than others, all expect to be challenged, and classes that move too slowly, focus on obvious points excessively, or are devoid of even occasional references to critical questions are likely to be dissatisfying.

Some students' need for mastery is indistinguishable from their need to surpass their classmates by receiving higher grades. Unfortunately, it is difficult to design a course that satisfies grading-oriented students' competitive needs without frustrating others' desire to meet individual learning needs—for example, focusing class presentations on specific facts and theories pleases those students who are most concerned about their grades, but frustrates those who are eager to consider the implications of the content. Teachers share with athletic coaches the dilemmas of handling students emotionally to avoid complacency among those who "win" and hopelessness among those who "lose," and to help students learn to see external challenges as opportunities to test their skills or assess their learning rather than as obstacles to be overcome at any cost. Grades are exceedingly important to most students, especially those who are accustomed to receiving high or low ones. Like good coaches, skillful instructors are able to motivate all students to improve their performance and to remain engaged when they are less successful than they might wish.

Because professors must evaluate students' work, they assume a role as symbolic parent figures, which makes students vulnerable to the belief—correct or not—that the teacher who evaluates their work negatively is rejecting or disapproving of them personally. Though less frequent than frustration of needs for control and mastery, the feeling of being personally rejected by a teacher can profoundly reduce motivation and satisfaction.

Students may be fully aware that they are not intellectual giants or especially hardworking, but they do not appreciate it when their teachers remind them of these defects openly. Neither do they need to be reminded that they have only a beginner's grasp of a discipline and are not yet professional scientists, artists, musicians, or writers. Students do, however, need accurate evaluations of the quality of their work. How can an instructor give accurate feedback without dampening students' self-confidence and motivation? The key is in the way criticism is given and the overall quality of the relationship within which it is given. Almost any student can benefit from an accurate evaluation of academic performance that is given with tact and affirmation of his or her basic worth as student and person.

Complimenting students' effort and enthusiasm before offering criticism reassures them that the instructor does not think them hopeless and helps them to hear specific suggestions for improvement without becoming defensive. Criticism also is more likely to be well-received if it is specific rather than general ("These two paragraphs are not connected" instead of "Your paper is disorganized") and if it criticizes the product rather than the producer ("This paper is poorly written" instead of "You can't write"). Carefully constructed criticism in which emotional support and specific feedback are combined will show a student how to improve without destroying his or her motivation to do so. Because most students consider teachers' critical judgments indisputably valid, they may be devastated by negative comments untempered by tact. These considerations all point to the special need for teachers to actively seek interpersonal rapport with students so that students will be able to use the criticism certain to come later on. An underlying reservoir of rapport can be drawn on throughout the course to mitigate the stress we place on students and the critical feedback we give on the quality of their performance. Even when positive interpersonal relationships are present, however, diplomatic skill is needed if teacher criticism is to have a constructive effect.

Evaluative comments by teachers are further complicated if such comments are made in the presence of other students. An instructor who openly criticizes any student—even if others can see clearly that the student deserves the criticism—risks decreasing the quality of his or her relationships with everyone in the class; by rejecting one student, the teacher introduces the possibility that all may one day receive similar treatment. Excessive praise can also backfire by creating resentment or jealousy among those not praised and by emphasizing the teacher's evaluative role. The instructor (or parent) who praises excessively raises the specter of harsh criticism that might be dispensed under different circumstances. Thus, college teachers must be skillful in the way they praise and criticize students, whether individually or collectively.

Instructors at times make evaluative statements about characteristics of students other than the quality of their work. Teachers who imply or state explicitly that individual students or the class as a whole are poorly motivated ("You are not applying yourselves fully to your studies"), superficial in their interests ("I find it hard to understand how you can get so excited about a mere basketball game"), or morally culpable ("It is elitist, racist, and sexist of you to support that position") are more likely to produce guilt and dissatisfaction in students than to change their attitudes. Even the clergy, who have a clear mandate to question others' values and behavior, risk preaching to empty pews if they do not temper their moral criticism with assurances to their congregations that they care about them, do not consider them despicable, and respect the difficult individual decisions everyone must make about ethical matters. College teachers who desire to improve their students' character in addition to teaching them face a similar challenge.

Types of Behavior Toward Teachers

Students are in no way passive pawns in the classroom game, doing just as instructed and keeping their emotions to themselves. Students communicate their personal feelings and expectations toward college teachers by their classroom behavior—the kinds of questions they pose, the ways they respond to an instructor's questions, and the readiness with which they smile or meet the teacher's eyes. Students also communicate a great deal in one-to-one encounters before and after class or during office hours. Much student communication is subtle, however, and college teachers must be perceptive and a little speculative to read the messages accurately. Instructors skilled at creating high interpersonal rapport with students are able to do this, whether their understanding is intuitive or acquired from deliberate study of the complexity of interpersonal communications.

The Mann studies (1970) described in the section on instructors present a rich portrait of the varieties of student feelings and behavior toward classroom instructors. Mann and his colleagues performed a cluster analysis of student comments to identify eight different types of students in terms of the emotional messages that the students expressed over a semester. Some students were compliant, some anxious, some oppositional, and a few independent. Because the classes were small and characterized by considerable discussion, most students (80 percent) made enough comments to be classified. Other data available on each student—SAT scores, overall GPA, and questionnaires about family background, personal feelings about the teacher, and preferences for different styles of instruction—showed other ways in which the students in each cluster were similar. Although few students will fit any of these types exactly, students resembling them can be found in every college class. The Mann group's student types and some techniques for motivating each are discussed in detail in the next chapter. Chapter Three also discusses other categories of students who may benefit from special understanding and motivational techniques.

Predictable Changes in Class Rapport over Time

Studies of group behavior have demonstrated that the ways in which people attempt to meet needs for control and affection in small groups are predictable. The kinds of groups studied have varied from work groups with highly structured tasks to unstructured sensitivity or self-analytic groups. A predictable sequence of phenomena occurs in the life of every group, structured or unstructured (Cartwright and Zander, 1960; Shaffer and Galinsky, 1989).

Regardless of who is officially in charge, all groups initially show great concern about leadership—about who is going to control whom and whether the methods used will be mindful of the members' opinions and feelings. Once an initial solution to the problem of leadership is made, group members then become concerned about how close they will let themselves become to each other. Although the issue of leadership may appear to have been settled, after a few meetings a minor revolt of the members almost always occurs, during which the initial solution is called into question. When an implicit system of leadership is worked out and accepted once again (even if the original solution is readopted, it will now have more genuine support), group members will be less distracted by emotional concerns and can devote more of their energies to the purpose of the group. For groups having a limited life, such as college classes, a period of heightened emotionality always occurs at the end. Sadness is common as members withdraw their emotional investment in the leader and each other.

A fundamental observation about the way groups function over time is that little stays the same for very long. One of the clearest explanations of the reason small groups change so regularly is Robert Bales's differentiation between *task* needs and *maintenance* needs in groups (Bales, 1950; Bales and Slater, 1955). Task needs relate to the work of the group, its external purpose. Meeting course objectives would be the task of a college class. Maintenance needs are the personal needs of the members, primarily needs for control and affection. This distinction between task and maintenance needs parallels the presentational and interpersonal dimensions of college teaching presented in Chapter One. Bales's critical points are that both types of need must be met and that groups vacillate over time between emphasis on task needs and emphasis on maintenance needs, each type always being met at the expense of the other. For example, a group that works exceedingly hard to meet a production deadline (focuses most of its energies on meeting its task needs) will necessarily create a relative deprivation of the members' needs for relationships with each other (their maintenance needs). After a long stint of heavy investment in the task, dissatisfaction will increase to the point that work effectiveness decreases greatly. (Employee slowdowns or strikes are extreme symptoms of maintenance deprivation.) At this point, the group must hear grievances or reconsider its operating procedures (systems of leadership and division of labor) to right the balance. When the group spends time on enhancing personal relationships, pressure for meeting its task needs increases, and the focus must swing back to the work at hand.

The implication of this theory for group and organizational leaders (including college teachers) is that the best way to avoid large swings back and forth—the kind of swings that wreck production schedules and lead to employee unrest—is to attend to the maintenance needs of groups at the outset rather than waiting until members force the leader to show concern for them. This book's emphasis on personal teaching is based on this well-accepted principle of organizational leadership: recognizing and attempting to meet the emotional needs of group members from the outset leads to greater work (or learning) in the long run.

Mann's group applied these group dynamics principles to time trends in their classroom data. They found remarkable similarity in the patterns of students' and instructors' feelings and control strate-

gies over the semester, even though the four classes differed in overall teacher effectiveness and student satisfaction. The Mann group's
description of "the natural history of the college classroom" rings
true for most experienced college teachers. Newer instructors can
benefit greatly from being aware of the predictable stages Mann and
his colleagues describe. The following discussion of the typical emotional progression of a college class over a semester has been adapted
from the Mann group's empirically derived stages.

Regardless of whatever underlying fears students and instructors
may harbor, college courses almost always start with a sense of optimism and positive anticipation in everyone. Students usually arrive
early for the first class meeting, and many hope that this course and
their own performance will somehow be different from their past
experience. Instructors commonly hope that they will teach effectively and be well-received by students. Those teaching for the first
time have an even richer array of initial expectations, many unfortunately based on unrealistic ideas about their role.

Beneath this surface excitement and anticipation are a number
of fears. Students fear that the instructor will be authoritarian and
rejecting and that they will fail to perform as well as they would
like. Concern over success on exams and papers is felt by all students, both by the consistently outstanding, who must once again
enter the fray and emerge with a high mark, and by those who have
not performed up to their own or their parents' expectations. College teachers know they must win their laurels with still another
group of strangers, no matter how highly their previous classes
regarded them. Even with these fears, however, the overall mood at
the beginning of a class tends to be positive for everyone.

The first few classes build on these initial positive expectations.
Typically, teachers are relatively controlling at first, and students
are comfortably compliant. Students suggest by their initial comments what impression they wish to make on the instructor and
their fellow students—whether they expect the teacher to structure
their learning or give them their head, for example. The initial
positive expectations of students and instructors lead to a brief

honeymoon period of good feelings: the college teacher is not as controlling as the students had feared, nor are the students as dependent or dull as the instructor had feared. However, these early positive impressions arise from initial expectations—from both optimism and disconfirmation of early fears—more than from actual experience, and so they must eventually be questioned.

The "era of good feeling" ends with a relatively sharp drop in satisfaction and rise in anxiety among students and instructors. In the Mann group's four classes, this occurred after six to eight meetings (about four weeks). Even the class that has been working well must now swing back to address emotional needs. This drop in morale occurs at four to six weeks, even in classes without an exam, though first exams are often given about that time and are frequently the focus of student dissatisfaction. Giving an exam or graded assignment speeds up the revolt by dramatizing the teacher's evaluative role. Grading students' work reminds instructors that student mastery of content is never as complete as they had hoped and that their relationship with students is unavoidably an evaluative one; thus, teachers' morale drops too.

Fortunately, college teachers can be assured that the drop in morale is usually brief and ushers in a more realistic period of satisfaction and independent work. The optimal work atmosphere, in which students more readily participate in discussion and show independent thinking and work outside class, falls in most classes in the middle third and last half and, according to the Mann group's thinking, could not occur without the emotional crisis that precedes it. This optimal work atmosphere can be extended by fostering positive interpersonal relationships, but it cannot be gained too quickly or by simple gimmicks such as class social events.

The end of a class is emotional for everyone. During the last few class meetings, students often become anxious about the final exam and course grades, but this anxiety rarely reaches the height attained just before the first exam. Students now are commonly sorry that the course is ending, even if it has not been particularly satisfying to them. College teachers may be disappointed that they were not able to present more material or to help students master it more fully. Though dissatisfaction expressed in the last few class meetings (especially the final meeting) usually concerns course content, students and instructors are also sorry to have their personal relationships come to an end. They shared an important common experience, the class, and are sad to say goodbye. In classes in which student morale has been high, it is not uncommon for students to ask the instructor personal questions during the last class, as if to make a final attempt to be intimate.

Some students in every course, to be sure, are happy to have the class end, to move on to a vacation or new courses. In highly unsatisfactory classes, the last few meetings are occasions for such students to express dissatisfaction openly. Teachers as well frequently feel the need to share negative feelings they have about the class. Regardless of the specific kinds of feelings expressed, students and instructors tend at this time to communicate their subtle emotions for one another, and the need to do this will take precedence over concerns about the course content.

Emotional needs during the last class meeting are so important that I strongly recommend against the common practice of covering one last topic or scheduling an exam at this time. Students need an opportunity to reflect emotionally as well as intellectually on the semester coming to an end (Eble, 1988). Because students' ratings of instruction are a major vehicle through which to communicate their feelings about the course and instructor, I argue in Chapter Ten that the last meeting is a particularly apt time to administer rating questionnaires.

In conclusion, college classrooms are rich laboratories of interpersonal psychology. Although students and instructor show characteristic behavior as all seek to satisfy the same fundamental human needs, considerable diversity in individual patterns is possible. Chapter Three applies what has been presented here to the practical demands of the classroom and suggests specific techniques for interpersonally skillful teaching.

Developing Interpersonal
Skills and Teaching Style

Social events early in the term do not harm the devel-
opment of rapport but have limited power to produce
it, are not likely to be attended by the students who
most need help forming relationships, and cannot off-
set distancing or rejecting remarks by the teacher in
class.

Some college teachers try to promote rapport and downplay their classroom image as authority figures by dressing casually, encouraging students to call them by their first names, or giving students considerable freedom to select the work they do. Others encourage informal interaction with students outside classrooms by scheduling conferences, sponsoring parties or picnics, inviting students to lunch, or holding class meetings outside on the grass or in their homes. Even though opportunities for student-faculty interaction have been identified as a major predictor of the overall positive impact of a college education (Astin, 1992), none of these strategies per se ensure satisfied and motivated students. Furthermore, none are necessary for interpersonal rapport to develop and for students to be highly motivated.

The students most likely to call the instructor by his or her first name or to accept social invitations are the ones who already feel relatively comfortable, not those who are most in need of special attention. Many students find the novelty of calling their instructor "Bill" or "Betsy" refreshing for a while, but like the honeymoon period near the beginning of a course, this comfort is superficial and is no quick substitute for a real relationship developed over time. As Kenneth Eble observes in *The Craft of Teaching* (1988, p. 106), the best strategy for developing rapport "may be no more formal than providing excuses and opportunities for easy talk." One-to-one interactions with students in the second half of a course are likely to be more meaningful than those that occur earlier. The subtleties of a college teacher's behavior toward a class throughout the term do more to produce an optimal class atmosphere than sweeping structural changes at the beginning ("Let's move the chairs back and sit on the floor"). This chapter suggests specific ways in which college teachers can foster relationships with students that promote motivation and satisfaction. The techniques presented here were collected from books on college teaching and observations of outstanding teachers. They are organized into groups of techniques dealing with:

1. Fostering personal relationships with students

2. Obtaining regular feedback from them

3. Motivating students to work by means of effective classroom leadership

4. Showing special attention to certain types of students

5. Handling miscellaneous interpersonal issues

Fostering Personal Relationships with Students

The easiest way to begin forming personal relationships with students is to have them introduce themselves and to learn their names (Duffy and Jones, 1995). Nothing so impresses students as a college teacher who makes a serious effort to get to know them as individuals. Engineering professor Mary Sansalone, 1993 CASE

Professor of the Year, is known for memorizing her students' names and using them regularly in and out of class (Shea, 1993). Any instructor can learn to match up to fifty students' names with faces in the first few classes (several hundred can be learned if still or video photographs are used) if he or she approaches the task with a positive attitude and commitment. Learning each student's name is so effective at promoting rapport because it begins personal contact immediately but does not seem forced, rushed, or intrusive. When we meet a new colleague, we learn his or her name as the first step in forming a working relationship; so it should be between college teacher and student.

The following paragraphs describe two name-learning strategies that have been successful for many instructors. The first lends itself well to classes with fifty or fewer students and the second can handle classes of several hundred. Other general techniques for improving memory can be used, but like the systems advocated here, any method will require effort to be effective.

Begin by introducing yourself on the first day of class and including a few personal facts (hometown, years at your school, major professional or personal interests, and so on). Then hand out index cards and ask the students to introduce themselves to you by writing basic descriptive information (name, student identification and local telephone number, e-mail address, major, and so forth) on the cards. Be sure to ask them to indicate what they would like to be called and to note if they object to your listing their name, local phone number, or e-mail address on a class roster to be distributed to the class. Then, ask them to add anything else they think you, the instructor, might wish to know, or that they might wish you to know. The open instruction to add comments pressures them politely to divulge a bit of themselves and makes it easy for students to alert you to any special needs. Many students will add nothing, but a few will dutifully list other courses they have had in the subject or their extracurricular activities; a few will attempt to show off their wit or political attitudes, demonstrating what interesting persons they are, and occasionally a student will use this medium to inform you of a visual or hearing problem.

It helps to have reviewed the names on a preregistration list beforehand, even though these lists are never completely accurate. Certain first names are common, so make a mental note of how many Bobs, Jims, Jennifers, Kathys, and so forth are in the class. You might also practice pronouncing unusual first and last names. Consulting "face books" (annuals or other directories with student pictures) beforehand will make learning the names a little easier, but it is ineffective to attempt to learn all the names in this way before the first group meeting. Learning names in class requires a large amount of eye contact, and this may contribute as much to the growth of the individual relationships as your permanent association of face and name.

After asking students to hand in their cards, explain that you would like everyone to learn each other's first name to facilitate class discussion and studying together out of class. Announce that you will be distributing a class roster containing names, local telephone numbers, and e-mail addresses alphabetized by first names. Then have each student stand up and slowly say his or her name and hometown while scanning the room to make brief eye contact with everyone else in the class. Repeat the name to be sure you (and everyone else) heard it and can pronounce it accurately and to keep students from going too fast. Concentrate on looking directly at the students' faces, forming a visual image of each face while silently saying the first name over and over. After the fifth student, stop and practice the whole set one or two times by calling students' names out loud in different orders to make it more likely everyone will associate names with the faces, not the order in which students identify themselves. When two students have the same first name, learn them as a group (for example, "Oh, you are one of our two Jennifers!"). When the entire class has been introduced, attempt to call each student's name. When you cannot remember a name (and you are sure to forget several), ask the class to help you out. When finished, ask for a student volunteer to lead the class through one more practice round. (Students usually miss fewer names than I do on this review trial.) At the end of the first class meeting, go over the names one additional time before students leave. You need make no effort to learn last names at this time; first names will suffice for calling on students in class and beginning personal relationships. You will learn last names almost automatically when you grade and record the first exams or papers.

As soon after the first class meeting as you can, go through the cards again, saying each first name silently and attempting to picture the face that goes with it. Repeat this process once more later in the day and once each day thereafter until the class meets next. Give yourself a final refresher just before going to the second class, but do not be disconcerted if you can remember only a few of the faces with confidence.

At the beginning of the second class, look at each face and try to call each student's first name. Though this is easier than trying to imagine the faces from the names, no more than fifty percent accuracy is normal. Once again, try to remain calm when you must ask the rest of the class for a student's name. When ending the second class meeting, call each student's name again. Most likely, you will do better now than at the beginning of class.

Continue going through the students' names at the beginning and end of each class and picturing the faces from the cards each day until you can say every name quickly and correctly the first time. By the third or fourth class meeting, it is usually no longer necessary to call every student's name; you can scan the room before class and call only those about which you are not completely confident. In addition to these steps, use students' names as much as possible when calling on them in class, answering questions after class, or meeting them on campus. This helps to solidify initial learning, and you will rarely forget the names during the rest of the semester.

Photography is essential for larger classes, because it does not take so much class time and lets instructors work on the memory task on their own over several weeks. Some instructors use still photographs of individual students or small groups (three or four), usually produced by instant cameras at the end of the first class meeting. I find video images more effective, because they provide additional memory cues from voice and facial expressions and allow more of students' personalities to come through. If you use instant photographs, simply have students write their names on the back of the picture. If you use video, have students line up, hand you their cards, and state their names and home towns in front of the camera as they leave. Be sure to keep the cards in order and to repeat the names slowly to be sure they are understandable when you play the tape later. A class of one hundred can be videotaped in about fifteen to twenty minutes. For bigger classes, a second (or third) video camera is needed. Larger classes will take longer to learn—several weeks or so—but the names can be memorized if worked on regularly and in small batches, and if you come to class early to practice names and use them often.

Whatever size your class and whichever method you use, tell the students that learning names is a difficult but important activity for all of you and suggest they greet you and each other by name, both in your class and around campus. If they do not recall a name, they should ask for a reminder. Assure them that you are going to keep practicing their names for a while during class until you learn them. Students are more likely to believe that you really do want to get to know them if you put this into practice.

This no doubt seems like a lot of time to spend on such a modest goal—and instructors who pursue it report that it does require effort and commitment, especially at first. Most find that their memory for names improves over successive semesters, however, and that the resulting rapport is well worth the investment. I believe that learning names is the most important single thing a college teacher can do to communicate to students that he or she values them as individuals. It also satisfies the instructor's need for personal contact with students and opens up other channels to personal relationships with them.

Another way to develop rapport with students is to come to class five to ten minutes early, especially before the initial class meetings. This conditions students to expect to start on time and also provides opportunities to chat informally with them before class or for them to approach you about their concerns. Similarly, staying after class accomplishes educational as well as interpersonal objectives by allowing in-depth discussions of the content just presented. However, many students will not come up after class, and contact with some of these individuals will be possible only before the class begins.

Announced office hours are a traditional way of communicating accessibility to students, though only a minority will use them, and it is rare for a student to come by during the early weeks of the term. Because students expect college teachers to post office hours and want to know that they *can* come by without an appointment, it is very important to do this. However, being available over a large number of hours does not necessarily contribute to student perceptions of personal interest on the part of the instructor; two or three hours per week is usually sufficient. The last section of this chapter offers specific suggestions on ways to achieve maximum interpersonal and educational value from individual conferences with students.

In addition to being available during regular office hours, offer to schedule meetings at other times as well. Some instructors pass around a sign-up list each week for small groups of students wishing to have lunch with them at the students' dining hall or a local eatery. Students will take your interest in being accessible to them for questions or discussions more seriously if your home telephone number is listed on the course syllabus and you encourage them to call you in the evening and on weekends ("But never after 10:30 at night!"). Few students will call, but all will view the invitation as a serious indication of your commitment to communicate with them. The accessibility you offer will take little time in actuality and will be more than repaid by the positive attitudes you will create in the class as a whole.

Anything you can do to show interest in students as individuals will help to promote rapport. For example, one outstanding teacher I interviewed reported that he regularly scans the student newspaper (especially the letters to the editor and sports news) for the names of any of his students so that he can congratulate (or console) them or merely acknowledge seeing their name or letter. Other teachers make a special effort to attend athletic and artistic events in which their students are involved. Of course, for these techniques to be effective, a teacher's interest must be genuine.

Soliciting Feedback from Students

Giving students many opportunities to communicate and listening carefully to them can be valuable for a number of reasons (Barnes-McConnell, 1978). Interpersonal relationships require a dialogue, a two-way communication, so any teaching method that encourages students to communicate will help to form personal bonds. instructors are more likely to know when to clarify content or give emotional support if students feel free to raise their concerns. Some students need little encouragement, but active solicitation of feedback from all students will help to form and improve relationships with those who are less comfortable or who avoid contact.

One effective method of encouraging student communication is to begin the third week of class by handing out index cards and inviting students to ask a question about you or the course content or make a personal comment—anything they want to say about you, the course, or the subject. Stress that they are free to ask questions or comment anonymously, but that you will write a personal reply if they sign their names. Circulate more cards than students, and point out they can send in two cards (signed and unsigned) if they wish. Offering great latitude in the ways that students may respond (or not respond) to this opportunity for personal communication says implicitly that you care what they think but respect their privacy. This method makes it very easy for students to say what is on their minds. By writing personal notes in reply, you will complete the communication circle, strengthening the personal relationship. Some college teachers who use this method hand out cards as frequently as every third class meeting, but students become less interested in filling them out as the semester progresses. Using the technique after about two weeks of class and once again after seven or eight weeks (or whenever class morale seems low) is usually sufficient.

My experience is that student questions and comments are commonly divided about equally between substantive topics and personal subjects. When you answer their content questions, you obviously aid their learning. When a student comments on your style of presentation ("You mumble at the end of phrases" or "You jingle your keys in your pocket and it's distracting"), paying attention to the comment may improve your teaching. Even if students write, "I can't think of anything at this time," they are still relating to you. Most will ask important questions and will greatly appreciate the notes you write in reply. Using this technique to actively solicit comments from each student (including the quieter ones) in a nondemanding way provides useful feedback on your teaching and establishes the personal relationships with a class from which satisfaction and motivation spring.

A variation on the card technique that has become increasingly popular in recent years is the "minute paper." Occasionally ask students at the end of class to take a minute or two to jot down the topic in today's class that is most confusing or about which they are most excited. Ask whatever questions you wish, but keep them brief and focused. Minute papers are but one of a comprehensive array of classroom assessment techniques (Angelo and Cross, 1993) discussed in Chapter Seven that can yield important information on what students are learning as well as helping promote effective working relationships.

As important as fostering personal relationships and seeking feedback from students may be, they are insufficient for interpersonal success. College teachers must also be able to control classroom proceedings and motivate students to work. Students will be more motivated to please those who they believe care about them, but instructors also need effective methods of classroom leadership. The following section outlines some ways for classroom instructors to control students subtly through careful attention to the language chosen when trying to influence them.

Indirect Classroom Leadership

Some instructors believe that being liked by students and being firmly in charge are mutually exclusive—that students do not like teachers who control them, assign them challenging work, and evaluate it rigorously. Not only is it possible for college teachers to demand a great deal from students and still have positive interpersonal relationships with them, but it is also *necessary* for students to view teachers as being in control if the students are to be maximally satisfied with their leadership (Kinichi and Schriesheim, 1978). The key here is the choice of methods. As we shall see, indirect methods are almost always superior to direct or autocratic ones.

Does indirect control mean indicating that students should not worry about grades or exams and should learn only what they see as relevant? Not at all. Such a laissez-faire policy of classroom management fails to recognize that all students have a modicum of grading and learning orientation, need to master challenges and compete with peers, and differ in the style of leadership to which they respond best. The section after this one details ways in which students with different emotional needs, levels of intellectual development, and patterns of dealing with authority can be optimally motivated by varying the teacher's interpersonal approach. Indirect methods are ideal for such individualization.

The key to using indirect methods is to select words carefully when attempting to control students, suggesting and implying rather than ordering or directing. Indirect control is similar to the covert control exercised by the hypnotist or Zen master in that a college teacher lays verbal traps that control students' choices of behavior while giving the illusion of personal freedom (Bandler and Grinder, 1975). This sort of control is advantageous because it leads students to take responsibility for their own behavior—to become controlled from within—rather than expecting others to exercise overt control over them.

How is indirect control accomplished? In Chapter Two, the example of the complex messages an instructor can give when announcing a term paper illustrated the importance of the way an assignment is presented. When announcing a course assignment, college teachers emphasize the formal dimension of their relationship with students when they say "I require," "I expect," or "You must." In contrast, saying "I would like," "It is my hope," or "You will probably want" emphasizes the instructor as person rather than as authority. Using these words implies that the students will choose to do something because it is what they, or someone they like, wants rather than because they have been coerced. Word choice may seem trivial, but research in human communication has demonstrated that subtleties of language strongly influence the leadership relationships that develop in a group over time; such subtleties particularly influence the amount of resentment felt toward individuals in positions of power (Watzlawick, Beavin, and Jackson, 1967; Cousins, 1984). College teachers who use more egalitarian language promote independence among students and are at least as likely to have assignments completed as those who are more authoritarian.

Another way to control students indirectly is to give a rational justification for assignments. If students see the work asked of them as consistent with their own goals, they are less likely to respond to it simply as a frustrating task imposed by an educational authority. There are many sound reasons for a college teacher to formulate course objectives (see Chapter Seven), not the least of which is that sharing objectives with students makes them more likely to see an assignment as something they want to do rather than as something the instructor says they must do. The grading-oriented student is the typical product of an environment where the sole motivation is to meet an instructor's most overt demands.

Giving students choices whenever possible also increases their feeling of freedom in the classroom. This does not mean devoting the first few class meetings to the formulation of course objectives or the building of agreement on assignments for the purpose of enhancing the group's ownership of the course. It means giving students choices about a few decisions of much smaller consequence, such as whether to have an exam on a Monday or a Friday or whether to schedule a film during class or in the evening. Giving students choices between options that are consistent with the instructor's objectives and the available time tells them that their preferences are recognized and will be considered whenever possible; thus, interpersonal rapport and a learning orientation are also enhanced. At the same time, the fact that the instructor exempts important decisions about requirements from a class vote communicates to students that he or she is firmly in charge.

A final principle of indirect classroom leadership is making sure the students can walk before expecting them to run. As Mann and his colleagues have demonstrated, students need more structure at the beginning of a course and are more capable of independent learning in the later portions. Requiring mastery of instructor-defined content at the beginning and more independent thinking and choice of topics at the end is a traditional academic arrangement consistent with what has been learned recently about the "natural history" of college classes.

Treating Students Individually

There are certain students with whom instructors should make a special effort to establish positive interpersonal relationships. The following suggestions about ways to do this should not be taken as sure formulas for achieving rapport and optimal motivation. Rather, they are illustrations of techniques that a college teacher can use to individualize his or her approach to certain students. Such individualization, far from being unfair or producing negative effects in response to "unequal" treatment, helps all students work up to their academic potential in a course.

The Mann Group's Student Types

The student categories described below are based on the Mann group's research (1970) and expanded by my own informal observations. Though some of the Mann labels ("hero" and "sniper," for example) may seem disparaging, they are retained and used here because they are easily remembered and aptly capture the key emotional concerns of each group. No lack of respect toward any students is intended.

The typical *compliant student* is notably teacher-dependent, conventional, and highly task-oriented. Unlike other types, these students are comfortable with being dependent and are content simply to learn what the instructor wants them to know. Compliants speak in class most often to agree with the instructor or ask for clarification. They rarely pose problems or question the teacher's control. They are in class simply to understand the material. They often prefer lecture to discussion classes. Because they always do what is asked, compliant students usually do moderately well on exams, but they are unlikely to show much independence or creativity. As might be expected, the percentage of compliants (10 percent in the Mann sample) is greater among freshmen and steadily decreases with age. The most important characteristic of these students is that they are content to support the status quo and never question authority.

College teachers can help compliant students become more independent by initially accepting their dependency. Once the students come to believe that the instructor accepts them, the instructor can ask them to show more independence. For example, the teacher might write on an exam or paper, "You showed mastery of the material presented in class and assigned readings. Good work! I think you are now ready to add some of your own conclusions and critical evaluations to what you are learning so well. Include one or two of your own views next time, in addition to presenting what others have said. Keep up the good work." This strategy supports what is admirable and effective about the students' preferred style while encouraging them to grow toward independence and maturity.

Anxious-dependent students are very common (26 percent of the Mann sample) and can be spotted early by their excessive concern about grades. Like compliant types, anxious-dependents want to learn exactly what the teacher wants them to know—but these fear that they will miss something. They are likely to ask the teacher to repeat definitions so they can get them word for word. Compliant students generally trust teachers and assume that the grades they receive are justified. In contrast, anxious-dependent students distrust teachers and expect trick questions or unfair grading practices. Their combination of high ambition, anxiety, and suspiciousness suggests that they feel angry about having less power in the educational setting than they would like.

Anxious-dependent types frequently hold low opinions of their own ability, an evaluation not entirely unfounded; their verbal SAT scores were the lowest of the eight types studied by the Mann group. It is perhaps this self-doubt that leads them to make a great show of their academic effort. These students commonly come to exams looking frazzled and stay until the last possible moment, rechecking their answers or adding "just one more sentence" here and there. Because of their excessive anxiety and relatively limited abilities, their work is frequently unimaginative, mediocre, or erratic. It may be packed full of memorized details and definitions, but lacking in conceptual complexity. However, having their work evaluated poorly merely confirms their pessimistic expectancy, their belief that they have little independent power to succeed, and reinforces this pattern of overly anxious and dependent behavior. It is easy to understand why such students prefer lectures to discussion.

A teacher may easily become frustrated, angry, and rejecting of anxious-dependent students. Still, when one of these students whines, "But how are we supposed to know which of these names is important?" the wise teacher counts to ten. Responding angrily with, "Come now, you should be able to figure that out for yourself" increases the student's anxiety and solidifies his or her belief that the instructor really does see some names as "important" and others as "unimportant." A better response might be, "That's a good question. I guess some of the people mentioned in the book have had more impact on the field than others and are more important, but I hope everyone appreciates that they are all notable authors (scientists, artists, philosophers, or whatever). I would rather that you decide how they are similar and different and what impact they have had on each other than try to guess how I might decide to rank-order them." The essential message in this lengthy comment is that there is no correct answer to the student's question, but that the question is relevant. The comment does not reject the student for asking the question, but rather suggests a way to evaluate the persons being studied—and the comment is one useful for the entire class to hear.

Anxious-dependent students have a penchant for black-and-white distinctions, for simple right-or-wrong answers; a college teacher who expands their range of options aids their intellectual growth. Rejecting their questions or refusing to acknowledge their concerns simply raises their anxiety further and increases their need for specifics from the teacher. Suggesting a less dichotomous way of viewing the material, on the other hand, gives anxious-dependents reassurance while stimulating their intellectual development.

Discouraged workers, the Mann group's third category, make comments in class that communicate a depressed and fatalistic attitude toward themselves and their education. Like compliants and anxious-dependents, discouraged workers see themselves as having little control over their learning. Some may have worked so hard to earn high grades in the past that they no longer find learning pleasurable; they have burned out. Often, they are older students coming back to school after a stint in the military or the workforce or as homemakers, who find it hard to regain their youthful enthusiasm. Some have jobs or families and are more likely to be physically tired and preoccupied than the typical "college kid." Any of these circumstances can dampen curiosity and lead to joyless learning. Though classes appear to offer little pleasure to this small group of students (4 percent in the Mann sample), they can be made into active participants by an inspiring teacher.

Recognizing that certain students are chronically discouraged or resigned calls for a special effort to pick up their spirits. Written compliments on their best work (admittedly a difficult task if they have done poorly) are good, but face-to-face conversations are even better. The instructor should look for some excuse to engage them in small talk before class or ask them to stop by for a conference during office hours. Openly acknowledging that he or she has noticed their low morale or is aware that they are older than many students and wants to understand them better may be the best help a college teacher can give discouraged workers.

Independent students, the prototypical learning-oriented students, take what instructors have to offer and pursue their own goals in equal measure. They are comfortable (perhaps even detached or aloof) in doing what is asked of them, usually prefer seminar to lecture classes, and do not balk when asked to formulate their own thinking about a topic. The majority of independent students are high participators, make friends with instructors easily, and identify with them to some extent, much as many graduate students relate to their professors. They are ideal, mature students, the ones a teacher can count on to discuss and to perform at a consistently high level. In the Mann group's population, 12 percent of the students were in the independent group and, not surprisingly, they were more frequently juniors or seniors. Independent students rarely present problems for teachers, but if the quality of instruction is poor, they are most likely to be selected as spokespersons for the group's grievances. Independent students do not require much special attention other than the just deserts of their achievements. The instructor should acknowledge their independence and encourage them to use it to go beyond what might be expected of others. However, in some cases apparent independence may be a cloak for rebellion, and an instructor needs to discern this in order to relate to such students productively. The best test is their performance on structured tasks.

Heroes resemble independents in their identification with the teacher and their preference for independent or creative work. They lack the detachment of the independents, however, and seem anxious to make the teacher notice immediately what great students and interesting people they are. Most critically, heroes routinely fail to deliver on their initial promise. They are the erratic, optimistic underachievers who initially excite an instructor with their intensity and grand plans for independent projects, only to disappoint later with poor execution. Heroes would very much like to be the independent, creative students they see themselves as being, but some underlying hostility toward authority figures or inability to maintain their commitment to a goal prevents them from playing this role to the end. Ten percent of the Mann group's students fit this classification, and in my experience, almost every class has one or two.

Heroes make certain that the teacher notices them very early. They frequently stop by after the first class to let the instructor know how interested they are in the subject and how much first-hand knowledge of it they already have from previous reading or work experience. Their initial comments in class may impress the instructor and raise hopes that he or she has run across an unusually outstanding student. Heroes love discussion; they can be annoyingly argumentative, never admitting that they have lost a debate. Reflection on their comments, however, usually reveals that they have not done the assigned reading and are simply showing off previous knowledge or posing tangential questions that occur to them in class. Inexperienced instructors may be quite surprised at these students' poor performance on initial exams or papers. Heroes typically miss class more often than others once the novelty of the semester has worn off or they have begun to do poorly.

These examples suffice to make the point: heroes promise much but usually deliver little. This is particularly sad because they are usually quite capable students with very high expectations for themselves. Their failure to live up to their potential often results from a fear that they might not be able to live up to their heroic ideal even if they try their best. Because they typically make friends with the instructor right off, they can be enticed to perform more consistently by skillful handling. Still, they are unlikely to work up to their intellectual potential until their impulsive temperament is stabilized by increased maturity. Though most heroes have poor academic records in spite of their high SATs, so-called late bloomers in this group sometimes settle down during their junior and senior years and receive better grades. Heroes occasionally drop out of school to work for a year or two and return as more mature and better students with high graduate or professional aspirations. Heroes typically have high, even grandiose expectations for themselves, and many are capable of outstanding careers if they lower their expectations slightly and resolve their ambivalence about authority and achievement.

Giving heroes the independence they claim to desire almost never improves their performance; it reinforces the special attitude they hold about themselves without making them responsible for living up to it. It is better to encourage heroes to channel their energies into meeting the more structured requirements of the course first. For example, instead of letting them select a term paper topic more ambitious than that assigned to the whole class, the wise teacher will suggest that they use their special skills or insights to produce a tightly reasoned, well-written, polished paper on the common topic. Such a suggestion reinforces the high opinion these students have of themselves but says that they will not be free from the limits imposed on others and makes them less likely to attempt more than they can achieve.

Heroes are more likely to produce good work if given such special handling. To be successful in motivating heroes, a college teacher must maintain a good relationship with them over the term. Heroes are very prone to withdraw their initial investment in the course and put their energies elsewhere. If heroes believe that an instructor expects great things of them, they are more likely to live up to their own billing—but only if the instructor keeps close tabs on them and applies persistent, soft control.

A *sniper* is a hero who is hostile toward college teachers, unlikely to approach them, and filled with cynicism. Like heroes, snipers (9 percent in the Mann group) have very high expectations and positive images of themselves, but they have little hope that the world will recognize their worth or give them a fair chance to demonstrate it. Their hostility seems untempered by positive feelings. They are habitual rebels who sit as far from the instructor as possible and often comment with cutting remarks. Because they apparently feel guilty or fearful about their hostility, they retreat quickly when questioned about their sallies. Unlike heroes, who never seem to tire of debating, snipers strike their colors after the first salvo is fired.

The instructor's first task in forming positive relationships with snipers is—as with anxious-dependents—to control anger toward them. Their hostile comments often should simply be ignored. However, ignoring snipers does not break through their hostility, permitting a relationship that is likely to lead to work or change on their part. A more fruitful, but more difficult, approach is to respond enthusiastically to the snipers' comments, emphasizing what is positive and ignoring what is hostile. For example, suppose a sniper criticizes a nineteenth-century political leader for having racist, sexist, or elitist attitudes. The instructor might say in response: "That's an interesting point, and it raises an important dilemma for the historian: How can we look at distant events through the eyes of the people of that era, rather than coloring them with contemporary values? We will discuss historical methods again in a few weeks. For now, let me say that I very much sympathize with your concerns and I suggest that all of us try to imagine why this leader did what he did, given the way that he and many others of his time viewed the world." This response relates to the student's hostile comment to a critical issue in the field without rejecting the student. By expressing sympathy with the student's concern and suggesting that the whole class try to learn from it, the instructor also recognizes the student as a valuable class member. Admittedly, it is hard to respond at length to frequent sniper interruptions without showing irritation. Responding to some sniper comments and ignoring or laughing off others can reduce these students' hostility and make it easier for them to put forth their best efforts.

A smiling offensive—eagerly seeking them out—does not generally work well with snipers, especially early in the term. Approaching snipers makes them more uncomfortable, so they become more hostile in order to distance themselves from the instructor. A better strategy is to praise their class comments as much as possible, make lengthy and careful notes on their exams or papers, and wait vigilantly for chances to start personal conversations with them later in the course. By that point, they can sometimes tolerate short conversations of a personal nature, but even then they will seek out the instructor only rarely. As the Mann study showed, snipers do respect authority, and they will become even more hostile toward a college teacher they see as weak. The snipers' hostility stems from discomfort with authority figures and protects them from close contact with them, but such students may actually desire closeness and welcome someone who makes contact without scaring them away.

Attention-seeking students (11 percent in Mann's group) enjoy coming to class mostly to socialize with other students or the professor. Like heroes, they are fond of discussion; they love to talk. For them, social needs predominate over intellectual ones. They are pleasant to have in class, and many will form close personal relationships with an instructor. Attention-seeking students are capable of good work if it is made clear that they must work well in order to be well thought of by the instructor or other students. These students like to organize group review sessions or class parties. Thus, they fill a useful role in class as what is known in group dynamics literature as "social-emotional leaders." Attention-seekers are no less intelligent than other students, just less intellectual. However, like discouraged workers, they are easily influenced by others, and a skillful instructor can interest them in intellectual as well as social discourse.

Because instructor attention is so reinforcing to attention-seekers, they are relatively easy to motivate. An instructor should give them ample attention with no strings attached at first to assure them that he or she thinks well of them. Then the teacher should reduce the level of attention and show it mainly for their academic work, especially good work. This strategy effectively motivates most socially oriented students to take intellectual content more seriously while maintaining their interpersonal engagement.

In the classes studied by Mann and his colleagues, *silent students* (20 percent) made so few comments that they could not be classified into one of the other seven mathematical clusters. The Mann group observed classes with heavy discussion formats, in which not speaking was a more revealing characteristic than it might have been in larger classes. Given this context, it is not surprising that the Mann group's silent students proved to be similar to each other in additional ways. For example, their personal questionnaires and teacher evaluations revealed that they were acutely aware of the way the instructor behaved toward them. Of all the types, these students most wanted a close relationship and were most afraid that the instructor did not think highly of them and their academic work. Silent students respond to this fear with silence rather than hostility. Unlike snipers, silent students are usually aware of their desire for a personal relationship with the instructor. This makes them easier to reach.

The easiest mistake a college teacher can make with silent students is to ignore them, for they will not attract attention or pose problems. To guard against this, a good teacher goes through the class roster every few weeks, noting how each student has been behaving in recent meetings. Any students who have not made comments or approached the teacher individually by the end of the first third of the semester should be earmarked for special attention. Smiling warmly at them, walking to their part of the room before class, and making eye contact with them during lectures and discussions can help to bring them out. Silent students are often receptive to the direct suggestion that they come by during office hours or sign up for a lunch group to get acquainted. It is preferable to let them approach first, but if they have not done so well into the term, it is appropriate for the instructor to take the initiative.

The Mann group's student types reflect what is probably a developmental progression common to many college students in that freshmen were more likely to be compliants or anxious-dependents than seniors, who were more likely to be independents. Others have studied developmental changes over the college experience that are relevant to how students approach their intellectual work.

Developmental Patterns During College

William Perry's classic 1970 study of cognitive (and accompanying ethical) development speaks to a common progression from passive, instructor-centered student to more independent student-centered learner over four years of college. Marcia Baxter Magolda's (1992) epistemological elaboration of Perry's system is particularly impressive. On the basis of her ambitious longitudinal study of 101 students over their four years of college (and beyond, for some of them), she details their various patterns of progression from students who believe in absolute knowledge handed down by an authority to those who see knowledge as something one constructs and evaluates independently or in interaction with others. Magolda's identification of gender-related subthemes within each of these stages—for example, a focus on receiving rather than on mastery of absolute knowledge, or on independent knowing acquired individually or in collaboration with others—are especially interesting.

She concludes from analyzing her numerous student interviews that just because females and males as *groups* develop along parallel and equally complex intellectual lines, many *individual* females and males will show opposite or mixed styles of thinking about knowledge as they progress through the four broad stages. Most significantly, Magolda's research suggests that the males and females who eventually show contextual thinking—the ability to critically evaluate knowledge from various sources, often in collaboration with others—come to resemble each other more than they differ.

The Mann group's system focuses on underlying emotional development (rather than the cognitive patterns studied by Perry and Magolda) and includes more than one immature pattern. Yet the parallels within the various studies of developmental changes suggest a coherence to the kinds of maturity many students show during their college experience. Like any developmental or personality typology, however, group generalizations risk glossing over significant individual variability. Every college instructor occasionally encounters an unusually mature freshman and all too often an immature senior.

Unfortunately, we do not have data that adequately address the question of what it is about the college years that accounts for these changes. Is it the teaching students receive? Is it the out-of-class social and leadership experiences? Or is it simply the maturing process of moving into young adulthood from late adolescence—the kinds of changes that would also be seen in young people after four years of military service or challenging vocational experience away from home? Magolda assumes teachers have some control over development when she suggests key instructor behaviors that should be beneficial for students at different stages of intellectual growth—for example, demonstrating helpfulness with students who still believe that they must master absolute knowledge, and creating opportunities for critical thinking and peer collaboration for independent-stage students. For each stage, she advocates teaching strategies that promote active involvement on the part of students, giving them opportunities to interact with the instructor and with each other. She also emphasizes the importance of demonstrating concern for students. Given the consistency of her recommendations and the mixture of students present in most classes, the strongest practical implication of her developmental categories is to aim for this kind of teaching in all classes.

Students Under Special Pressure

Some students enter classrooms under considerably more pressure than others. Though few college teachers advocate assigning less work to such students or grading their work differently, these students do require special understanding if they are to perform maximally. Regardless of the source of the pressure, the instructor's strategy should be the same in all cases: recognize the added challenges these students face and communicate empathy with them. The teacher should not think of them as victims needing remediation or reduce requirements for them; students are likely to be insulted by such stigmatization (Steele, C. M., 1992; Steele, S., 1990). Forming a good relationship with them, being a willing listener without dwelling on their specific condition or asking less of them, and communicating genuine confidence in their ability to succeed is normally all the teacher needs to do (Davis, 1993).

Which students are under unusual pressure? In the following, I have expanded on a list proposed by Barnes-McConnell (1978). Students with chronic physical disabilities, diseases, or learning disabilities are obviously overcoming a greater number of obstacles to attend college (see Davis, 1993, for a comprehensive treatment of disabilities). At some point early in the semester, the instructor may ask if these students will need special consideration in connection with examinations, laboratory work, or field trips. Students under treatment for emotional problems also may need an especially understanding relationship, though it is important not to reinforce their symptoms by offering to exempt them from requirements.

Other high-pressure groups to consider are identifiable minorities in class or on campus. Students of minority races, genders (that

is, men on predominantly female campuses and women on predominantly male campuses), sexual orientations, or religions greatly
appreciate an instructor who acknowledges them as individuals.
They are *not* likely to enjoy being called upon in class to speak "for"
their group. Even students who choose to emphasize their minority
identity in their class comments wish also to be seen as capable of
contributing ideas about other issues. A survey of faculty behaviors
most important to the quality of student-professor relationships
showed that students ranked "treating students equally regardless of
sex and race" at the top (Walsh and Maffei, 1994). Most minority
students want simply to be treated like other students, to be given
an equal chance to participate in classroom discussions, and to
receive appropriate attention in the curriculum.

Freshmen are under unusual pressure, too. They are especially
likely to feel uncertain at first and to need extra structure and reassurance from teachers. At the other end of the age dimension, older
and single-parent students with family or work responsibilities also
typically face added challenges. They greatly appreciate the instructor's recognition that by their greater maturity and experience they
can make a valuable contribution to the class. Some faculty rank
the opportunity to form mentoring relationships with the growing
numbers of older students on their campuses among their greatest
sources of teaching satisfaction (Daloz, 1987). Other groups to keep
in mind are upwardly mobile students who are the first in their families to attend college, students on athletic teams (which require
extensive time commitments and occasional missed classes), and
students supporting themselves financially.

Students with Unusual Academic Abilities

It is especially important for college teachers to form personal relationships with students at the extremes of academic ability. Identifying such students is rarely easy, but the level of complexity and
abstract thinking displayed in class comments and on exams provides
useful clues. Especially bright students—the truly gifted, not merely
the high-achieving "grinds"—are vulnerable to boredom and apt to

slack off if they fail to find a class intellectually challenging. Besides offering stimulating lectures, instructors should actively cultivate personal relationships with these students and encourage them to think independently or creatively about the subject. They will resent extra make-work assignments, but they may welcome recognition of their talent and encouragement to read advanced works on their own. Some instructors invite very bright students to come by regularly to discuss their independent reading or ideas on the common work. Grades should not be given for such work; the teacher should let the students' satisfaction of their own curiosity and the pleasure of discussion suffice as reinforcement (Lowman, 1990b).

It is equally important to pay special attention to the student who finds college work extremely challenging or even overwhelming. Such students almost always work hard at their studies, and they are not likely to be helped by admonitions to work harder. Specific guidance on ways to study and organize material is more likely to support their struggle (Davis, 1993). The instructor should recognize their difficulty and empathize with their fear of flunking out of school but reassure them that doing well in college is not the only important thing in the world. He or she should teach these students as much as they can learn and support their efforts to survive this demanding enterprise. For some students, eventual failure may provide the needed understanding that higher education, or at least some aspects of it, is not for them.

In sum, when forming personal relationships with different kinds of students, college teachers need to apply a variety of interpersonal strategies, even though all students are assigned the same work and graded using identical criteria. To motivate each student fully, we must necessarily modify the approach we use.

Other Interpersonal Issues

Three additional topics, loosely related to each other and all within the interpersonal realm, are presented in this section: relating to students during office hours, especially those students asking—

implicitly or explicitly—for extended counseling; the ethics of teaching, including the question of love and sex between teacher and student; and the importance of teacher tolerance of adolescent behavior. Some of the suggestions given here are adapted from Wilbert McKeachie's *Teaching Tips* (1986) and Barbara Davis's *Tools for Teaching* (1993).

Individual Meetings with Students

Even in small classes, most students will not drop by during office hours or call on the telephone. When one does, the way the instructor reacts will determine whether the student finds the venture satisfying or feels frustrated, even punished, for risking a one-to-one encounter (Eble, 1988). To begin with, an instructor should *always* be present during his or her posted office hours. Dropping by a professor's office is rarely a casual action for a student. To prepare oneself to appear "between 1:30 and 2:30 on Wednesdays or Fridays" and then find the door locked or standing open with no sign of the instructor or an explanatory note is disappointing, if not anger-provoking.

Nonverbal communications to students in the office are even more important than those in class. Offices are seen by students as very much "teacher territory," and entering them often stimulates authority conflicts. Consequently, it is imperative at least to *seem* eager to see a student, even if one is preoccupied with a research project or must leave for a committee meeting in fifteen minutes. Some instructors act impatient or irritated when a student interrupts their work. I had a colleague several years ago who was fully aware of this behavior and remarked that he used it "to make the students more independent and keep them from bothering me too much." Instructors may fear that students will take inappropriate advantage of their time, but if they wish to maintain high interpersonal rapport with students, college teachers must be skillful in the ways they limit accessibility.

How can an instructor seem eager to see a student who drops by right at the end of, or even outside of, office hours? The teacher might say something like, "Hi, Josh, I'm glad you stopped by. I'm sorry I only have a couple of minutes right now. Which would you rather do, talk briefly now or longer in a couple of days?" If given such a choice, the student is much more likely to feel that the instructor is in fact interested in talking with him than he would be if the instructor simply said that office hours were over or that he or she did not like to see students outside posted hours. A pleasant message is at least as likely to control a student effectively as a curt one. Similar considerations apply to telephone calls received at inconvenient times. Obviously, no one can be available any time a student wishes, and limits must be imposed. But there are many ways to set appropriate limits without appearing to reject students for wanting to see their instructor and taking the (for them) big step of stopping by.

What are some things to consider when meeting with a student when ample time *is* available? Two aspects of the instructor's behavior are especially important: whether the instructor relates to the student as superior to subordinate or as adult to adult, and whether the instructor assumes that the student's chief purpose in coming is revealed in the first topic he or she brings up.

College teachers may unknowingly emphasize their power over students during office meetings. A common way of doing this is by appearing indifferent when students drop by to see them. Some teachers avoid eye contact as a student stands at the door or enters. Some provide a place for students to sit that is distant from them or across a large and imposing desk. Answering phone calls or responding to colleagues in the hall as if the student were not there or without saying, "Excuse me" also tells a student that he or she is not considered important.

To de-emphasize status differences and promote a sense of confidentiality, some instructors stand when students enter their offices, show them to a seat, offer to take their coats, or practice other common courtesies of our culture, and close their office doors as they would during any important meeting. Others find such actions too formal and prefer to behave more casually. Any courteous style that is personally comfortable for the instructor is likely to be effective. A conference in the atmosphere created by such behavior facilitates the development of a person-to-person relationship by downplaying the elements of hierarchy.

Reasons that prompt students to visit a teacher vary immensely. Many students are concerned about their performance on exams or papers. Occasionally, students drop by in anticipation of doing poorly, but more usually they come after graded work has been returned. Anxious-dependents are especially likely to come by to express concern about grades, almost regardless of what marks they receive.

Other students may visit for a variety of reasons. Compliant students, for example, may come by to have the teacher check the outline of a term paper; independents or heroes may come to share some insight they have had about the subject or a proposed project; and attention-seekers may want to chat or reveal personal things about themselves. By their choice of ostensible reason for coming, by the confidence or anxiety they show, and by the dependence or independence they assume, students will reveal what they expect from the instructor in a given meeting. They may also attempt to maneuver the teacher into treating them as they expect.

How can a teacher best handle these hidden agendas in student conferences? It is best to be accepting and egalitarian and also not to assume that a student's first statement about why he or she has come is a sufficient reason for the call. If the teacher waits patiently and lets a student talk or ask questions freely, he or she may be able to guess the student's underlying concern or interpersonal strategy. Then the teacher can respond in a way that both affirms the legitimacy of the student's desire and gently pressures him or her toward a more independent and assured attitude.

A teacher should not let an emotional response to a student's remarks dictate his or her behavior. The instructor who becomes angry or defensive about grading practices when a student questions a grade does not foster a relationship that is conducive to good work or aid the student's subsequent study. Those who calmly listen to the student's complaint, indicate that they can see why the student might feel that way, and then reread the answers or paper in question communicate to the student that his or her concerns are taken seriously—even if the grade is allowed to stand as originally given. It is important that a teacher not feel guilty about a student's failure or identify to excess with a hardworking student's desire for an A. As has been stressed throughout this chapter, an instructor's ability to be aware of and control his or her personal feelings is the first ingredient in fostering interpersonal rapport with students.

The emphasis throughout this book is on warm interpersonal relationships with students, but instructors still should set limits on recurring personal conferences. Students may on occasion raise topics of immense personal concern with their college teachers. For example, they may express the fear that they are going crazy or will kill themselves, or they may report serious incidents or describe ongoing conflicts with roommates, dates, friends, or family members. Troublesome eating or sexual behavior or substance problems also are sometimes revealed. Students talk about their personal troubles primarily to instructors they like and trust, so a teacher should feel complimented if a student brings a personal concern to him or her. A college teacher needs no special training or professional skills to listen to what are usually transiently troubling problems (Strupp, 1980). The teacher should encourage students to talk about what is bothering them, but only on one or, at the most, two occasions.

An instructor should advise students to speak with a professional counselor if their problems are interfering seriously with their academic functioning, if they want to change their behavior or improve a conflicted relationship, or if their health or lives are in danger from suicidal impulses, drug or alcohol difficulties, or physical or sexual abuse by another. In order to deal with such problems, a student needs to form a specific counseling relationship. Even instructors who are trained as therapists or counselors avoid becoming involved in recurring counseling sessions with their own students. If counseling sessions are to be helpful, the counseling relationship must be clearly defined by both participants as existing *only* for that purpose, and the evaluative role of a college teacher rules out completely the possibility of formal counseling.

Ethics of Teaching

College teachers are responsible for controlling the considerable power they have over students and ensuring that it is used only to achieve educational objectives. Not surprisingly, written ethical codes for college teachers do exist. For example, the ethical guidelines of the American Psychological Association (APA) include codes designed to protect students from various forms of abuse or exploitation, such as requiring students to reveal personal information that might be used selfishly by instructors as research data (although having students collect or generate data in order to teach research methods or content is deemed appropriate). The deciding question should be, "Does the activity (laboratory or library research, field observations) fulfill *educational objectives* for the students?"

An excellent case book on teaching ethics prepared by the APA's teaching division offers illustrative examples for teachers of any discipline (Keith-Spiegel and others, 1993). Ethical guidelines do *not* set limits on instructors' ability to give disquieting information to students for the purpose of stimulating them to think about both sides of complex issues, but they do urge college teachers to respect students as persons and avoid being gratuitously shocking or provocative.

Most college teachers could state their personal ethical admonitions, and I will propose two. The first is that teachers should ensure that evaluation and grading are as fair and objective as possible. The second is that it is *under no circumstances* appropriate for a teacher to become romantically or sexually involved with a student, even if the relationship is initiated by the student or the contact comes within a year after the end of the course. Here are my reasons for taking this position.

All students are prone, and some students especially so, to react to college teachers—even youthful graduate instructors—as symbols of authority figures in their lives, notably their parents. Though no teacher-student relationship is likely to have the intensity of a psychotherapeutic transference relationship, romance between instructor and student is no more likely to be mutual or rationally chosen than is romance between therapist and client. The difference in power is simply too great for a truly mutual relationship to develop. The student is responding to the instructor more as a powerful symbol than as an individual, and the instructor is likely to be using the less powerful student to meet a variety of selfish needs such as distraction, denial of aging, or affirmation of attractiveness.

An instructor implicitly or explicitly requesting sex for a grade would be rightly damned in anyone's ethical code, but as Eble (1988) notes, this is much less common than romantic involvement between discrepantly powerful participants. The most common type of attachment is one-sided: a student develops a crush on a professor or has frequent sexual fantasies about him or her. If an instructor suspects that a student has such romantic feelings, he or she should try to limit individual contacts with that student and discourage a more involved relationship. However, the teacher should not respond by giving the student less attention in class than is given to others. College teachers may also have romantic or sexual fantasies about students on occasion, but private fantasies need not lead to overt behavior. The best ways to prevent a blurring of professional and personal relationships is to avoid any personal interest in a student that might be misinterpreted and to meet with students outside of class in small groups (Davis, 1993).

Certainly, lasting and satisfying relationships have been formed between individuals who originally met as student and teacher, and this fact makes controversial the attempts on some campuses to proscribe any romantic contact at any time. However, even if an instructor believes that he or she has found in a student a potential life partner, the worst possible time to begin the relationship is when the student is enrolled in that teacher's class, or in the immediately ensuing months. Both should wait until well after the end of the professional teacher-student relationship before exploring the personal relationship further. Each person will then be in a position to respond freely as an adult and to avoid misinterpretations of innocent behavior as sexual harassment. Waiting also allows for the "glow" of the professorial relationship to fade, ensuring that a romantic relationship can then begin on a firmer ground.

Teacher Tolerance of Youthful Behavior

Between the ages of eighteen and twenty-one, most men and women complete the process of separation from their families that was begun in their early teens. The open struggles with parents during early adolescence result in increased physical freedom, but it is the private skirmishes of late adolescence that free individuals from the emotional vulnerability of childhood. Relationships with other adults during this period (teachers, military officers, work supervisors) provide a useful setting in which to learn how to relate to important others as an adult.

Outstanding teachers have often expressed the sentiment that to be a great classroom instructor one must genuinely like college-age students and identify with their interests, both serious and foolish (Highet, 1950). Appreciating the emotional tasks facing students puts their sometimes inappropriate, immature, or even self-destructive behavior into a perspective that makes it more tolerable. Remembering personal excesses when one was at a similar age can curb tendencies to judge students too quickly. An instructor who likes college students and accepts their interests will find enjoyable the time he or she is required to spend with them and value even more the greater time needed to have a significant impact on their lives.

The suggestions presented in this chapter are based on the position that common emotional reactions will appear in college classrooms regardless of what the instructor does. Instructors familiar with these phenomena, aware of their own expectancies and contributions to them, and skilled at communicating will be able to individualize their approach to students so as to avoid stimulating negative emotions and to promote warm and work-conducive relationships with all. Knowing what emotional phenomena are likely to occur in the classroom over a term also prevents the dissatisfaction that results from incorrectly labeling transient behavior as permanent. The ultimate argument for interpersonally skillful teaching is that most college teachers enjoy classes more when they have good personal relationships with students, and this satisfaction has a beneficial effect on the quality of their instruction.

The preceding two chapters have dealt exclusively with maintenance or emotional concerns in classroom groups. The next two chapters deal with task concerns: the techniques of speaking before groups that teachers need to learn in order to utilize the classroom as a dramatic arena; and ways of organizing lecture content for maximum impact and learning.

4

Analyzing and Improving
Classroom Performance

*Drama critic John Lahr (1973) argues that drama
encompasses more than plays on the conventional
stage; in his view, drama also includes the highly
engaging and emotionally stimulating performances
witnessed by thousands in the form of sports specta-
cles, rock concerts, or symbolic political gestures such
as draft card burnings and self-immolations.*

This chapter is based on the premise that college classrooms are
dramatic arenas first and intellectual arenas second. Its objectives are to sensitize the reader to the critical importance of communication skills in college teaching, to describe those skills fully,
and to help an instructor evaluate and improve his or her performance in this area. Mastering traditional stage skills is in no way
sufficient to attain excellence in teaching, but it is impossible to
attain such excellence without considerable practice and comfort
with these skills. The chapter that follows (Chapter Five) deals with
the specifics of choosing and organizing lecture content and should
be read in tandem with this chapter.

College Classrooms as Dramatic Arenas

The fundamental structure of drama—speaker or speakers before an audience, captivating their attention and stimulating their emotions—is universal in human experience. The spell of drama has been wielded in innumerable ways, both formal and informal. It has worked through the tribal storyteller and epic poetry, through Greek comedy and Elizabethan tragedy, through nineteenth-century opera and modern existential theater.

Even when the purpose of a gathering is not explicitly dramatic, speakers require the skills of the stage in order to be successful. Religious, military, and political leaders must be able to attract and hold an audience's attention if the message they convey is to have its desired impact (Stevens, 1966). If the speaker's skill is great, his or her presentation will create the involvement and feeling of suspense associated with theater. College teachers, too, need dramatic skills to ensure that students become fully engaged in class presentations and find them memorable as well as instructive.

In what ways do classrooms resemble theatrical settings? Many classrooms have stages or raised platforms in the front of the hall, and there is frequently some kind of overhead stage lighting. Furthermore, the overwhelming proportion of college teaching follows a lecture format in which the instructor stands before an audience of up to several hundred students. Although teachers of large classes are relatively more dependent on speaking skills than are leaders of seminars, all college teaching is fundamentally public speaking.

College teaching is different from religious, military, or political leadership, but it is leadership nonetheless; and though it is far more than dramatic entertainment, it should resemble drama in being engaging and pleasurable. College teachers develop more involved relationships with their audiences than is possible from single appearances on the theater or lecture circuit, and instructors play themselves rather than having assigned roles. Still, teachers share with other speakers a fundamental reliance on an ability to engage an audience and to stimulate emotions.

Effective communication in no way ensures that a college professor will promote wisdom or stimulate intellectual growth in students. Professors—and the public at large—rightly have long distrusted speakers who appeal to the emotions for the purpose of closing rather than opening avenues of inquiry. But distrust of demagoguery does not require that the college teacher avoid developing the skill to speak powerfully and persuasively to students. Sound arguments are the prime ingredient of a fine lecture, but the skill with which they are delivered should be equal to the skill with which they were prepared if they are to have maximum impact on students.

Using Emotion in Lecturing

Capturing an audience's attention—or "taking hold" (Balthrop, 1993)—is the first thing required of any performer, college teachers included. Almost all students will pay attention to an instructor for a few minutes, but most students will not continue to listen actively to a mediocre lecturer, any more than they would be responsive to a mediocre theatrical performance beyond the opening moments. But eliciting and maintaining attention is only a first step.

College teachers need to stimulate emotion, but their purpose in doing so differs from that of entertainers. The entertainer's goal is to stimulate emotion for its own sake, while the classroom instructor uses emotion to engage students' attention fully in the content or learning exercises selected for consideration and to transfer to them his or her own passionate interest in the subject.

Like most of us, college students remember images longer than they remember words, and instructors can aid recall by pairing abstract content with emotionally tinged associations and vivid images whenever possible. Expressive speech, including changes in facial expressions and in voice volume, also helps to punctuate a presentation and emphasize the organization of the lecturer's ideas.

In addition to using positive emotions, skilled instructors avoid stimulating negative emotions such as anger, anxiety, or—perhaps especially—boredom. The best way to keep students from being bored by a subject is to show them that *you* are not bored by it. Some professors can make anything interesting, primarily by conveying their own excitement about the topic. At the other extreme, some instructors show so little emotion when discussing their subject that their students may wonder why the professors bothered to learn it themselves. College students, like most other reasonable adults, are generally able to spot the shallow or fraudulent instructor who relies on emotional appeals to gloss over a superficial understanding of content or to present information or arguments in a slipshod manner. They will, however, respect and respond to a teacher's genuine enthusiasm.

Improving Classroom Communication Skills

College professors can be effective classroom teachers in spite of physical disabilities. Most could continue to teach from a wheelchair or even after losing sight or hearing. However, unless a teacher had students who understood signing, it would be almost impossible to continue teaching after losing his or her voice. Yet almost all instructors take their speech for granted. Unless they have a significant speech problem such as stuttering or speaking too softly to be heard, few college teachers evaluate the effectiveness of their speaking voice or actively work to improve it.

Instructors may also be unaware of the importance of their gestures and movements to their communication effectiveness. Students respond to what they see as well as to what they hear and, like speech, body movement can enhance or distract from the intended message.

The purpose of this section is to present a framework within which an instructor can evaluate his or her speaking voice and movements before groups and to suggest exercises that may help in overcoming common weaknesses. The aim here is not to give professors the expressive range of James Earl Jones or Vanessa Redgrave but merely to describe what ordinary teachers can do to improve their communication skills in the classroom.

Increasing Sensitivity to Others' Speech

The first step in improving one's own speaking voice is to pay serious attention to the ways others use their voices in group settings (Machlin, 1966). Notice the variety of others' speech. Some people speak slowly and deliberately and others with speed and impetuosity; some speak softly, others with loud projection. Still others present great variety and change between these extremes. The tone of speech probably varies most, from deeply resonant to high or shrill. Tune, the musical quality resulting from patterns of rising and falling tones, also varies. More than anything, you will notice differences in the amount of energy speakers convey. Voices and speech styles are almost as unique as physical appearance.

You are also likely to notice how certain speech habits distract you from the ideas being presented (Satterfield, 1978). Some speakers habitually begin sentences with meaningless vocalization such as "Uh," "Well," "You know," or "Okay," as if their vocal cords could not begin to vibrate without a warm-up. Speakers are often unaware of how much their speech is interrupted by such unnecessary sounds. When observing one novice college teacher, I was so struck by her habit of beginning sentences with "Okay" that I made an informal count over the remainder of a fifty-minute class. In discussing her lecture afterwards, I commented on her use of "okay." She agreed that she said it a lot, estimating that she had used the word "about ten times" during her talk. The actual count was over seventy-five!

Other speech qualities also distract listeners. For example, some instructors speak in such low tones or with such poor articulation that listeners become fatigued from the effort needed to grasp what is being said. At the other extreme, rapid speech or speech delivered in staccato bursts also can be tiring to the hearer, especially if no breaks occur. Others reveal a lack of confidence by frequently ending sentences with a drop in volume to an inaudible level or with an elevation in emphasis and pitch that implies they are asking a question. Anything about vocal delivery that takes the listener's attention away from the content of the speaker's remarks will distract from the overall effectiveness of the communication (Sprague and Stuart, 1992).

You have probably noticed that some speakers' voices are easier and more enjoyable to listen to than others. From the first few phrases, some voices capture the ear and produce a warm glow of anticipated pleasure, while others create almost a dread of what is to come (Machlin, 1966).

What voice qualities contribute to these markedly different effects? Foremost among them is *pitch*. The degree to which the voice varies in pitch is critical to engaging speech. A voice ranging melodically between high and low tones is much more likely to keep listeners' attention than a monotonous voice that merely uses one or two notes. The way a speaker uses *inflection*, giving more emphasis to some words than to others, also contributes to audience interest. Speech with little or no emphasis is unlikely to engage and retain attention.

Even something as subtle as the timing of a speaker's breathing can contribute to the overall quality of the speaking voice. Silent or barely audible inhalations occurring at the ends of major phrases are less likely to interrupt the flow of ideas than noisy inhalations occurring in the middle of important sentences. Ironically, some political speakers seem especially prone to break up their speeches with unnecessary pauses (Henry Kissinger is one example).

Though more difficult to pin down than other characteristics, the degree to which speech conveys a sense of relaxed energy contributes significantly to its overall effect on listeners. When speakers have a relaxed or flowing style, when their speech seems to come easily, we say they are fluent. Energetic speech shows more than smoothness, however. Words delivered with energy convey a sense of purpose, or focused movement, which engages listeners' attention to follow wherever they lead. Hesitant or jerky speech does not show focused energy and is more likely to cause listeners to share the speaker's tension, discomfort, or lack of confidence.

Noticing how differences in others' speech affect you is the first step in improving your own speaking voice. Next, shift your focus to the visual dimension and note the role of gesture and movement in presentations.

Increasing Sensitivity to Others' Movements

If we can "turn off" our hearing while observing college instructors, we are certain to see individuals whose movement styles are almost as varied as their speech styles. Starting with the face, we are certain to note differences in expression ranging from stiff poker faces to exaggerated mugging. Extent of eye contact will also vary: some teachers appear to look mainly at the ceiling, the walls, or the floor—anywhere but at their students—whereas others meet their students' eyes frequently. We might see stiff, wooden figures solidly planted for long periods at single spots on the floor, with arms locked behind in a parade rest position or folded in front in a perpetual self-hug. Or we might see fluid figures step out from behind the lectern and stroll purposefully across the front of the classroom, stop occasionally and turn to face the audience, even dart down the middle or side aisles. Speakers' gestures are also certain to vary: arms and hands move away from the body for emphasis, or hands are stuffed in pockets or appear stiffly frozen to the body or lectern. Simply by the way they stand—shoulders back, head erect, eyes looking directly at students' faces—some instructors convey confidence in what they have to say. In contrast, a slumped-over posture and avoidance of eye contact communicate uncertainty and discomfort. At times subtle, at times sweeping, speakers' movements and gestures can be coordinated with their speech to communicate as eloquently, and with as much energy and expressiveness, as their words—or they may be random or unconnected.

Gesture and movement can also be distracting, however. Most of us are unaware of the habits most of our students notice and some find annoying (Sprague and Stuart, 1992). Common examples are rattling change or keys in pockets, fiddling with jewelry or hair, nervously smoothing wrinkles from skirts, or frequently scratching ears or noses. Several years ago, my wife presented me with a nice new pen with a cap, on condition that I throw away my ballpoint pens with "clickers" on the top. She had decided it was time to rid me of my bad habit of clicking my pen rhythmically when speaking before groups, an annoying habit of which I was totally unaware. Fortunately, we need not depend on others' helpful concern to eliminate distracting communication habits. All we need do is analyze a videotape recording of ourselves speaking before a group.

Recording and Analyzing Your Speech and Movement

Communication teachers agree that a detailed analysis of a videotape recording is an essential step in deciding how one's voice and gestures can be improved. The following method is adapted from those advocated by others (for example, Machlin, 1966) and refined on the basis of my experience with college instructors. (Chapter Ten presents additional suggestions on how to use videotape recordings of actual classroom teaching in self-assessment and development. The discussion here deals with recordings of short, practice communications.) I recommend that you make *two* video recordings of yourself speaking to a friend, one in conversation and one in role-played teaching. In a small or moderate-size classroom, assemble basic video recording equipment—or ask staff running your faculty taping service to do it for you—and ask a friend to join you there. If your friend also wants to study his or her communication, you can take turns.

For the first tape, start the recorder, face your friend, and begin a simple conversation by stating your name, your age, and where you were born. Then pick some topic that interests you—a recent movie, book, or sporting event you liked or hated, for example— and for four or five minutes tell your friend how you feel about it. Instruct your companion beforehand to ask short questions or respond briefly to what you say if he or she wishes, especially if you stop talking. The objective of this exercise is to record yourself talking in a natural, conversational style for a few minutes. (If both of you are participating in this self-assessment, put in a new cassette and reverse roles.)

For the second recording, stand about fifteen feet from your seated partner and give a short lecture of five to ten minutes' duration on some topic you might cover in a college course. If each of you is making a recording, be sure to put your second session on the same cassette as your first.

Do not listen to either of your recordings right away. A few days later, set aside an hour for your analysis. The following steps may be useful in structuring your assessment of the recordings:

1. Watch and listen to each recording without stopping to take notes.

2. Afterward, note your initial reactions to hearing and seeing yourself speak. What are your feelings (puzzled, pleased, ashamed, pessimistic, defensive, critical)? Try not to let your initial reactions, whatever they may be, discourage you.

3. Turning away so that you cannot see the television screen, *listen* to the first (the conversational) recording a second time and jot on a piece of paper the words that seem to best describe your voice. Try to think of it as a voice you have never heard before. *Stop at the end of the conversational recording.*

4. Rewind the tape and listen to the conversation segment for a third time. Using the Communication Assessment Rating Form (Exhibit 4.1 at the end of this chapter), rate your speech along each of the eight voice dimensions. Do not be too concerned about selecting a particular number on the scale, but note where in general you believe your voice fell on each dimension.

5. Now, rate the lecture segment using the same listening-only procedure.

6. Consider differences in your speech in the two situations. Was it more relaxed and spontaneous when in the informal setting? Did your speech become tighter and higher-pitched when you were lecturing? Was it louder and more precisely articulated when you lectured? In which setting were you more fluent, more enthusiastic? Any differences you note will help you decide how to improve.

7. Rewind your cassette to the beginning and turn down the sound on the monitor. Watch the silent first segment, stop the machine, and rate your gestures and movement using the six visual dimensions on the rating form.

8. Observe and rate the second segment using the visual dimensions.

9. Contrast your movement ratings for the two segments. Were your facial expressions more natural, did you make more eye contact, and was your posture looser when engaged in conversation? Did your hands and arms move in close to your body and become less expressive when you lectured? Did your whole body seem more involved in one setting than in the other? As with your speech ratings, differences you note between the two segments may help you decide what can be improved.

10. Finally, wait a few hours—even overnight—and watch both segments again back-to-back. Rate each segment on the

global dimensions of energy and involvement. Note: (1) any distracting or annoying speech or movement habits you would like to reduce, if not remove completely; (2) any voice patterns, facial expressions, or gestures you especially like and may want to use more often; and (3) the speech and movement qualities you would like to change. For example, you might be disappointed to hear how often you say, "you know," or to see how infrequently you make eye contact with your audience. But you may really like the way you sometimes pause, tilt your head to one side, and raise your eyebrows to communicate a questioning attitude and will want to include this gesture more often. You might also decide that your speech needs to sound more relaxed and that your posture needs to become straighter and more confident.

For your self-assessment to lead to improved communication, you need to formulate a specific plan for improvement. There are several ways to do this. The best method is to take the tapes and rating forms to a speech coach or faculty development staff member at your teaching center for review and critique. You might also work with another instructor whom you consider to be an especially effective speaker. You can even work with a colleague who also is interested in improving his or her communication—perhaps the person who helped you with the taping exercises.

Regardless of who else listens to your recordings, *you* must make the final decision about what, if anything, needs improvement. It is important to note that no *single* voice or movement quality (other than distracting habits, perhaps) will determine listeners' interest when you speak. Rather, the overall energy, variety, and expressiveness seen in your communication is the critical thing. A speaker whose voice is sometimes loud, sometimes soft, sometimes fast, sometimes slow, sometimes sharp and crisp, and sometimes mellow and melodic is more likely to keep an audience's attention than one whose voice has any one quality for too long. Similarly, the speaker who is sometimes stationary and sometimes moving, or the one who uses a variety of genuine gestures rather than a few taken from stock, is more likely to engage and keep an audience's attention.

Remember that the impact of your communication on your audience may have as much to do with what you are feeling when you speak as with the technical qualities of your presentation. If you are enthusiastic and eager to tell your audience what you know, they are more likely to be enthusiastic about hearing it. If you are fascinated by the topic at hand, they are likely to have their curiosity aroused, too. If you are confident about a group discussion topic or in-class writing exercise and eager to see how your students handle it, they are more likely to participate actively. In addition to selecting specific speech or movement characteristics to change, it is wise to attempt to experience what you wish your students to feel and trust your voice and body to model it for them.

The following section discusses a number of common speech weaknesses that can be improved. Most college teachers report feeling anxious on occasion when speaking to their classes, especially early in the term and early in their career (Gardner and Leak, 1994), so do not be too concerned about what may be simple nervousness. For best results with serious problems such as stuttering or extreme or persistent stage fright, you should consider consulting a speech therapist. However, the self-improvement techniques that follow are helpful remedies for the most common minor weaknesses observed in the speech of college teachers. A final section covers common movement problems.

Voice Improvement Exercises

Though you may not be fully aware of how often you use unessential words or phrases, it is relatively easy to increase awareness of their use and to eliminate them from your formal speech. Ask someone in the audience, such as a friendly and trusted student, to count your uses of certain words for a few days and report at the end of each class. Knowing you are being observed and receiving the resultant information can help you gain control over a distracting habit.

Many college teachers speak too quietly. Developing a speaking voice that is strong and energetic enough to be easily heard and understood by students in the back rows is essential. Speaking loudly enough is especially important at the beginning of a class when the students have not yet settled down and become caught up in your ideas or made an aural adjustment to your voice. Once you have their attention, you can deliver a dramatic point with a whisper, but initially you must speak loudly, at one step above a conversational tone (Balthrop, 1993).

Projection refers to the combination of volume and energy that makes the voice carry well to the back of a room or auditorium. As any actor knows, speaking with projection is more than simply speaking loudly. The following exercise can both illustrate voice projection and, when repeated on several occasions in increasingly large rooms, provide a technique for increasing it.

Position yourself and a companion in the middle of a room about the same size as those in which you typically teach. Standing only a few feet from one another, take turns reading several lines from a book. Speak your lines expressively, opening your mouth wide and saying them with vigor and conviction. Notice the sound of your own voice as it reverberates around the room and compare it mentally with that of your partner as he or she speaks to you. Each of you should then take two or three steps backward and repeat the procedure. Even though you are now farther away, continue to speak directly to your friend as if it were critically important that he or she hear and understand what you are saying. Repeat this process until the two of you are standing against opposite walls.

During this exercise, you probably noticed the need to take much bigger and deeper breaths as you moved farther away from your partner. You may have also noticed that you needed to open your mouth considerably wider to project your voice over a greater distance. The speed with which you spoke may also have decreased slightly. You may have become aware of a tightening in your throat as you were required to speak across a larger distance.

If this was the case, your voice quality and comfort probably decreased as well.

A well-projected voice requires a sufficient volume of air to generate the vocalization and still have a reserve to support the sound. You must fill your lungs with more air than you need, because lungs are much less efficient balloons when they are only partly inflated. To fill your lungs completely, inhale from your abdomen rather than your chest. Your "stomach," not your chest, should rise when you take a deep breath. (This is far easier to do if your posture is good—spine straight, shoulders back.) Singers and wind players learn "belly breathing" early in their careers.

Voice projection is aided by opening the mouth wide enough to allow the sound to escape easily. Singers know well the importance of adequately opening their mouths to deliver a relaxed-sounding voice with high volume. The key to opening the mouth wide while keeping the throat (and therefore the sound) relaxed is to lower the jaw as far as possible rather than stretching the cheeks sideways. Making a wide, exaggerated smile ruins voice quality by creating tension in the mouth and throat. To feel how far your jaw will hinge downward comfortably, yawn several times. This is the type of mouth opening to use when you are trying to fill up a room with the sound of your voice. Except when speaking in very large halls, it will not be necessary to project to your maximum potential, but developing such power makes it unlikely that your voice will ever be underpowered in less demanding classroom settings.

No matter how well you project your voice, there are situations in which other factors will work against your being heard. Power to project your voice is especially important in poorly designed classrooms with less than optimal acoustics. Because bodies and clothing absorb sound and thus reduce distorting reverberation, a room full of people will have better acoustics than an empty one. Avoid classrooms with especially poor acoustics if possible, and schedule your classes in rooms only as large as the number of students enrolled; decline the option of a larger but half-filled room.

It is almost impossible to be heard in some teaching situations. For example, on one of those first few lovely days of spring, students may persuade you to let the class meet outside. With no walls or ceilings to reflect your voice, it will be practically impossible for students spread out on the grass to hear you—even assuming that they are looking in your direction and not watching the passing campus scene. Giving in to earnest requests to hold class outside is inadvisable for a number of reasons, but the near-impossibility of being heard is foremost among them.

To increase your voice projection, there is no substitute for practicing in actual classrooms. Begin in small rooms and gradually work your way up to the largest ones at your school. Bring along a friend or two to sit in the back row, if possible; they can tell you how well your voice is carrying. Whether you are alone or accompanied, the key to projection is speaking directly to a real or imagined person sitting in the back row. Some college teachers have learned to do this in actual classes by picking one or two students in the rear and occasionally pretending that they are speaking only to them.

Learning to speak with sufficient projection is relatively easy if practiced with commitment, but a few college instructors who have used these exercises still have had difficulty in making themselves heard. Discussions have revealed that the source of their difficulty is an underlying inhibition about speaking loudly. When they first tried the exercises, they were quite uncomfortable about speaking with such vigor and volume. The origin of this anxiety about hearing themselves speak vigorously may be excessive demands from parents and elementary schoolteachers that they speak softly. Do not be concerned if your voice sounds different or displeasing to you as you begin to project more. Such a reaction may simply reflect deeply ingrained conditioning to speak softly, even in front of groups. Luckily, such maladaptive conditioning (maladaptive for a college teacher, that is) can be modified with practice.

Next to speaking too softly, poor articulation is the most common speech problem I have observed in college teachers. Speaking crisply and clearly takes considerably more effort than speaking conversationally. Speaking before others, especially as the size of the group and the necessary projection increases, requires proportionately more distinct and energetic articulation.

Well-articulated speech results primarily from the way the speaker sounds consonants, especially those that begin and end words. Such sounds result from lip movements to some degree, but primarily they result from the way the tongue touches the roof of the mouth and the back of the teeth. You can demonstrate for yourself how much activity occurs in your mouth when words are well-articulated. Read any short passage out loud, slowly and with deliberate pronunciation of every syllable. Notice how much your lips and tongue must move to make all the consonant sounds. The consonants that precede and follow open-mouth vowels make possible the large number of sounds human beings can make.

Increased attention to forming consonants and to speaking more deliberately in front of groups is probably all you will need to overcome poor articulation habits. However, some instructors have also found it useful to practice saying tongue twisters that focus on different consonant sounds such as "p," "t," "s," "ch," and "ing." More than anything, a college teacher must make the conscious decision to speak as distinctly as possible.

Anyone can learn to speak with sufficient projection and articulation, but tonal quality is more difficult to improve. Voice quality is largely the result of the physical properties of the throat, mouth, sinus cavities, facial bone structure, and chest, none of which can be changed easily. There are, however, certain unpleasant and distracting voice qualities that college teachers can and should reduce or eliminate.

The first of these is *stridency*, speaking with a hard, metallic (usually loud and shrill) tone. This voice quality typically results from trying to speak loudly without breathing deeply. The attempt to gain volume in this way constricts the throat and produces the strident sound. Breathing deeply to achieve projection will usually help to produce a more relaxed, less strident tone. An additional voice exercise to reduce stridency is to yawn a few times and then make an "ah" sound for ten seconds or so, letting your voice gradually fall in pitch to produce a long, sliding sound. Stridency comes from tension in the vocal apparatus, and this tension will disappear when you learn how to produce volume while maintaining relaxation.

Excessive *nasality* or a twangy quality results from directing too much sound through the nose. It is normal to send sound in this direction when we make "mmm" or "nnn" sounds, but doing so with other sounds, especially open vowel sounds, such as "ah," produces an unpleasant result. Practice making long vowel sounds through the mouth rather than the nose to eliminate this problem.

Winter colds or excessive strain can give the voice a hoarse, breathy sound. College teachers should know a few stage tricks for speaking well in spite of a cold. Singers and actors learn to spot the beginnings of a sore throat and to avoid speaking or singing any more than they must at such times. It is also common practice for them to gargle with a mild soda and salt solution or to suck a lemon just before performing. This can reduce unpleasant voice tone and provide relief for an hour or so. Keeping the voice apparatus moist by regular sips of water helps one speak well at any time, whether one has a cold or not.

Gesture and Movement Improvement Exercises

Other than good posture and the practice of standing when in front of a class (it is much more difficult to breathe deeply or to capture students' attention when sitting), there are few formulas to offer for developing effective movement before a group.

Nonetheless, the most common problems with gestures and movement may be improved by following a few simple suggestions. For example, if you notice that you are prone to random movements or to keeping your hands together or making abortive gestures, consciously decide to keep your hands free and away from the sides of your body and concentrate on using them to make smooth and flowing movements. You might also practice retiring to a comfort-able place—preferably one with a mirror—where you can play music and move your hands and arms along with the melody, as you are trying to express the emotion of the music to someone who can-not hear. Expand your potential repertoire of gestures by trying to see how many different ways you can move your arms, hands, and fingers to make an important point in a lecture.

Improve your pattern of movement before your classes by con-centrating on two features: (1) how you stand when not moving and (2) how you move when you decide to change position. Try to do most of your talking to the class while standing still in a platform position—facing your students squarely, with your feet shoulder-width apart and your knees bent slightly. Speaking from a stable platform allows you to gesture and lean confidently, knowing you will keep your balance no matter what. When you do move, do so decisively and go from one platform position to another. Talking while wandering aimlessly around the front of your classroom and letting your feet get tangled or your body off balance is not nearly as engaging as working from a series of powerful stationary positions (Balthrop, 1983).

More than anything, you will increase your skill at using the visual dimension to teaching if you try to increase your overall energy level and relax whatever inhibitions you may have about throwing yourself into a classroom presentation. If instructors are genuinely excited about the business of communicating to students, their bodies will automatically become involved in the process. There is no need for every movement you make before a class to be totally fresh and original, any more than there is a need to replace clever phrases or illustrative anecdotes that have worked well in the past. When you find a movement that is effective, by all means make a note of it and hold it in reserve for another appropriate time. Accomplished actors have a variety of expressions and gestures that they use to communicate emotions, and the best players have the largest repertoires to draw upon. Actors typically experience the emotion first and let the movement follow naturally. The prevailing school of theater in America (and to an increasing degree, in Britain) is one emphasizing the actor's experience of emotion as opposed to skill at mimicking it (Linklater, 1976). (Much modern stage training resembles experiential encounter groups more than speech classes.) Similarly, the accomplished teacher may have a large repertoire of gestures and movements, but the pantomime is more likely to enhance the point being made if it occurs spontaneously.

There are some exceptions to the general rule that gestures are more effective if they are natural rather than planned. Many excellent instructors step to one side of the lectern or table when expressing one side of an argument and to the other side when presenting the opposing view (Harris, 1977). Because the presentation of contrasting views is so common in teaching, this staging can be used by instructors of most subjects. Such side-stepping not only catches the students' eyes but also emphasizes an important logical relationship in the material and probably aids recall as well. College teachers who use this device are frequently unaware of it, but most do so deliberately. A similar tactic is to advance close to the front row when discussing administrative details, making anecdotal illustrations, or leading discussion, and retreat nearer the board when presenting new content. One professor I observed sometimes sat on a tall stool placed within a yellow square when he wished to speak as an individual rather than as a scientist.

In summary, learning to move well in the classroom is a matter of involving the whole body, in a relaxed but energetic manner that is consistent with one's personal style of communication. Natural and appropriate movements and gestures support the oral presentation.

Many static characteristics of classrooms have significant power over students' visual attention, and college teachers can increase the overall quality of their performance by being sensitive to these characteristics. The next section deals with some of these factors.

Sensitivity to the Classroom as a Stage

A number of physical features of classrooms enhance or detract from an educational experience. Taking stock of the physical classroom and making whatever adjustments are possible will not offset unclear content or poor delivery, but it can make a significant if admittedly small contribution to your teaching performance.

Make a special visit to the classroom you are going to use, to examine its theatrical characteristics. This is especially important during course planning, because you may wish to modify your initial plans after you have seen the room in which you will teach. Evaluating the hall increases the precision with which class presentations can be accurately planned.

Size is surely the first attribute to consider in evaluating a room. Compare the actual number of seats with the expected enrollment to determine room density. If you have many more seats than students, the acoustics will be poorer and your presentations will have less sense of intensity and intimacy. When faced with such a situation, use strands of crepe paper to close off the rear rows, so that students are encouraged to sit nearer the front. Alternatively, you can hand out hard candies during the first few classes to students who followed your request to sit in the first four rows. Young adults can be as responsive to such incentives as grade school students.

Some beginning teachers are initially distraught to find seats bolted to the floor in their assigned classrooms, believing that they must be able to move chairs into small groups for discussion to occur. As Chapter Six shows, movable chairs are not really a prerequisite for effective student interaction. Still, if you think your teaching plans require movable seats, a visit to the classroom will reveal whether you have them.

A room's acoustics are important, and it is a good idea to practice a bit of lecturing during your visit, even though you cannot make a final evaluation of the room's acoustics until it is filled with students. Also note other physical characteristics (room shape, distance between speaker and students, ceiling height, lighting, availability of overhead projectors, video-players, or computers) that will influence the ease with which you will be able to communicate with your audience. Most classrooms are adequate, but an early scouting trip can help to anticipate possible problems while there is still time to complain and have them corrected.

When entering a classroom to teach, note the presence of anything that may distract the students' attention. Are the chairs in a state of disarray? Are there pizza boxes or coffee cups scattered across the floor? It is also a good idea to make sure that all the lights are on and that the area in front of the blackboard across which you will be moving is free of anything that might get in your way (chairs, electrical cords, trash cans). As a matter of routine, erase the board completely before beginning to teach, to ensure that students are not distracted by the remains of someone else's outline and that you do not have to take time while in the middle of a lecture to clear a space to write.

Any good actress or actor knows the importance of entrances and exits in capturing the audience's attention. College teachers should also note the way they enter a classroom. (Exits are unimportant because professors in American colleges rarely leave before their students.) Noting by which doors you can enter the classroom and deciding on the mood (optimism, friendliness, intensity, seriousness) with which you wish to begin will help you create an air of expectant excitement among your students from the very beginning. Though there are interpersonal advantages to arriving early for class, I have observed excellent teachers who habitually arrive a few minutes late: with a flourish, they begin to lecture as they dash down the aisle or in from stage left. Think about the way you begin a class to see if it is consistent with the effect you wish to have on your students.

Like actors on a stage, college teachers can effectively use various props on which to focus students' attention. Books are the most commonly used. Students are more likely to remember a book's title if the book is held up and passed around. Reading quotations directly from books also has a greater authenticity than reading the same quotations from lecture notes.

Books are not the only props that can be used effectively. Especially in science and art courses, numerous objects can be brought in to illustrate topics and break up the routine of lecturing, note-taking, and discussing. Passing around a fifty-seven-caliber minié ball from a Civil War musket will dramatize a presentation on the horrific casualties at Shiloh and Antietam. Props do not have to communicate anything directly; it is not even critical that students see them closely. Their primary value is a dramatic one: they add visual variety and refresh student attention. Slides, films, video clips and other electronic props are a common means of increasing visual attention and emphasizing organization (see Chapter Five).

Even though college teachers cannot easily leave the classroom with flair, they can end their classes decisively. Stopping on time and with a strongly inflected concluding comment is far superior to yelling out a few additional points or suggestions about an assignment as the students file out. Conditioning students to expect a class to end as emphatically as it began will keep them from becoming restless when their watches (or stomachs) tell them the end is near.

Actively Engaging Students

Speaking clearly with variety and projection helps to engage an audience; so does movement. An additional quality that is easily as important as these is *eye contact* (Sprague and Stuart, 1992). Except for stage asides, actors are taught to speak their lines as if the audience is not present. College teachers, by contrast, have a powerful additional resource in the opportunity to look directly into the eyes of their listeners.

Our faces reveal more about what we are thinking than any other part of our bodies. Though our eyes may not be literal windows into our souls, they do mark the spot of closest outside contact with our consciousness and emotions. Some instructors avoid looking at their students' eyes, habitually gazing to one side, the ceiling, or the floor after a quick, unfocused glimpse at the class. Even if they gaze out at the students, they rarely focus on single faces and allow that little spark of human contact to pass between them. Many students are equally uncomfortable with direct eye contact and will avert their eyes if the instructor looks directly at them. Over time, however, students can learn to be more comfortable with instructors who look them directly in the eyes. Making frequent and direct eye contact with individual students is as important as anything else discussed thus far in engaging their minds. Eye contact is also invaluable because routinely scanning students' faces is the best way to assess the impact of what you are saying or doing so that you can make small adjustments in your presentation.

An outstanding literature professor said that what contributed most to her teaching effectiveness was "where the students are sitting. I can capture the full attention of anyone who is seated in the first ten rows, but I will hook only some of the students seated farther back." Her rationale was that it is difficult to catch an individual student's eye beyond the distance usually covered by ten rows. So certain was she of this physical limit that she taught classes in rooms larger than this with great reluctance. When I asked how much of the time she was making eye contact, she looked puzzled and replied, "I suppose I'm always making eye contact—with someone."

Even though actors cannot focus on individual sets of eyes, they are acutely aware of the necessity of maintaining that fragile connection between themselves and the audience. By "losing the house," stage directors and actors mean breaking or weakening that gossamer but all-important bond between audience and performer. Actors are taught the importance of keeping their faces directed toward the audience as much as possible. Directors block actors' movements on stage so that they almost always face the audience (or are sideways to it) whenever they are speaking or are the center of action. The ancient admonition to "never turn your back to the audience" is no longer observed rigidly in contemporary theater, where thrust or round stages are common, but it is still followed more often than not.

In college classrooms, the traditional rule still holds. Every time instructors turn their backs to the class, they risk "losing the house"; if they stay turned for more than five seconds, they will find most of their students looking elsewhere or thinking about something else. The theatrical tradition suggests that college teachers should maintain face-to-face contact with their students *at all times*. You can do this by turning your body no more than ninety degrees from the front when writing on the board, regularly looking toward the class, and glancing around the classroom when a student is making a long discussion comment. When reading quotations, you can also read a phrase to yourself quickly and then deliver it with expression while looking directly at your audience, rather than keeping your eyes fixed on the page. This ability to read with what is called a leading eye can be developed by anyone with practice and was taught routinely to schoolchildren in nineteenth-century America (Machlin, 1966). The delicate visual bond so critical to facilitating understanding between instructors and students requires constant cultivation and protection.

College teachers must give exciting and moving performances day after day (though at least, unlike actors, they are not often required to give the *same* lecture every day—with two presentations on Wednesdays and Saturdays). Like other performers, college teachers will find it difficult at times to "get up" for teaching. Being excited and fully motivated to teach is much easier at the beginning of a term than after the novelty has worn off and other demands on one's time increase. Luckily, college teachers can benefit from some of the techniques that professional actors use to give their best performances time and again.

The single most useful technique is to recognize that you must prepare yourself emotionally as well as intellectually before your "performance." No instructor is likely to go into a class without some idea or specific plan of what he or she wants to do and the necessary materials (books, props, maps, slides) to carry it out. Many college teachers, though, walk directly from parking lot or committee meeting into a classroom, with only a short pause to collect their thoughts. The outstanding professors I interviewed typically set aside from five to thirty minutes beforehand to think about the class they are going to teach. Some close their office doors and hold telephone calls; others walk a longer route to their classroom building than necessary. However you can manage to find a few minutes of solitude before class (in the bathroom, if necessary!), recognize the importance of emotional preparation in ensuring a high-quality performance, especially if you are tired or depressed.

If you are emotionally prepared, you will possess the energy to model the intellectual attitude you want your students to have. If you want them to be excited about the ideas you are presenting, you should be excited by those ideas as well—no small task when presenting fundamental concepts you first learned years ago and may have taught numerous times. If you wish your students to think, to push aside their emotional reactions and prior views to consider a problem objectively and rationally, you must wrestle again through your own reactions as well. If you wish your students to respond with emotional sensitivity to art, then you must be able to portray this response for them. Another literature professor I interviewed remarked that when he reads lines in his Shakespeare class, he tries to do so as if he has never heard them before. Students will learn more about the emotional attitude they should (or could) have about a content area from what their instructor models than from anything else.

Several years ago, I inadvertently learned the importance of preparation time when growing enrollments in psychology courses forced one of my classes, which met at a popular hour, to be moved to a building some ten minutes' walk across campus. As the semester progressed, I noticed that I was able to *begin* teaching this class with the energy and concentration I had come to expect only five to ten minutes after a class period had started. In effect, I had been warming up at the students' expense in the past. When I mentioned this to one of my students, a drama major, she said that no actor or musical performer would ever fail to prepare emotionally before going on stage, and she wondered where I had gotten the idea that college teachers were exempt from this rule!

Creating Dramatic Suspense

How can college teachers infuse their presentations with suspense, with a sense of dramatic tension and the excitement that comes from expecting something important or unusual? Instructors can create this sense of anticipation in their students by giving presentations as if they were telling a story, ordering and presenting their topics in ways that stimulate in their listeners a sense of unfolding and discovery.

To tell any story well, the narrator must become almost as caught up in the plot as the listeners. Even if they have told a story countless times, masters of the ancient storyteller's art grow excited at hearing the tale once again. They save the big surprises until the end, laying the groundwork early by posing questions from the opening moments and dropping clues along the way. The storyteller must approach the well-known plot as if telling it for the first time, so that listeners will experience it afresh, even when they, too, have heard it before.

Superb lecturers share many qualities with storytellers. They, too, save the conclusions or most crucial points until the end, having teased the students along the way with key questions and preliminary findings or interpretations. Such instructors seem genuinely moved by the story they are presenting, the excitement of scientific discovery or historical events or the pathos and beauty of literature or art. These teachers have a well-developed empathic sense, the ability to imagine accurately the thoughts and emotional experiences students are having as they listen to the story. Award-winning historical filmmaker Ken Burns shows that he understands this well in his comment, "History is not *was*, but is. The challenge is to bring it to life" (1994, p. 7E.)

Some college teachers are natural storytellers who add a sense of drama to anything they talk about. But almost *any* instructor can learn to be a good storyteller if he or she relaxes inhibitions and reacts to the suspense inherent in most content. Practice in telling traditional stories to children or adults can help college teachers add a sense of immediacy, spontaneity, and dramatic suspense to their teaching.[1] Teachers who have tried this have reported good results. As noted psychology teacher James McConnell quotes an influential professor as saying, "If you want to capture the imaginations of young people, you have to tell them stories!" (1978, p. 4).

Exhibit 4.1. Communication Assessment Rating Form.

Speaker's Name_____Date_____

Instructions: Watch the entire taped segment first to become familiar with the content and to gain a general impression of the speaker's voice and movement. Then read the rating form and keep the dimensions in mind as you watch the tape a second time. Note the descriptions at the extreme ends of each dimension when marking a point on the line that best represents the characteristics of speech or movement over the entire segment. You may want to rate the voice qualities by listening to the tape without looking at the monitor. Similarly, you may want to rate the movement dimensions by watching with the sound turned down. <u>Hint: Try to ignore the content and pay attention only to the speaker's voice and movement.</u>

1.   Materials helpful in developing one's storytelling skills are available from the National Storytelling Association, P.O. Box 309, Jonesborough, TN 37659 (800/525–4514).

What do you hear?

1. How frequently does the speaker begin or break sentences with unnecessary words or sounds (such as "uh," "you know," or "well")?

1	2	3	4	5	6	7

Such words
or sounds are
used very
frequently.

Few, if any
unnecessary
words or sounds
are uttered.

2. How relaxed is the speaker's voice?

1	2	3	4	5	6	7

Voice sounds
very tense
and tight.

Voice sounds
very relaxed
and free from
tension.

3. How rhythmic and fluent is the speech?

1	2	3	4	5	6	7

Speech is very
halting, jerky
and broken by
unnecessary pauses.

Speech flows
in a naturally
rhythmic manner.

4. How noticeable or distracting is the speaker's breathing?

1	2	3	4	5	6	7

Inhalations
are noisy and
occur at distracting
times (in the middle
of phrases).

Inhalations are
barely audible
and are well
timed (between
sentences or
phrases).

5. How varied is the pitch of the speaker's voice?

1	2	3	4	5	6	7

Voice is
monotonous.

Voice uses a
wide range of
pitches, from
high to low.

6. How appropriate and varied is the rate of speaking?

| 1 | 2 | 3 | 4 | 5 | 6 | 7 |

Speech is
too slow,
too fast,
or too unvarying

Appropriate
rate—speech
shows varied
speed and is
easy to follow.

7. How meaningful is the stress put on different words?

| 1 | 2 | 3 | 4 | 5 | 6 | 7 |

Stress is
distracting—
too light, too
heavy, or
inconsistent with
meaning.

Stress enhances
rather than
distracts from
meaning.

8. Are the words clearly articulated?

| 1 | 2 | 3 | 4 | 5 | 6 | 7 |

Words are
frequently
slurred or
sloppily
pronounced.

Words are
sharply and
clearly
articulated.

What do you see?

9. How frequently are distracting mannerisms or habits shown?

| 1 | 2 | 3 | 4 | 5 | 6 | 7 |

Distracting
mannerisms
are shown
frequently.

Few, if any
distracting
mannerisms
are apparent.

10. How much does the speaker's face enhance the communication?

| 1 | 2 | 3 | 4 | 5 | 6 | 7 |

Face is lifeless,
shows anxiety,
or contradicts
message.

Facial
expressions
communicate
involvement.

11. How often does the speaker make eye contact with the audience?

1	2	3	4	5	6	7

Very little eye contact—
usually looks up, down,
or to the sides.

Usually looks
directly at members
of the audience.

12. How smooth, natural, and varied are the speaker's gestures?

1	2	3	4	5	6	7

Hands are "tied"
or make random or
abortive gestures.

Hands move
smoothly and
expressively.

13. How much does the speaker's posture communicate
   confidence and involvement?

1	2	3	4	5	6	7

Posture shows
rigidity, slouching,
swaying, or
too much leaning.

Posture is
erect—feet
usually in
"platform" position.

14. How purposeful and varied are the speaker's movements?

1	2	3	4	5	6	7

Speaker remains
in the same place,
shuffles, or paces
too much.

Frequently
and purposefully
moves to
different locations.

What are your overall reactions to the segment?

15. How much energy does the speaker show?

1	2	3	4	5	6	7

Speaker
seems flat
and lifeless.

Speaker shows
high level
of energy.

16. How involved did you feel in the presentation?

1	2	3	4	5	6	7

I felt uninvolved—
time passed
very slowly.

I felt highly
involved—time
passed quickly.

Note: Movement dimensions adapted from Balthrop (1993).

5

Selecting and Organizing Material for Classroom Presentations

*Scholarship must be accurate, whether it is interesting
or not. But teaching must be interesting, even if it is
not 100 percent accurate.*

—*Highet*[1]

To many people, the college lecture is a dinosaur, a holdover from a pretechnological age when books were scarce or nonexistent and the lecture was the primary means by which students could gain information. For some, it represents some of the worst moments in their college education, evoking images of fighting to stay awake while a distant professor droned on and on, his or her head buried deep in yellowed lecture notes.

There is surely some merit in these points. The lecture is no longer needed for the purposes for which it was first created, and it can be an unsurpassed soporific for students when it is poor. Still, unlike the dinosaur, the lecture thrives as the dominant form of college instruction today. Why has the lecture survived?

Lecturing occurs whenever a teacher is talking and students are listening. It flourishes in an age of cheap paperback books and affordable videotape technology (Howe, 1980). Its survival is not

1.   G. Highet. *The Art of Teaching*, 1950, p. 219. Reprinted by permission of Alfred A. Knopf, Inc.

due solely to the old-fashioned preferences of conservative college faculties. Many students, especially those who seek information and high marks, also prefer lectures. Innovative course formats eventually fade from listings of departmental offerings when students are given a choice between them and traditionally taught courses. The lecture also survives because at its best it can be *magnificent*. And at almost every school, there are enough lecturers demonstrating this for the form to remain the norm in spite of poor practitioners. Furthermore, the economic advantages of teaching classes by means of the lecture, especially those offering very large sections, are numerous, though they are insufficient to account for the lecture's popularity.

The model of teaching effectiveness on which this book is based suggests that lectures survive because, like bullfights and "Masterpiece Theatre," they satisfy the need for dramatic spectacle and offer an interpersonal arena in which important psychological needs are met. These assumptions suggest that an appropriate way to improve college instruction, even in these technologically rich times, is for professors to master the enduring and traditional skills—the art form, if you will—of lecturing.

The Many Forms of the Lecture

A graduate instructor I once supervised eschewed lecturing in favor of discussion. He said he did not believe in lecturing. Asked to describe the lecturing he did not believe in, he realized that lecturing symbolized for him a rejecting, dominating attitude toward students, not a variety of presentation.

What are the major types of lecture? At one end of a continuum is the formal oral essay, the tightly constructed, highly polished lecture that presents information primarily to support a summative point or conclusion (Kyle, 1972). In this kind of lecture, the professor has reviewed and selected from a large body of knowledge the theories, research studies, and arguments that support his or her conclusion. The most formal of such lectures are written out and read to the students.

At their best, oral essays are by no means boring. Listening to one can be an emotionally and intellectually significant experience. However, lectures such as these rarely occur in college classes, for a very practical reason. A formal lecture for a fifty-minute class needs to be about 7,500 words long (Satterfield, 1978). At three classes per week for a fifteen-week semester, a teacher giving only oral essays would have to compose 337,500 meticulously chosen words, yielding over one thousand pages of typed manuscript—a feat well beyond the powers of most faculty members.

There are other problems with this kind of lecture. Formal essays can achieve the highest level of Dimension I teaching, but a course consisting exclusively of such lectures fails to meet educational objectives that require dialogue with students. Because formal lectures ignore the interpersonal dimension, they are not likely to fully motivate or satisfy most students. A long series of such lectures would wear out students' ability to concentrate, as well as the teacher's ability to prepare material. However, there are times in any course when formal lectures are needed. Tight, integrative presentations are especially useful near the end of a course, when the fundamental content has been mastered and the desired interpersonal climate of the class has long since been established.

The most common type of college lecture is called the *expository lecture*, because it primarily defines and sets forth information. Most students think of this sort of lecture when they hear that a professor "lectures a lot." In such lectures, the instructor does most of the talking, interrupted only by occasional questions from the bolder students. Such lectures are less elaborately planned than oral essays, but nothing prevents them from being outstanding and satisfying to students if they are skillfully prepared and delivered.

A related form is the provocative lecture. As in formal and expository lectures, the instructor does most of the talking, but here there is a greater intention to provoke thought. In such lectures, the teacher challenges students' existing knowledge and values and helps them to form a more complex and integrated perspective. Provocative lectures are better suited to the humanities than to the sciences, but lectures that challenge and question student assumptions are appropriate in any discipline, especially near the end of a term, by which time a common body of knowledge has been shared. Instructors rely more on discussion than on lectures to help students question their personal values and attitudes, but a first-rate provocative lecture can achieve the same objective. If the class is large, a provocative lecture may be more effective than discussion, unless active or cooperative learning techniques are used.

Most college classes are variations of the type of lecture in which the teacher does more than talk. A common variant is the *lecture-demonstration* class, in which an instructor uses props to illustrate the subject at hand. Such classes are essential in most music, art, engineering, and science courses.

In a *lecture-discussion*, the college teacher encourages students to comment or express concern rather than simply raise questions. The typical lecture-discussion class begins with the instructor speaking for five to fifteen minutes and then stimulating a few minutes of discussion around a key point in his or her remarks. During such discussion, the instructor offers brief clarification or integration between student comments, but students do most of the talking. Discussion skillfully interspersed with lecture need not interrupt the flow of the lecture organization, and it encourages students to think about the content being presented as well as heightening their involvement in the lecture part of the proceedings.

The *punctuated lecture* technique described by Angelo and Cross (1993) goes a step further by occasionally asking students to write down their reflections on lecture points and submit them to the instructor.

Another common variation of the formal lecture is lecture-recitation, in which the teacher stops to ask specific questions or request students to read prepared material aloud. Class time in

American colleges was once spent almost exclusively on recitation (Kyle, 1972), and some teachers and subjects (especially languages) still use it heavily.

A final variation is the *lecture-laboratory*, in which students follow short lectures by making their own observations, conducting experiments, or doing other independent work. Science courses most often use this method, but studio art and writing classes can be lecture-laboratories as well.

What the Lecture Can and Cannot Do Well

A common criticism of lectures is that if a speaker does not write out a lecture beforehand, what is said is likely to be inferior to something already written in a book; and if a lecture is already written, why bother to read the words aloud rather than simply assigning students to read the text?

This is indeed a conundrum if one accepts the premise that the sole purpose of a lecture is to present information. Available research consistently concludes that lectures are one of the *least* effective methods of conveying information (Bowman, 1979; Thompson, 1974). Though lectures sometimes produce better immediate recall than reading, tests of recall several hours or days later indicate that a single lecture does not produce more learning of information than a single reading of the same material. Since most students can read faster than a lecturer can talk, it is easily argued that lectures are an inefficient use of students' and teachers' time. Individualized teaching methods were developed in part because of this evidence of the lecture's relative ineffectiveness at transmitting information.

Fortunately, this narrow view of the objectives of the lecture is neither universal nor necessary. Lectures do much more than readings. I believe that a first-rate lecture is better than written material at emphasizing conceptual organization, clarifying ticklish issues, reiterating critical points, and inspiring students to appreciate the importance of key information. The high clarity of an excellent lecture aids understanding, as do the emotionally tinged associations created when students learn in a state of intellectual excitement.

The lecture is probably most effective at motivating students to learn more about a topic. Good lectures are very difficult to ignore. They are, above all else, *engaging*. Any student's mind wanders more often while reading assigned chapters or articles than when listening to an instructor who makes his or her knowledge about a subject seem exciting and important. The intellectual excitement resulting from good lectures can make students more likely to read assignments attentively and to talk with one another out of class about their studies. Thus, lectures can be very effective at creating an emotional set that aids students' learning indirectly by motivating them to apply their energies fully.

Lectures, then, are not superfluous. When formal essays, expository lectures, or provocative lectures are combined with any of the modes requiring active student participation, such as discussion, writing assignments, or laboratory, a number of educational goals can be accomplished. Students can question their values and attitudes and increase their problem-solving and thinking skills. A professor can model the kind of thinking he or she wishes students to emulate and then give them an opportunity to try it themselves.

To organize lectures well, teachers must consider how students learn. The next section contains a brief summary of what psychological research has demonstrated about learning. These general principles apply to all human learning, but they are especially relevant to the way content should be selected and organized for presentation in a college lecture.

What We Probably Know About Human Learning

While many theorists stress the importance of events outside individuals for learning, the position taken here is that human learning is heavily mediated by internal events—thoughts or cognitions, that occur as students actively construe meaning from what they see and hear rather than passively soak up information. The following principles of human cognitive learning are sufficiently well-established to be used by a college teacher desiring to organize and present lectures in ways most likely to produce learning (Bugelski, 1964; Duffy and Jones, 1995; Eble, 1988; Smith, F., 1990):

1. It is better for college students to be active seekers than passive recipients of learning.

2. For students to be fully engaged in learning, their attention must be focused on the material.

3. Differences in intellectual ability among college students will influence their speed of learning; these differences will be more noticeable when the information to be learned is abstract and complex than when it is simple and concrete.

4. Students increase their effort if rewarded rather than punished; however, students differ in the teacher behaviors they find rewarding.

5. Students will learn and remember information better if they have many cognitive associations with it; learning of isolated information is more difficult and less permanent than learning of information that is connected to a network of other material.

6. It is difficult to learn ideas that are very similar unless the differences between them are emphasized. Conversely, it is easier to learn disparate ideas if their similarities are emphasized.

7. Students learn images as well as words, and images are more easily remembered, especially if the images are vivid and emotionally tinged.

8. Students enter every class with positive and negative emotional attitudes that can interfere with learning or can increase motivation and provide an associational network for new learning.

9. A moderate amount of anxiety or challenge activates most students and increases learning; however, excessive anxiety interferes with learning.

10. Students differ in how much anxiety they can tolerate before their performance becomes impaired.

Choosing What to Present in a Lecture

This section deals with ways of organizing outstanding lectures. The preparation is the same whether the instructor lectures only or combines lecturing with other activities. My recommendations in the remainder of this chapter concern both *what* a college teacher chooses to present in a lecture and *how* he or she presents it.

Deciding How Much to Present

As instructors quickly learn, only a small number of major points can be presented effectively in a single class meeting. Research on what can be remembered following classes indicates that most college students can absorb only three to four points in a fifty-minute period and four to five in a seventy-five-minute class, regardless of the subject being taught (Eble, 1988; McKeachie, 1986). Students can remember details about each point, but the number of general ideas that can be absorbed is limited. Attempting to cover too much causes the coverage of each point to be superficial and the pace to be rushed for the instructor and frantic for the students. Time to answer questions or to pause so that individual ideas can sink in will be eliminated. Most critically, squeezing too much into one presentation will reduce the amount of learning, because people store information much less efficiently when their minds are temporarily overloaded.

Selecting Points for Presentation

Since relatively few major points can be presented in each lecture (and in a semester), choosing what to present is critical. A first choice is whether to survey course content comprehensively or select only key topics for presentation. Though most teachers, in theory, endorse concentrating on points of fundamental importance, in practice they seem to believe that if they do not cover everything, their teaching is somehow suspect, shoddy, or superficial. Introductory or survey courses particularly evoke this feeling. When, as is common, beginning college teachers fall hopelessly behind schedule near the end of the term, they wrestle in obvious discomfort with the question of which important topics to omit. Without guidelines on ways to select material, the easiest course for an instructor to take is to attempt to present it all, however sketchily. Neither college teachers nor students, however, are likely to be satisfied with this solution to the problem.

Experienced instructors know that lectures cannot carry the primary responsibility for conveying information or imparting skills. Readings or problem-solving assignments should do that. Points for lectures should be chosen using the following criteria:

1. *Central points* or *general themes* that tie together as many other topics as possible should be presented (Highet, 1950). Details will then be easily associated with the central points. The lecturing practice of placing topics in brief historical perspective is common because of this advantage of overall organization.

2. Points should also be selected for their *high interest* to students. If the most provocative topic in the assigned reading for a given class is ignored in favor of more theoretically critical topics, students are likely to be disappointed. Satisfying students' initial curiosity about certain topics is a good way to lead them to appreciate the importance, beauty, or relevance of other ideas that seem less appealing at first and to motivate them to read assigned materials outside of class.

3. A teacher should occasionally choose a topic because it is *especially difficult* for students. Though class time would be drudgery if it were spent only on the most difficult or abstract points, selecting commonly misunderstood topics is frequently appropriate.

4. Of most importance in choosing what to present is the *depth* and *complexity* of a given topic. A lecture should not be so simplistic

or obvious that students are unlikely to learn anything new from it (especially if they have done the assigned reading); neither should it be so sophisticated and dense that many will be overwhelmed with the intricacy of the remarks. Finding the appropriate depth of presentation for a group whose members differ significantly in ability and background is one of the greatest challenges in giving fine lectures. Experience can help a teacher calibrate his or her presentation, but careful observation of student reactions is the most effective way to fine-tune the level of complexity on the spot. The best exposition will be fully comprehensible to most listeners, and will involve some new thinking or reorganization of what they already know.

Organizing the Lecture

A lecture should begin by stimulating students' curiosity. Any playwright, screenwriter, or novelist knows the importance of starting with a "grabber," a tension-producing statement or juxtaposition that attracts the audience and holds their involvement as the plot and characters are developed further. The opening of a lecture should also create in students an expectation that something important will follow.

Many lecturers begin with a key question or paradox that the day's lecture will attempt to answer or explain ("What can we learn about changes in British images of the heroic through comparison of nineteenth- and twentieth-century novels?"). Another option is to call attention to an intriguing example of or exception to a general phenomenon ("What does the treatment of immigrants at Ellis Island who brought less than $50 with them suggest about class and race attitudes and political power in early twentieth-century America?"). Sometimes, lecturers approach a familiar concept from a fresh direction ("Today we will examine evidence supporting the idea that our culture's emphasis on romantic love is a major cause of divorce"). Lectures aimed at students who have had considerable prior coursework in a subject are especially appropriate for beginnings that reexamine familiar ideas.

After the attention-getter is chosen, there are several options for organizing the remaining points in a lecture. A common method is to proceed in a linear and logical fashion, gradually building to a final concluding point. Some lecturers, however, prefer nonlinear organization, in which students may not understand at the beginning where the lecturer is heading. In his television series "The Ascent of Man" (1974), Jacob Bronowski typified nonlinear organization in that one could not be sure of his conclusion until near the end of an episode. Another common tack is to present two separate topics in some detail and conclude by contrasting and comparing them. Proceeding chronologically is often appropriate in history courses, but in other subjects this approach can bore students unless the chronology is important in its own right. And in organizing any subject, time makes for a weak glue.

Whatever the organization of a given lecture (and one should vary the approach from one class meeting to another), it is advisable to approach the structure of the formal lecture as much as possible. Ploughing through loosely related topics without emphasizing the relationships between them promotes neither understanding nor satisfaction. When organizing a lecture, the instructor should remember that it is a dramatic presentation needing boundaries: an engaging beginning to take hold and a conclusion that drives home the major points. The acronymic "SADTIE" technique makes use of statistics, analogies, demonstrations, testimony from some specific person, incidents, and exhibits in support of major points (Balthrop, 1993). The best lectures can be completed in a single class, but if a lecture must be continued, the speaker should bring the first installment to an end decisively.

Lecturing to Promote Independent Thinking

The professor who wants students to be active learners, to think and reach conclusions on their own, should first model such thinking for them (Browne and Keeley, 1986; Satterfield, 1978). Explicitly pointing out the thought processes involved helps to ensure that all students will be aware of them. Students should be told *how* conclusions were reached or theories constructed rather than being given only the finished products. Students can also be encouraged to think by asking them how they would interpret given data and by putting conflicting ideas before them for debate or consideration whenever possible.

Students will think more critically about a subject if an instructor exhibits a healthy skepticism at times about the field's assumptions and methods (Woditsch and Schmittroth, 1991). One outstanding instructor told me, "I always begin the semester with optimism and enthusiasm about the material and usually have the students well enough informed by about two-thirds of the way through that I can be more skeptical and show them the limits of our methods, can bring them down to earth a bit. It's hard for some of them to take—a few become disillusioned—but it's the best way I know to teach them to think critically on their own."

Finally, college teachers can encourage independent thinking in students by addressing value issues directly rather than shying away when they appear. An instructor who openly admits that his or her conclusions are at times influenced by personal values is more likely to encourage students to examine value influences on their own conclusions than one who perpetuates the myth that knowledge can be value-free.

What an instructor chooses to present in a lecture and the way the material is organized will affect students' understanding of what they read and their eventual sophistication in a subject area. The *way* the teacher gives the lecture will affect the students' motivation to pay attention in class and to complete assigned work.

Presenting Content Effectively

This section focuses on general lecture style and the use of audio-visual technology to enhance interest and organization. Carefully selected and organized points, however laudable, constitute a lecture of only moderate quality unless they are delivered well. Increasing the interest value of a lecture is the best way to prevent students from dozing off in classes or staying away altogether.

Lecturing with Immediacy and Spontaneity

Classical Greek orators spent an amazing amount of time preparing their speeches for contests (Highet, 1950). Every word, every gesture, and every inflection were planned and practiced beforehand so that they would have the desired effect on the audience. Yet the effect the orators sought was the appearance of speaking extemporaneously to express genuine emotions. In effect, Greek orators worked exceedingly hard to appear not to have prepared at all! Contemporary college teachers can learn a useful lesson from them.

Regardless of how carefully a teacher has prepared a lecture, the actual delivery should have a sense of immediacy, as if the speaker were having for the first time many of the thoughts he or she is sharing with the students. This quality of conversational intimacy involves the students more readily in the flow of ideas than does a didactic style. The instructor should avoid at all costs the stern, moralizing tone commonly associated with a lecture from a disapproving superior. Instead of speaking *at* or even *to* students, the teacher should strive to speak *for* or *with* them (Satterfield, 1978). This approach is more likely to sweep them along in the interesting story that the instructor has to tell.

Beginning college instructors sometimes indicate that they intend to prepare for their courses by writing out all their lectures beforehand. Such energy would be highly misplaced. The elegance of written lectures is admirable, but such lectures take too much time to prepare and cannot seem spontaneous when delivered. Rather, teachers should think first about the major points they wish to present. If they want to plan specific classes ahead of time, they should write brief outlines for *at most* the first three class meetings.

Because most beginners fear they will not be sufficiently prepared and will run out of content before the class hour is up, they almost always prepare too much and write notes in too much detail.

After a few months' experience, they gradually shorten their lecture notes and come to realize that their initial fantasy about writing out all lectures ahead of time was foolish.

Lecture notes should contain in outline the major topics selected for presentation and the key points under each (Highet, 1950; McKeachie, 1986). Experienced instructors know that complete sentences in notes are both unnecessary and difficult to read quickly. Words or brief phrases suffice. Any formulas or definitions to be read to the class may be written out, though quoting from memory is often more impressive to students, and reading them from a book may add credibility and authority. If you find it convenient to type your presentational outlines, you might try using a large computer font for improved legibility. Wide margins will enable you to write comments about intended delivery, key words, and visual aids. And leaving the lower half of your pages blank will limit the need to look down, away from your audience (Balthrop, 1993). The purpose of lecture notes is to remind the instructor of what he or she planned to say or do, not to provide something to read. There are no definitive criteria for the length of lecture notes for a single class, but less than one page is probably too short and more than three is surely too long. To achieve a sense of immediacy and spontaneity, a college teacher must *create* a lecture to some extent while presenting it, and writing notes out in too much detail risks sapping creativity and making the speaker too dependent on them. Many outstanding teachers report that they commonly have new ideas or insights into their material while actually giving a lecture. They also rarely consult their notes during their better lectures. The notes are there if needed, but the presentation comes from the teacher, not the notes.

Introducing Variety

An instructor must not only capture but also hold students' attention throughout each class meeting (Duffy and Jones, 1995). "Never do any single thing for very long" is a good rule for keeping attention. Students will tire of anything, even humor or anecdotes, if it is extended for too long without a change of pace. A lecturer should plan for some change in format every ten minutes or so. The organization of content need not be broken, only the manner in which ideas are presented.

An instructor might vary a presentation by giving a specific example of the topic under consideration, asking a series of rhetorical questions, or saying something humorous. Humor is an especially good way to introduce variety and let everyone (the instructor included) relax a bit. A teacher should note, however, that the best humor in college classes is not canned jokes; satirical, ironic, or witty comments about the subject, individuals studied, or oneself are more appreciated. Not all instructors will be fluent enough to engage in clever wordplay or spontaneous enough to present a brief impersonation of a famous individual during class, but everyone can think of humor as a learnable skill, keep a humor file of illustrative and amusing cartoons or stories, and apply course concepts to unusual situations (Cartwright, 1993). (Humorous comments about students are not advised, because some students may well take them as hostile unless they are delivered sparingly and with just the right touch.)

Seeking Feedback During Class

Fortunately, college teachers need not worry about knowing when to shift gears to maintain the class's interest—the students will tell them. All that instructors need do is note the messages that students send their way. Students' faces give the best indication of the way a presentation is being received (Highet, 1950). Students signal when they are no longer caught up in a lecture and are having to work to pay attention.

Yawns, chair shuffling, sighs, or whispered asides to fellow students clearly tell an instructor that it is time to do something different. More subtle cues give the same message. Students who are no longer fully engaged develop the proverbial glazed look. The wise instructor looks for it constantly to fine-tune the pacing of a lecture and to indicate when it is time to ask a question, give an example, or in some other way break stride for a short while.

Another technique to solicit feedback from students is to ask questions such as "Am I going too fast?" or "Should I slow down a bit to let all this sink in?" Highet (1950) suggests maintaining a running joke with the students in the back row of a large room: every week or so, the teacher can break up slow spots in a lecture by suddenly asking, "Can you people in the back row still hear me okay?" Occasionally instigating feedback from students keeps them alert and lets them know the instructor is concerned.

Feedback about what students are learning can also be solicited. Minute papers collected near the end of class can be focused on course content. For example, "What was the muddiest point?" in a statistics class or "What important question did the novel make you ask of yourself?" in a literature course (Angelo and Cross, 1993, p. 371). Instructors can also ask students to evaluate the usefulness of assignments. In whatever way faculty ask students to comment on their learning experience, the responses can be used to fine-tune teaching.

Emphasizing Organization

A traditional adage is that a good lecturer tells the class what he is going to tell them, tells them, and then tells them what he has just told them. Though boring if used to excess, previews and recapitulations are particularly helpful ways to emphasize organization and key points. Students have thought about many other things since the last class meeting and can benefit from brief statements connecting today's topic to what went on before. Mentioning the objectives for the day's lesson provides a context within which students can organize what they hear, especially if a major shift in the course has occurred.

A college teacher can also emphasize organization in a lecture by reviewing at the end of major sections and at the end of each class. A few sentences of recapitulation can help students notice that a transition is occurring and a somewhat different point is now going to be addressed. At the end of class, the teacher should take five minutes to tie things together and anticipate what will happen next time (Eble, 1988). The best lectures are well enough paced and include few enough points to allow an instructor to put what has been said into perspective in the last three to five minutes, rather than desperately trying to cram in a few more details while the students are disengaging mentally, if not filing out the door.

Excellent students can take useful notes from the lectures of almost any professor, but the best lecturers are those from whom it is easy for every student to take well-organized notes. Lectures that emphasize organization and connections between concepts and provide frequent pauses so that less intelligent or well-prepared students will not miss additional points while writing are more likely to promote learning. Better students do not attempt to transcribe everything the lecturer says, but distill organized information in notes (McKeachie, 1986).

Students should be encouraged to take their own notes rather than relying on other students or commercial note-taking services. Even though many students believe that the main purpose of coming to class is to have a record of what went on, possessing an archival record is not the main goal of note-taking. It is the *process* of taking notes that is most important, though the notes do have some value as later reminders of what went on. Just as a teacher's notes are no substitute for mental activity on the part of the instructor during a top-notch lecture, so no student's notes can completely capture the experience of hearing and responding to a lecturer's words in "real time."

Using Visual Aids

Listening and thinking activities are the primary activities by which students learn during class, yet students learn most from what they see.

Handouts

Many college teachers distribute handouts such as lecture outlines, chronologies, listings of definitions or formulas, or diagrams. Because the teacher prepares them, they are more accurate than what some students would record in their notes. Little time is required to produce handouts, and they can be sold to students via course-pack services, which makes them cost-effective.

Some ways of using handouts are better than others. If given a detailed lecture outline at the beginning of class, many students simply examine the handout, develop a false sense of security, and pay little attention to the lecture, knowing they can refer to the outline if they miss something. Handouts, like students' lecture notes, should provide organization and a reminder of what the students heard in the lecture. Thus, the teacher should distribute handouts when presenting the material to which they relate. They are no substitute for a clear and engaging lecture from which a student actively creates a personal set of notes, but they do constitute useful souvenirs of the experience (that is, they have more symbolic and reminiscent value than practical value).

Blackboards and Flip-Charts

Whether green, beige, or white, blackboards are a universal feature of classrooms and are easily taken for granted. Because using them can soil hands and clothing, many teachers disparage and sometimes avoid them, but their educational value is substantial even in our electronic era. Nineteenth-century educators appreciated the blackboard's value. In 1841, Josiah Bumstead wrote, "The inventor or introducer of the blackboard deserves to be ranked among the best contributors to learning and science, if not among the best benefactors of mankind." Boards are still one of the most effective visual aids available.

The act of writing on the blackboard focuses student attention on the lecture. Research indicates that most college students will copy into their notes virtually everything the teacher writes on the board (Howe, 1980). The blackboard is an excellent place to write key words or names, if for no other reason than to increase the likelihood that students will learn to spell them correctly. Unfortunately, students sometimes omit key words when they take notes, especially "no," "not," and the prefix "un," and miss completely the meaning of a lecture point. It is therefore best to beware of writing negative statements on the board.

Writing a definition on the board draws students' attention to it and is most appropriate if the teacher wishes to comment on various words and components of the definition in some detail. If the instructor's sole purpose is to be sure that students write a long definition correctly, class time can be better spent dictating the exact wording. Writing on the board takes time (especially if material is written clearly enough to be read easily by students in the back rows), and it is possible to use the technique to excess. Basic rules are to write nothing unimportant on the board, nothing that one does not refer to in some detail, and nothing overly lengthy.

Many excellent teachers routinely write an outline or a list of key terms for the day's lecture in one corner of the blackboard before class begins. This provides a useful preview of what is to come. A teacher should not write a great deal on the board before class, however. Students will simply copy it all down at the beginning of class, sit back, and relax. It is the process of writing on the board *during* a lecture that keeps students' attention and prompts them to organize content.

Flip-charts of newsprint are another popular method of accomplishing the same ends. They allow different colored marking pens to be used (colored chalk is difficult to read), and the notes can be taped to the wall rather than erased during class.

Electronic Aids

Electronic audiovisual aids in college classrooms can greatly enrich a lecture, but they are neither necessary nor sufficient for lecturing virtuosity. Essentially, electronic devices are previously prepared blackboards with a greater range of sensory stimuli and greater power to attract students' attention. Their additional power results from the use of sound, color, and moving graphic images. Such enrichment is especially needed in very large classes (over 120), where the impersonality of the situation makes students less involved. The decision of most importance concerning any audiovisual aid is whether its advantages outweigh its cost and justify its use in place of handouts and blackboards.

Overhead transparencies are the most common electronic aids, because they are so easy to prepare and to use. Many teachers routinely employ them in place of the blackboard, using photocopy machines to transfer material to transparencies before class or writing directly on clear transparencies with specially designed pens. Experienced users put few items on a single transparency and point directly to the previously prepared transparency using a pen or pencil rather than stepping into the light to point to information projected on the screen. Overhead projectors can also be used to aid student note-taking by having student volunteers sit at the front of the class and take their class notes on transparencies so that others can see them. You can photocopy their transparencies to give recorders a permanent copy for their own records. Pass around a sign-up sheet on the first day of class to identify students interested in serving as scribe for a class or two. Ask students to sign up who believe they take good notes, expect to do well in your course, and have legible handwriting. Use the roster of volunteers to schedule students to play this useful role for the group and provide opportunities for others to sign up after they have seen the function and usefulness of the scribe's role. Once exams or papers have been graded, you might directly approach additional students who performed well and with good penmanship and ask them to take a turn as scribe.

Slides are much more difficult for most teachers to produce, because support personnel must photograph materials and develop film, but their visual quality is superior to that of transparencies and when projectors with properly working remote controls are available, they are easy to use. When the course content requires photographs of important objects or scenes (paintings, buildings, villages, geological features), 35mm slides are indispensable. Like transparencies, however, they are sometimes used to present electronically what could have been just as easily written on the board.

Motion pictures illustrate content vividly, and the best contemporary educational films are conceptually complex and of high interest to students. Showing a long film takes up scarce class time, however. Given the relatively limited educational benefits of most films, many teachers choose to show them at night or have film clips produced by media centers showing just the part needed to illustrate a lecture point. Even though almost all 16mm motion pictures are also available on more convenient videocassettes, some instructors still prefer the higher-quality images provided by film, especially when the audience is large.

Videocassettes have many of the advantages of motion pictures, although the sizes of television screens severely limit the number of students to whom such tapes can be shown effectively. Modern video projectors are a decided improvement over standard monitors, but are still inferior to movie projectors. Nevertheless, cassettes are very popular in college classes, primarily because they permit instructors to show the segments of their choice and to create their own collection of brief illustrations copied from different videotapes.

An ideal method of making films or videotapes available is to have them housed at the library (typically in the reserve or nonprint section), where staff can show them to students individually or in small groups during regular library operating hours. Some library media centers will tape selected lectures for students as well.

Computers and multimedia displays are the newest visual aid available in the college classroom. Chapter Eight discusses ways of using computers in out-of-class assignments (McGraw-Hill Primus, 1993). Computers also play a valuable role in focusing student attention, presenting content, and facilitating student understanding in the course of a lecture (Graves, 1989; Herman, 1988). Computer programs designed to present information on a screen before a group—in effect, an electronic blackboard—allow instructors to present the same kinds of information as when using handouts, overhead transparencies, or 35mm slides. When large-enough monitors or high-quality projection devices are available, the rich color graphics and eye-catching fades between one image and another are much more engaging than what can be achieved with still images. However, although presentational software offers tremendous power to an instructor seeking to produce vivid and varied images before a group, it has been superseded by a generation of multimedia equipment and software that offer even more possibilities.

Multimedia technology is, in effect, a collection of video and audio equipment linked together by a small computer. The computer is programmed to display still or moving images, to play sounds ranging from music to human speech, and to integrate these with more traditional computer-generated text or graphics displays on multiple-window screens (Hodges and Sasnett, 1993; Iuppa, 1993). The technology, which is capable of processing huge volumes of digitized images and sounds, combines the flexibility of computers with the fidelity of compact disk players. If a school is willing to spend a little money on equipping its classrooms for high-quality multimedia display and if faculty members are willing to spend a little time learning how to use the equipment—even perhaps preparing their own programs with the help of authoring software designed to be used by classroom instructors—the educational benefits can be enormous. The fact that many small computers now come equipped with compact disk players guarantees that there will be an increasing supply of materials designed for them. Textbook publishers envision the day in the not-too-distant future when textbooks will be delivered via multimedia equipment rather than paper and print. Unfortunately, multimedia displays are limited by the educational materials currently available on compact disks and by the willingness of faculty to modify their teaching to take advantage of this new technology. Like most educational technology, the multimedia variety is unlikely to rescue a poor teacher but will be most effective in the hands of an already proficient instructor who is able to weigh its advantages over simpler methods and who also recognizes the importance of the interpersonal dimension of teaching.

Advantages and Disadvantages of Visual Aids

An instructor must consider a number of things when deciding which visual aids to employ and how frequently to use them. *Availability* is a primary concern. Blackboards are almost always present, and flip-charts are inexpensive and easy to carry. However, unless a classroom is permanently equipped with a transparency, slide, movie, video, or computer-driven projector, using these teaching aids requires prior scheduling, transportation, and setup in the classroom. Audiovisual equipment is not difficult to operate, and every college teacher should be willing to make the small amount of effort required to learn how to use each kind of visual aid. But something *will* go wrong on occasion—someone else will have taken the overhead projector without checking the reservation list, the bulb will blow out on the slide or movie projector, the videocassette will jam, or the computer software will show an uncorrected programming error. Purchasing one's own equipment to ensure its availability when needed is expensive, but instructors who have come to depend on these devices sometimes take this step. The alternative is to expend time and energy on careful logistical planning—and still to run the risk that the equipment may not materialize at the appointed time. (The availability of chalk in classrooms cannot be assured either, but it is easy to carry chalk to class routinely.)

Another consideration is the amount of *advance preparation* required. All visual aids call for some advance planning; even diagrams drawn on the board must be planned beforehand. Films, film clips, and 35mm slides require more lead time—frequently weeks, sometimes months—because of the assistance that is needed from others.

A final consideration is the degree of *disruption* in lecture delivery resulting from the use of audiovisual aids. Turning to write on the board disrupts the proceedings little if the teacher does not lose eye contact with the class, but writing out a lengthy chart is guaranteed to lose students' attention. Turning on a videotape player already wound to the desired segment also introduces little disruption. The major disruptions caused by electronic aids are the noise they make and the necessity to dim classroom lighting. Both make it more difficult for a teacher to keep students' attention. Disruption will be reduced if the instructor turns off the machines and returns to full lighting whenever possible.

Some teachers must lecture almost exclusively with the lights off while students look at slides. One teacher of introductory art history whom I interviewed believed that her success resulted in part from her ability to maintain involvement by conveying emotion in her voice and skillfully coordinating the flow of slides and the lecture. She did express regret at feeling more distant from such in-the-dark classes and not getting to know as many students personally. Though it is possible to teach effectively in the dark with the noise of equipment in the background, a heavy use of audiovisual aids makes interpersonal rapport more difficult to achieve because of the loss of eye contact. However, spending as much time as possible at the beginning and end of class with full lighting and encouraging out-of-class contact with students help offset these liabilities.

General Principles of Using Visual Aids

The first principle of using visual aids is to employ them frequently enough to keep student interest high but not so often that students become distracted or have no time to think about what is being said. One outstanding college instructor I observed has perfected a lecture style that uses a dazzling array of media, primarily alternating between 35mm slides and film clips. His presentations sometimes average one slide or short film clip for every ninety seconds of class time. Though his classes are highly engaging, students in them may not have sufficient time to think about the implications of what they have observed. Many may simply sit back and wait for the next display. This particular style is most effective with extremely large classes (over three hundred) and cannot be used without considerable technical expertise or support personnel. In deciding on the appropriate amount of visual stimulation, an instructor should remember that the thoughts that go through students' minds are of more importance than the artful displays passing before their eyes.

A second general principle is to reveal visual material gradually, as it is referred to, rather than displaying it all at once. This keeps students' attention focused on one major point at a time. Even when using the blackboard, the teacher should write concepts one at a time to stimulate student thought and memory rather than putting them up all at once and then commenting about each individually. With overhead transparencies, many instructors use a blank sheet of paper to cover the parts not yet discussed. The same kind of thing can be done by preparing a series of 35mm slides, each identical to the one shown before except for the addition of one new topic at the bottom. However, using slides in this way requires considerable advance planning and cannot be modified easily during a presentation. Some instructors use an alternative to gradually revealing information that is sometimes called the "drain then explain" technique, which involves showing and mentioning all points briefly before concentrating on each in turn (Balthrop, 1993).

This section has touched only briefly on the possible ways that diagrams or outlines can be presented by using visual aids. The educational applications of electronic technology—especially multimedia materials—are expanding rapidly and will undoubtedly become even more sophisticated in the future. Some classrooms now have linked computers for all students; these allow many creative forms of student-teacher interaction as well as instructor presentation. If a computer display device is available—the simplest rest on top of a high-intensity transparency projector—there is nothing except expense and effort to prevent college teachers from using a small computer to create, store, and display everything they might write on a blackboard. The computer can be easily carried to class, where information can be presented to the class as the instructor wishes, and modified on the spot if desired.

Regardless of the specific methods used to present material visually, the psychological and educational purposes of the lecture remain the same: to ensure that students concentrate fully on the presentation, that they understand and organize it maximally, and that they are motivated to learn on their own outside of class. It is important for a college instructor not to let "gee-whiz" technology obscure these fundamental and traditional purposes—objectives that can also be accomplished by an exemplary teacher equipped with a single piece of chalk, a board, and a reasonably quiet place in which to talk with students.

Intellectually Exciting Lectures: A Recapitulation

An outstanding lecture is many things. Primarily, it is content that has been carefully selected and organized to capture the essence of a topic, complement what is presented in readings, and motivate students to learn the rest. The best-planned content, however, will have little impact on students if it is not delivered well. To achieve all the potential of a lecture, the instructor must use variety and energy in his or her voice, expressiveness in his or her face and movements, and visual enrichment to keep the audience captivated and stimulated and to aid the remembering of what went on.

Two short lists loosely adapted from Kenneth Eble's *The Craft of Teaching* (1988) conclude this chapter. They are sets of guidelines on how to be, respectively, a particularly bad lecturer and an especially good one. They summarize by negative example and by explicit suggestion many of the fundamental points of this chapter.

Suggestions for Bad Lecturing

1. Begin a course with no introduction to the subject or to your own bias. Simply start with the first topic you wish to represent.

2. Make no references to the broader context of the specific topic being considered.

3. Do not acknowledge the students' interests or previous knowledge and experience.

4. Become preoccupied with the historical context of a topic, neglecting the central subject of the course.

5. Give excessive attention to the trivial details of the subject or to those parts that most interest you; omit topics of more central importance or interest.

6. Dwell extensively on your private scholarly quarrels with other authorities over esoteric points, without showing how your concerns relate to the larger subject.

7. Qualify terms so excessively that students will not be able to explain them to a friend immediately after class. Be so specific and sophisticated in the definitions you present that students will have to memorize what you say word for word and will be unable to define terms meaningfully in their own language.

8. Present learned quotations without connecting them to the content.

9. Justify conclusions on the basis of tradition or authority, without explaining why the authorities believe as they do.

10. Use arcane terms and make no attempt to define them; do not acknowledge that students may not know what you mean.

11. Rarely look at your audience. With a fixed posture, keep your eyes on your notes, the floor, the ceiling, or the side walls.

12. Speak in a monotonous voice, showing little emphasis, force, or enthusiasm.

13. Hesitate frequently in the middle of sentences, but rarely pause at the end of major lecture sections.

14. Show little sense that time is passing and insist on presenting points in the orderly manner you planned, even if individual classes end in midtopic or you fall far behind the course syllabus.

15. Indicate that you know the students are confused or impatient, but then do nothing differently.

Suggestions for Good Lecturing

1. Fit the material you present to the time you have available.

2. Seek concise ways to present and illustrate content. Express concepts in the simplest terms possible and define technical terms when using them.

3. Begin each course and class by pricking the students' interest, expressing positive expectations, and sharing the objectives you have for them.

4. Follow a prepared outline but include improvised material or illustrations. Appear spontaneous even when you are following the outline closely.

5. Break up the monotony of lectures by varying your methods of presentation.

6. Use a wide range of voices, facial expressions, gestures, and physical movements, but be yourself. Develop a varied and interesting style consistent with your values and personality.

7. Give students regular places to catch their breath and ask questions. It is "better to talk too little and stop short than to go on for too long" (Eble, 1988, p. 81).

8. End each lecture with a conclusion that connects what has happened today with what will be covered during the next meeting.

9. Be guided by your students during your lectures. Continually observe their reactions, acknowledge them, and modify your approach when indicated.

10. Remember in your relationships with students that all of you are persons first, students and teacher second. Remember that you, as a teacher, "are both host and guest" (Eble, 1988, p. 81).

6

Enhancing Learning
Through Classroom Discussion

*A useful classroom discussion, unlike a dormitory bull
session, consists of student comments separated by
frequent probes and clarifications by the teacher that
facilitate involvement and development of thinking by
the whole group. Dynamic lecturers captivate a class
by the virtuosity of their individual performances.
Exemplary discussion leaders accomplish the same
end by skillful guidance of the group's collective thinking processes.*

College teachers who lead successful classroom discussion say
much more than "Any questions?" or "What do you think
about this?" In their hands, discussion is an active intellectual
process as emotionally involving as the most dynamic lectures.

Discussion requires interaction between student and teacher, so
its effectiveness depends heavily on the quality of student-teacher
relationships. Discussion also promotes a sense of intimacy in lecture classes (Meredith, 1985). Because discussion is much more
unpredictable than lecturing, it requires considerable instructor
spontaneity, creativity, and tolerance for the unknown. Whether
it is held in small seminars or in larger lecture-discussion classes,
discussion requires a teacher to have excellent communication
and interpersonal skills. If managed well, discussion can promote

independent thinking and motivation as well as enhance student involvement.

Like the lecture, discussion produces in many college teachers (and students) strong positive and negative attitudes that are based more on philosophical or political values than on experience. For many, discussion seems desirable because using it implies that students have important thoughts and experiences to contribute. An instructor who allows classroom discussions recognizes students as active participants in their own learning as well as passive recipients of the information and insights that the teacher has to share. Some people value discussion because the instructor seems more egalitarian or democratic during discussion exchanges than during lectures (Christensen, 1991b). A few go as far as to denounce other forms of instruction—especially the lecture—as insulting, even dictatorial. For many advocates, discussion embodies the humanistic educational philosophy (Brownfield, 1973). However, not all college teachers are so enthusiastic.

Faculty members who view education as the acquisition of information or explicit training rather than the development of thinking skills or critical perspectives find discussion of little immediate value. These instructors believe that the positive motivational benefits of discussion are overrated, and that it is more appropriate, given limited class time, to let the person speak who has the most to say: the instructor. Others see discussion as an abdication of teacher responsibility to share superior knowledge or as a shortsighted pandering to students' need to feel important and desire to hear themselves talk.

Though there are valid philosophical objections to classroom discussion, many college teachers have negative views of discussion simply because they have never observed good discussion or been able to use it effectively themselves. Like the lecture, discussion at its worst is painful and frustrating for all involved. Long silences, averted faces of students fearing they will be called upon or pressured to volunteer comments, or angry outbursts toward other students or the instructor so commonly characterize poor discussions that many college teachers abandon the technique after one or two unsuccessful attempts, rationalizing that their students "just aren't interested in discussing."

Discussions must be well-planned in order to be effective, but their quality also depends greatly on how well the instructor performs. Leading an excellent discussion demands just as much stage presence, leadership, and energy as presenting a lecture—and considerably more interpersonal understanding and communication skill. Because of these additional requirements, some educators believe that leading an outstanding discussion is more difficult than giving a lecture of comparable quality (Eble, 1988).

In this chapter, the many ways of using discussion in college classes are considered, and instruction is offered on developing discussion skills. Topics covered include educational objectives that can be achieved by discussion, the varieties of classroom discussion, general characteristics of outstanding discussion, specific instructor skills that facilitate dialogue, and ways to handle special discussion problems.

Educational Objectives for Discussion

Before an instructor can effectively master discussion skills, he or she must be cognizant of what these skills can and cannot accomplish.

Course Content

As McKeachie notes, "Discussion is probably not effective for presenting new information which the student is already motivated to learn" (1986, p. 27). Though not effective for presenting content per se, discussion does aid its mastery by encouraging students to actively process what they learn as they sit in class. Asking a few students to think and speak out loud encourages all students to think more fully about content. Discussion helps students assimilate and integrate information they have initially acquired from readings or lectures.

A skilled lecturer can walk the class through an application of a general concept to a specific problem or example, but this can also be done via group discussion. Though the students' solution may not match the instructor's, it is more likely to be at a level of understanding appropriate for the class as a whole. Lecturing to students about a method of literary criticism, research design, or computer programming is fine as far as it goes, but asking them to apply in class what they have learned requires them to demonstrate understanding, not merely memorization. The application of general ideas also promotes independence and is good practice for the time when students will be expected to work on their own. Class discussion is a safe way for students to try their wings while the instructor hovers close by.

Students can also be asked in discussion to compare and contrast different concepts. Focusing on the similarities and differences that always exist between specific ideas helps to link the ideas in an associational network (Smith, F., 1990). Such networks are remembered far longer than isolated concepts. Discussion is useful for emphasizing the connections between new and old knowledge.

Though each of these content objectives can be achieved to a similar degree with a skillful lecture, discussion is desirable because of the other objectives that it can meet, some of which it meets more easily than does lecturing.

Thinking Skills

The objectives discussed thus far deal with knowledge as product—with *what* students learn (Axelrod, 1973). Discussion is most useful as a way of teaching the *process* of learning, that is, thinking. A rhetorical question in a lecture may stimulate students to think for a few seconds, but a provocative question that sparks a group discussion can stimulate thinking for several minutes. Discussion is especially stimulating for students who speak, but thinking is also stimulated in those who merely listen to their classmates and consider what they might have said themselves.

What can students learn about thinking during class discussion? They learn to approach a problem or topic rationally, monitor their own thinking processes, and question their implicit assumptions. As with learners exposed to the Socratic method, they may discover that they are not as open-minded or rational about some topics as they had thought. By modeling a desired way of thinking within the content area, a skilled discussion leader can gently guide and shape students' thinking. If the questions asked have no clear right or wrong answers, the tendency to see knowledge as individual conclusions based on evidence—what King and Kitchener (1994) call reflective thinking—is enhanced. College teachers thus prompt students to think like literary critics, biologists, political scientists, or mathematicians. Practice in "as if" thinking can lead to better and better intellectual discourse.

Because discussion requires some students to demonstrate their understanding of concepts, it also tells an instructor how completely the information he or she has presented has been absorbed. Feedback from discussion is less systematic and representative than feedback from exams, minute papers, or other classroom assessment techniques (Angelo and Cross, 1993), but it is more immediate and enables the instructor to correct, expand, or reiterate important material on the spot. This is another, indirect way in which discussion aids student mastery of content.

Attitudes

Discussion is particularly good at revealing students' attitudes. The question presented by the instructor as a stimulus for discussion—the probe—frequently focuses on students' emotional predispositions or values. For example, a teacher might ask, "Are you or are you not in favor of abortion on demand, and how did you arrive at your position?" or "Do you believe the ideals of socialism can be put into practice, given human selfishness?" Whether they participate in the discussion or not, students become more aware of their own attitudes and values by comparing them with the values and attitudes expressed by others. Exposure to different views can lead some students to question or change their implicit assumptions.

Though especially useful in the humanities and social sciences, discussion is an ideal way to demonstrate to students of any discipline how knowledge may be evaluated. For example, students can be asked to assess the social benefits and problems resulting from basic research and technological innovation, or how one theory or observation leads to fruitful subsequent inquiry. Because evaluation is personal, discussion is ideal for encouraging it.

When students have strong and differing opinions about course concepts, it is relatively easy for a college teacher to bring these out in discussion. Students are more likely to jump into discussion when a distant or historical topic is connected to a local or contemporary issue about which they disagree. Skilled discussion leaders heighten differences in any group and use them to teach valuable lessons about the role of affective judgments in intellectual endeavor.

Student Involvement

In addition to clarifying content, teaching rational thinking, and highlighting affective judgments, discussion is particularly effective at increasing student involvement and active learning in classes. Some instructors believe that only those few students who get a chance to speak become involved in discussion, while others are left out. If discussion consists only of isolated student and instructor dialogues, this point may be valid, but for the kind of group discussion featured in this chapter it is not.

When a college teacher initiates discussion with a provocative comment or question, every student must shift gears. Discussion breaks up the lecture routine, increasing involvement by its novelty alone. Students pay closer attention for a while, merely to see what the instructor is going to do or what others have to say. They probably will think about what they *might* say if they were to enter the discussion, even if they do not actually speak out. Those who comment receive a lot of attention, and many of their classmates enjoy this vicariously. However, discussion in itself increases involvement only briefly. A discussion leader who lets students talk on and on with little control or direction will soon lose the group's attention.

Interpersonal Objectives

Discussion can promote student-teacher rapport and student independence and motivation in ways unattainable by lectures alone. Motivation to learn is increased because students want to work for an instructor who values their ideas and encourages them to be independent. An instructor who, by means of discussion, asks for students' opinions communicates that he or she cares about their reactions to the course.

Discussion enhances rapport between student and teacher partly because it gives instructors so many chances to show acceptance of student ideas. When students offer comments or raise questions, they risk being judged critically by their professor and their classmates. Student comments are offered to the instructor in the hope of approval and verification of their academic competence. The quality of the instructor's response potently influences both the student offering the comment and those observing the interchange.

In the course of an academic term, interactions between college teachers and students during class discussion reflect the morale of the whole group. Early in the term, discussion gives students an opportunity to determine how much to fear their instructor. A few will bravely test the waters, offering questions or comments whether the professor invites them to or not. Most students will simply stand by and watch what happens to those who invite dialogue with the lecturer. During periods of lower morale, all students will be less willing to participate, and especially provocative questions will be needed to stimulate discussion. Because it is decidedly interpersonal, discussion becomes a focus of the class's shared emotional concerns about the instructor and each other and an arena in which the group's development is demonstrated.

Discussion is also important because it requires students to demonstrate independence. For the most part, students must come up with responses on their own during discussion. They may say how they feel about a topic or give specific arguments supporting or opposing those presented in readings, by other students, or by the instructor.

Instructors who are skilled facilitators achieve both educational and interpersonal objectives with discussion. If they are perceptive of student communications and skilled in the specific techniques of leading discussions, they can both offer constructive criticism of students' contributions and demonstrate appreciation of students' individual worth. Instructors who reinforce student comments while correcting their errors educate as well as reassure and make the individual attention that students receive during discussion something to be sought rather than avoided. Skillful discussion leaders recognize that their behavior has much more power to affect their implicit contract with their students about what is expected of them than what is stated in the syllabus or opening class meeting (Hansen, 1991).

Types of Discussion

The ways college instructors use discussion vary in the amount of time students talk and the number of students involved. Some instructors allow only one or two students to respond to a question before changing the focus or resuming their lecture. Others give up to six or seven students a chance before moving on. All successful discussion leaders direct the group's thinking by following a series of student comments with brief remarks or additional questions that build on students' comments.

Though it is difficult to make generalizations about the optimal length of discussion, I believe ten to fifteen minutes per class meeting suffice to achieve most of the potential benefits. More than thirty minutes of discussion at one stretch can develop greater intellectual independence among the few speaking students, but extended discussion can also frustrate the majority, especially the more conventional and dependent students, unless the cooperative learning techniques described in Chapter Seven are used. The type of discussion and the attitude with which it is conducted are more important than the length of time spent on it.

Discussion also takes different qualitative forms. In one, an instructor listens to student complaints on administrative matters. Gripe sessions give the teacher important feedback and promote interpersonal rapport by letting students "blow off steam" and showing the teacher's interest in their problems (McKeachie, 1986). However, because this kind of discussion deals exclusively with group maintenance concerns, frequent use of it can be counterproductive, as it takes time away from the group's task.

Two types of teacher-student interchange are sometimes called discussion. In one, the instructor gives students an opportunity to clarify content or ask for the instructor's opinions on related issues. In the other, the instructor asks questions requiring specific knowledge of course content, frequently from the readings. In isolation, neither question-and-answer form is really discussion, because students are likely to simply record and memorize what the teacher says, and because remarks do not build on one another. Isolated dialogues or recitation can, however, be used as a springboard for additional discussion or explanatory comments by the instructor; thus, questions and answers can be the start of involved and thought-provoking sessions. College teachers using this approach should remember that the questions they or the students ask are of much less importance as ends than as beginnings.

Because discussion is more difficult in classes of over fifty, a common practice is to divide the class into small groups of four to five students, each of which discusses questions or issues separately for several minutes before the class focus is restored. This practice allows many more students to talk, but the instructor needs to sample group comments and integrate them into general points if learning is to be optimized for the group as a whole. Small groups can be especially useful when an instructor wants students to get acquainted or to consider personal values or attitudes.

Students get into discussion more quickly if someone, whether appointed by the instructor or selected by the group, acts as a leader. Asking group leaders to give summaries of their deliberations usually results in repetitive and time-consuming comments devoid of spontaneity and involvement, unless the instructor limits their number. Whether two or three groups volunteer to respond or are selected randomly, instructors should actively process and integrate the group comments, just as they would during any class discussion. A useful way to end small group reports without excluding important information is to ask if other groups have additional comments to add before moving on. Because moving chairs to form discussion groups takes several minutes, many of the same purposes can be accomplished with "pairing," a less time-consuming technique.

Pairing is a combination of discussion and cooperative learning that can be applied to classes of any size, from very large sections of several hundred to small seminars. Announce to your students early in the term that you will on occasion be asking them to pair, or discuss points with a neighbor for a minute or so. I try to include a pairing exercise the first day, to give students a taste of what is to come. Also explain the importance of stopping promptly when you are ready to go on and announce your preferred method of letting them know when to stop. The traditional technique is to ask students to stop talking and raise their hands whenever they see you or anyone else raise a hand. This works as well to rein in college students as to quiet unruly youth groups. Pairing works well with open-ended discussion probes, but the technique also lends itself to focused questions about content. For example, a mathematics instructor deriving a proof stops at a critical point in the process and asks students to work in pairs to come up with the next step. After a few minutes, students are polled on their proposed solutions and the various options are used as the foundation for comments by the instructor on the consequences of the various strategies used. A variation on pairing is to ask students to write down on a piece of scratch paper an example of a specific phenomenon, such as self-fulfilling prophecies, and after a minute, ask them to pass their example to a neighbor. After another minute, ask students to pass on the example they now have to yet another student. Then, ask students to share with the group favorite examples they have seen. Students are much more likely to volunteer someone else's comment than their own, especially if the task is controversial or requires creativity.

If a substantial portion of a class session is to be devoted to a controversial issue, a short role-playing activity may be especially effective. The instructor describes a setting and gives volunteers characters to act out. One popular form of role-playing is a "mini-debate" between students: those sitting in one half of the room argue for one position, and the rest assume the opposing view. If a show of hands indicates an equal split on an issue initially, one variation is to have each side assemble and argue for the position they do *not* endorse, *against* their own beliefs. This is guaranteed to produce a lively exchange and a fresh consideration of the topic by all.

Although students enjoy occasional role-playing immensely, getting them started requires instructor confidence as well as skill. The teacher should announce the activity in earlier meetings and assume that many students are secretly eager to participate and will volunteer if he or she expects them to and waits them out. An instructor should avoid communicating doubt or uncertainty by making jokes about student eagerness or the lack of it ("Don't everyone rush to volunteer at once!"). Above all, the teacher must not give up. Students resent an instructor who gives up on getting volunteers, "drafts" students to participate, or lets students volunteer each other.

Students will volunteer more quickly if told at the start of class that role-playing is going to occur ("Some of you will get to role-play an interesting situation later on today").

Some college teachers engage the class in an extended group problem-solving discussion that is designed to teach decision making. The case method of instruction popular in management, medicine, and the law (Boehrer and Linsky, 1990; Christensen and Hansen, 1987; Vance, 1993) is a notable example of extended discussion. Regardless of the specific method of problem-solving that is taught, this discussion format requires considerable time (part or all of several class meetings) in order to be effective. Most problem-solving methods are complex, with a number of separate steps, from "identify the problem" to "check the results" (for example, Wales and Stager, 1976). Less involved discussion can model and promote problem-solving without occupying so much class time, but more structured methods should be considered if the primary objective of a class is to teach decision making.

The most common type of discussion is the kind in which instructors ask in the midst of lectures for student comments on specific issues. From thirty seconds to five minutes may be spent in such discussion before the lecture is resumed. Simple discussion like this is common because it is so flexible and, depending on the specific questions asked, can meet most of the objectives discussed in the preceding section. A teacher can decide on the spur of the moment to give a breather in a fast-paced lecture, to focus on a particular paradox in the content, or to increase students' involvement by asking them to guess what happened next. Discussion generally should be planned, but this type can be introduced spontaneously when it seems needed. Brief periods of discussion scattered throughout help to give a lecture variety. Instead of changing voice characteristics, bodily movement, or pacing, a lecturer can use student comments to enliven a presentation. Particularly effective college teachers commonly use this form of discussion.

Techniques for Leading Discussion

However a college teacher uses discussion, a common set of fundamental communication skills is required (Neff and Weimer, 1989). Some of these are general principles that apply to most situations, while others are quite specific and have more limited value. In the following section, general considerations are presented first, followed by specific techniques for starting, shaping and guiding, and ending discussion.

General Considerations

Discussion techniques should fit desired objectives; brief discussion suits limited objectives (Tiberius, 1990). For example, if an instructor sees the class's attention waning, he or she might say, "Can anyone guess what happened next?" or "What might be the next point in the argument?" Even if no one responds, encouraging students to anticipate in this way increases their involvement.

Sensing student discomfort or confusion, an instructor might remark in a slower, more reflective voice: "We've covered several important points today. What do you think of them thus far? Are you persuaded or troubled by this line of thinking?" Such questions let students relax, and they communicate the teacher's concern about reactions to the content of the lecture.

A similar tack is to make a transition to a new topic by saying, "Any questions about these ideas before we move on?" Raising your own hand slightly and slowly scanning the room for about five seconds lets students know that the teacher seriously wants to hear their questions before proceeding. Knowing this is their last chance, students with genuine questions will ask them; but even if no one responds, as often happens, the pause for questions punctuates organization, gives everyone a breather, and demonstrates instructor concern for students.

When classroom discussion occurs for more ambitious purposes than these, the specific technique used must still fit the desired objective. For example, an instructor wanting students to appreciate the human qualities of a famous person they have studied might ask them to imagine the person's thoughts about some of his or her actions ("How might Charles Darwin have felt when, after delaying publication of his theory of natural selection for twenty years, he saw Herbert Spencer's paper proposing the same idea?", "What thoughts and fears might Martin Luther King, Jr., have had when he expanded his established position as a national civil rights leader to become an early critic of the Vietnam war effort?", or "How might Margaret Sanger have reconciled her early strong belief in radical politics with her open courting of wealthy women and conservative male physicians as supporters of her women's health clinics?"). This technique, which can also be the basis of a writing assignment, increases empathy and identification with the persons whose lives or ideas are being studied.

When using discussion to promote independent and critical thinking, an instructor should stimulate objective thinking rather than personal identification. He or she should ask questions such as "What are some problems with that line of reasoning?" or "If we assume that the author had these two purposes, how else might she have brought the plot to resolution?" Such discussion promotes general reasoning and can teach the type of scholarly arguments favored in a discipline.

Asking students to compare and contrast concepts, theories, and individuals orally in class helps to clarify the relationships within a content area. This discussion technique is highly favored because it encourages students to form associational networks, thereby increasing understanding and retention of details. For example, an instructor might ask, "How does the French Revolution illustrate the influence of both Enlightenment and Counter-Enlightenment ideas?", "How were the themes of early twentieth-century American artists of the 'regional schools' similar and dissimilar to those of

American composers of the same period?", or "How were American attitudes about expanded roles for women in the labor force similar and different during World War II and the mid-1960s?" Questions that students may not have considered before promote understanding of content as well as critical thinking.

Different discussion questions stimulate different kinds of thinking processes. For example, asking students to draw conclusions from a data set promotes diagnostic thinking; challenging students about why they concluded what they did promotes independent thinking; asking students to make predictions about future events or data stimulates "as if" thinking; and asking students to propose solutions to the problems under study encourages problem-solving (Christensen, 1991a). Good questions can prompt students to become more aware of how they feel about content in addition to what they think about it.

College teachers who want to increase students' awareness of value controversies relevant to content should design discussion to reveal differences in student beliefs. Such discussion is most effective when students are already aware that they disagree about a topic, and a skillful discussion leader will phrase the question to maximize disagreement. The instructor both stimulates controversy ("Let's you and him fight!") and creates an atmosphere of acceptance that promotes tolerance ("Is it necessary that we all agree on this?").

To illustrate, suppose a sociologist wants students to recognize that the benefits of affluence and membership of the middle class often come at the expense of underclass labor. The heavy use of Mexican laborers as migrant farmworkers in the fresh fruit and vegetable industries is chosen as a notable contemporary example. If the instructor simply assigns readings and discusses the economics of migrant labor, little disagreement is likely to ensue. A more effective approach would begin with the question, "How does each of us benefit directly from the cheap labor of people of different races or nationalities?" Some students may note the affordable grapes and apples they buy in the grocery store or their fashionable running shoes, sewn by poorly paid Asian workers. Some may even think of examples closer to home, such as the proportions of African, Mexican, Asian, or Native Americans or Appalachian whites working as housekeepers or groundskeepers at their school. The teacher should have a few examples in mind, in case they are needed to get the students going, but students can usually think of their own instances quickly.

Students will try to relieve the class discomfort generated by a personally relevant discussion in a number of ways. Some will justify the class system in this country, using standard notions of individual initiative in a democratic society; others will argue against such points. Personalized discussion forces students to encounter the inconsistency between their social values (especially as applied to distant, largely symbolic examples) and their personal behaviors and interests. Students are not likely to change their values overnight because of such a discussion, but they will gain a fuller appreciation of the concepts under study and may become less smug about their moral superiority.

The first general principle of discussion, then, is to use it for an intended purpose, not simply because there is something inherently beneficial about hearing students' voices. A second principle is that the advantages of discussion must be weighed against what can be accomplished, given a number of realistic constraints.

Discussion always represents a tradeoff of time and objectives; the instructor must decide if a particular objective is better met through discussion than through lecture, demonstration, or some other activity. Class size is one of several constraints that influence this decision: the number of possible objectives satisfied with discussion decreases as the number of students increases. In classes of less than twenty students, discussion can fulfill any purpose. Extended problem-solving sessions, case analyses, class projects, or student presentations are easy in a small class. Discussion can be used even in larger classes to increase student involvement, emphasize times of transition, promote critical thinking, and increase value awareness.

Physical space can be an inhibiting factor. Discussion is easier when all students can see each other and the instructor. Many teachers arrange classes in circles or horseshoe formations to facilitate eye contact. Because extended group problem-solving or value clarification sessions require that students make eye contact with each other easily, a course with such objectives should be taught in a classroom with conducive seating. However, seat arrangement affects the quality of discussion less than does the instructor's skill in eliciting and guiding it.

The largest constraint on the use of discussion is time. The most satisfying college classes are painfully fleeting for students and instructor alike: there are so many ideas to present and things to learn, and so little time. College teachers must judiciously weigh the task against the maintenance objectives that can be met in a given period. Lecturing in every class might give students more short-term knowledge of principles and facts, but it would also dampen motivation, satisfaction, and higher-order learning over time. On the other hand, designing entire courses around group discussion might promote high emotional involvement and independent thinking, but it would frustrate more dependent students and would create uncertainty for the instructor about whether essential content would be mastered, especially in introductory or survey courses.

Most outstanding college teachers resolve the time dilemma by mixing their objectives and methods in varied and interesting sequences. Their students learn facts and principles, improve critical thinking and problem-solving skills, and assess subjective judgments through both lecture and discussion. The specific combinations of these methods that an instructor uses are determined by his or her sense of what the group needs at the moment, which is weighed against the amount of time available.

How can a college teacher create an atmosphere conducive to discussion? First, he or she should formulate questions that give students as much permission to be wrong as possible (McKeachie, 1986). Questions such as "How does the text define entropy?" or "What is the definition of existentialism?" leave little room for error. Even if a student is fairly sure of the correct answer, he or she may not feel certain enough to respond. Instead, the teacher should ask, "What is your first association to the word, 'entropy'?" or "What does existentialism mean to you?" or "Are you an existentialist?" Including qualifying terms such as "what you know," "what stands out," or "mean to you" emphasizes that it is students' personal thoughts the teacher is interested in, not their ability to produce a "correct" answer. For every objective discussed in this chapter, it is more desirable for students to give their personal opinions or arguments than factual answers. Phrasing questions so that students have little to lose by speaking removes much of the anxiety that students have about responding to requests for discussion.

The way college teachers respond when students offer comments has an even more critical effect on students' anxiety. Every student should be reinforced or treated positively for making a comment in class—even if the comment seems dead wrong. The key to doing this is to select and emphasize the parts of what students said that were insightful or creative, so as to reinforce them for making the comment, while indicating that it was not quite what was expected. For example, a student might respond to the question, "How does the Fed regulate the money supply?" with "They print more money and burn less." The teacher might smile and say, "Yes, in a way that's the basic idea; they allow more money to be available by letting more out and calling in less. But they do it through their power to regulate loans to other banks, not through control of the United States Mint." When responding to students, an instructor should always reward them for trying ("Thanks for taking a stab at it") or highlight something positive about their contribution, even if he or she must reinterpret it a bit creatively to do so. The class has a common stake in knowing how much to fear the instructor, so all students will notice closely how each other's comments are treated. Because of this, the way an instructor handles a seemingly stupid comment is more critical to communicating an accepting attitude than the way he or she responds to an apparently brilliant comment.

Nonverbal messages also influence the way students feel after offering comments. Instructors need not scowl or throw up their hands to leave an impression of displeasure. Merely looking away when the student is speaking or sighing slightly afterward gives the same message. An instructor should make eye contact when listening to student comments and display whatever nonverbal cues (smiling, nodding) he or she habitually uses when showing interest in what another is saying. Instructors should also pay attention to which students they most often recognize and ask for follow-up comments to be sure all students are encouraged to participate.

More than anything, instructors should make participating in discussion a voluntary activity, not something done for a grade (Tiberius, 1990). Some college teachers include participation credit when computing final grades. This is a poor practice. Not only is it almost impossible to assign the credit objectively and fairly—except for the most and least talkative students, instructors are unlikely to remember accurately how much an individual has talked, much less the quality of their comments—but doing so encourages a grading orientation. Chapter Nine on evaluation argues against giving grades (or points) for any activity most students would do for intrinsic reasons and presents techniques for using grading in ways that promote a learning orientation. Letting students choose to participate in discussion promotes an atmosphere of mutual inquiry rather than competition.

In addition to showing that students have little to fear and much to gain by participating in discussion, college teachers should show that they themselves are participating as well. Instructors can strengthen a spirit of mutual inquiry by de-emphasizing as much as possible the hierarchical relationship between themselves and their students. Questions that indicate, or even hint, that the professor already has a good answer and that the students must guess what it is should be avoided. Instructors who respond with "No, that's not quite it" may inadvertently convey this attitude. In mutual, egalitarian discussion, the topics and issues are important to all concerned (Barnes-McConnell, 1978); they are not contrivances that the powerful teacher has deployed to test the students' mettle. A teacher might begin with something like "Let's see what we can discover about . . ." or "What are we to make of this?" to emphasize that he or she, too, is participating in the process. Skillful discussion leaders also encourage a spirit of mutual inquiry and discourage competition among students by not encouraging students to show off what they know or that they have complied with the reading assignment. Discussion also should not be allowed to become an avenue for students to demolish each other's comments. If discussion is mutually affirming inquiry for everyone, it can be exhilarating for teachers and students alike.

It is important that students be conditioned to participate in discussion from the outset of a course. The instructor should indicate during the first class that a number of provocative issues will be coming up and that he or she is sure the students will have something to say. This works much better than simply announcing that he or she "wants to see a lot of discussion." I believe that if teachers plan to use discussion during a term, they should devote part of the first two classes to discussion in order to condition students early to respond when asked. Because discussion promotes student-teacher rapport better than lecturing, using it early on also helps to put the class on a good footing.

The techniques presented in the following section are some of those used by especially skilled discussion leaders. But the general points just described are more important, and they should be kept in mind regardless of the specific techniques a college teacher uses.

Specific Techniques

College teachers commonly complain about the difficulty of beginning discussion. Not surprisingly, many instructors attempt discussion less and less often when they find they are unable to elicit it reliably. Actually, starting discussion is relatively easy if an instructor sets the stage in the general ways discussed in the preceding section and applies a few key techniques.

First, ask for discussion when the class is emotionally involved. Students are far more likely to want to respond to an instructor's probe if they are emotionally aroused (Barnes-McConnell, 1978). Stimulating students' emotions "primes the pump" and motivates them to vent some of their emotional energy. Giving the class a common emotional experience (via demonstration, case study, news clipping, provocative film, or intriguing reading assignment) is the most reliable way to ensure that they will be ready with something to say. Students' emotions can also be activated by reference to common experiences. For example, ask them to think for a minute about a relevant contemporary event or common personal experience. Alternatively, ask students to think about the way they might feel in certain circumstances. Whatever method is used to provoke emotions, remember that emotions are fleeting (discussion must follow immediately) and have little educational value in themselves. They aid learning by enhancing students' involvement in subsequent discussion and making what is said seem more salient.

Class discussion need not always be a major production. Once students have become accustomed to frequent discussion, an engaging lecture will suffice to create the necessary emotional involvement. Asking students to write down their reactions to the probe before sharing them out loud helps to initiate the process. Using cooperative learning groups—pairing, especially—also prepares students to speak in front of the whole class. The optimal level of emotional arousal depends on the reason discussion is used. Brief discussion requires little emotion, but if you wish to spend a considerable portion of a class in discussion, the strong emotional involvement produced by a provocative stimulus may be required. A corollary is that students will want to discuss more following a particularly arousing experience than following a mild one. Thus, you should stimulate students to an appropriate level and allow enough time for the energy created to be expended.

The second skill essential to eliciting discussion is wording the query appropriately. Experienced instructors avoid questions that can be answered with short factual statements or with yes or no responses. They also keep their queries short and simple. There is generally an inverse relationship between the number of words in an instructor's probe and the length of subsequent student comments. If students must work to decipher your question, they are less likely to respond to it. Avoid especially the common habit of asking a second (or third) question before students have responded to the first. Neither new questions offered in succession nor the original question reworded and prefaced by "In other words . . ." is likely to elicit productive discussion. Discussion questions should be easily understandable by students, put forth decisively, and followed by silence.

Even if an instructor follows these first two suggestions carefully, student discussion may not be assured. You must also learn to *wait* patiently for the first student response. Here, class conditioning becomes especially important. If a class knows that the teacher will pause only three or four seconds before going on to something else—and many instructors stop no longer than that—students are likely to wait it out, certain that the pressure to respond will soon be over. If a class sees from the instructor's worried or uninterested expression that little discussion is really expected, they are also unlikely to respond. If the instructor is openly angry at students for not discussing, responses are even less likely to occur. Several instructor behaviors, then, tell students not to respond to discussion. Fortunately, it is quite easy to replace these behaviors with more effective ones.

The following method of training a class to respond to well-phrased questions has been successful for a large number of college teachers. Begin by stating your question in a relaxed and confident manner. When you finish, start counting silently to yourself: "one thousand and one, one thousand and two," and so on until you get to "one thousand and ten." Ten seconds is *not* a long period of silence, though it will seem like an eternity unless you mark its passage. Scan the room slowly, remaining calm and relaxed, as you count. If students are in an aroused state or you have just used the pairing technique, you will not have to wait long for the first response, but you can expect to get all the way to ten several times during a term, especially during the first few classes when your control over the class is not yet well-established.

If it seems that no response is going to come before you get to ten, begin moving slowly toward a table, chair, or wall. When you finish your count, remain calm and repeat the question in a shorter and slightly modified form—a "reprobe." If you wish, you may reduce even further the students' fear of giving a wrong answer ("Give any associations at all"). As you finish the reprobe, calmly, patiently, and slowly lean or prop yourself against whatever solid object you have maneuvered near and begin your silent count once again. You can be confident that your nonverbal message—"See how comfortable I've made myself; I can wait here all day!"—will prompt students to respond. Teachers using this two-probe technique almost always see students respond before they pass "five" on their second count. Once the class has become conditioned to discuss when you ask for it, you will rarely need to use this maneuver again.

The first student comment is by far the most difficult to obtain; after the first student breaks the ice, others are usually eager to jump in. Once discussion is under way, a number of techniques are useful to keep it going and guide it gently. As has already been noted, using eye contact, smiles, and gestures to reinforce student speakers makes others more likely to offer comments. The following suggestions illustrate other ways to encourage student response.

After the first response, summarize the student's comment and say something mildly positive about it ("I hadn't thought of it in quite that way before"). If you are uncertain about the comment's meaning, add a questioning inflection to your voice or qualify your summary with something like, "If I understood you correctly, Janice, you are saying that . . ." You might also ask the student to expand on the comment, but do so with utmost care so as not to make the student feel that he or she is being examined, especially early in the term or if the student rarely speaks in class.

It is important to summarize students' remarks in order to be certain that everyone heard them clearly. One of the biggest drawbacks to discussion is the difficulty students often have in hearing each other's comments. The summary also encourages students to listen to each other's points before firing off rounds of their own. Although summaries are necessary early in the term—and at all times in larger classes, where hearing is difficult—an instructor can easily turn off students' motivation to speak up if he or she talks for more than fifteen seconds between their comments. Thus, make your summaries very brief, and avoid launching into comments of your own unless you are ready to shift focus or bring discussion to a close.

Many college teachers habitually arouse their students with an engaging example and initiate discussion with a well-formulated question, only to frustrate them by delivering a spontaneous two- to three-minute minilecture after the first student comment. They do not realize that the reason they rarely get a second response is because the readiness to talk that they created in students was dissipated during their own lengthy response. Instructors should wait for at least two or three student comments before moving the discussion along with another query or shifting back to lecture. On the other hand, a class's enthusiasm for responding usually wanes after five or six comments, and the instructor must then exert leadership once again.

For discussion to progress smoothly toward thoughtful conclusions, the teacher must control the proceedings: sometimes overtly directing traffic, sometimes subtly encouraging students to interact with one another by saying little. There are times when silence is the best instructor behavior. More than anything else, control during discussion should be indirect and lightly delivered.

I believe that the single most useful technique for controlling student discussion is the age-old practice of having students raise their hands to speak. This method lets you decide who will talk and makes it less likely that only the loudest and most assertive students will get the floor. In large classes, students will need to raise their hands throughout the semester, because it is hard to maintain adequate control without this procedure, but hand-raising can be phased out in smaller classes that have been conditioned to discuss in an orderly manner. Hand-raising also reminds students that the instructor is in charge and will decide who will talk and when.

A few principles are important to remember when calling on individual students. It enhances morale to use students' names when recognizing them. (It also provides good practice for remembering their names.) Morale is seriously harmed, however, by calling on students who have given no indication that they wish to speak. Unless you are giving a recitation class or a class in which students are supposed to learn to think on their feet (as in law school), calling on students takes away far more than it adds. Even if you force only the outgoing students to talk, others will become anxious about being called on. All students prefer to choose when they speak, and for students who are fearful about speaking out, worrying about being called upon can seriously impede motivation and learning. If a student is looking puzzled, you might observe, "Dina, you look perplexed," and ask if she has a question, but otherwise I do not believe you should call on individuals who have given no indication that they wish to speak. The interpersonal costs of this intrusive behavior more than outweigh any possible educational benefits.

Scan the classroom frequently to be sure you notice students who wish to speak. Many will raise their hands high, even wave them, but others, especially quieter students, raise their hands tentatively. A few raise only a single finger in front of their questioning faces. Unless you watch students and monitor your own behavior closely, you are likely to miss subtle cues or hands in the rear of the room and to unintentionally slight some students.

Get as many students as possible to participate in the discussion by recognizing students who talk infrequently before those who have little hesitancy about speaking up. In almost every class, a few students can come to dominate discussion unless the instructor actively recruits other speakers. When asking a question, scan the entire room before calling on the first person whose hand went up. Delay recognizing a frequent contributor in the hope of a sign from a quieter student. When several students raise their hands at once, always pick the one who has spoken the least. However, also remember which students were not called on and go back to them when the first student is finished, even if they no longer have their hands up. Even students who like to talk respect an instructor who lets as many students participate as possible.

College teachers should control group discussion to make it as easy as possible for every student to participate. Once students are talking, instructors must use their control to shape and guide individual student comments toward common intellectual conclusions. Steering discussion is clearly the most difficult part of leading fruitful classroom discourse. How can it be done?

Instructors to a large extent must let the discussion develop in its own way (Eble, 1988). You can set the stage and focus attention on a provocative issue, but then you must wait for discussion to begin and to develop. Because they are anxious for students to reach certain conclusions and want them to realize the logical problems of an argument, college teachers sometimes force the process, state their own position too quickly, and deny students the chance to come to independent conclusions. Thus, requisite skills for teachers in guiding discussion are patience and willingness to let students think on their own.

You must also listen carefully to what students say in order to comprehend what they really mean (Christensen, 1991a; Eble, 1988). Without listening closely, it is difficult to remember and summarize student comments for the class. Give careful and complete attention to discussion, noting the essential point(s) in each comment and, from associated nonverbal messages, the way the student feels about the topic.

In guiding a discussion, you should organize individual student comments into a mosaic of related ideas, into themes meaningful to the group as a whole. Teachers commonly do this by jotting comments on the board as students offer them and indicating later how the different ideas illustrate the overall dimensions of the topic or varying theoretical approaches to it. Student comments that reveal underlying assumptions may be highlighted to promote thinking.

The following example illustrates both methods. In a course on social deviance, the instructor asks students at the first meeting to suggest examples of behaviors they would call deviant and lists them on the board. Within five minutes, the board has ten to fifteen examples. The instructor points out that several of the examples given represent groups who violate social or moral norms and asks if the board entries might be compressed into general categories such as political extremists, religious eccentrics, or those with alternative sexual orientations. After students have worked for a few minutes at combining individual examples into categories, the instructor summarizes the dimensions they have generated and points out that these are similar to what experts in the field usually see as important. Students are certain to remember the groupings better now than if they had simply heard them in a lecture and copied them down.

To follow the example further, the instructor could then ask *why* each category is considered deviant. As the students struggle with this question, the instructor can help them discover their underlying assumptions about deviance, sometimes asking them to say more, sometimes exaggerating a point to emphasize difficulties ("So you're saying that our society considers everyone a deviant who believes they have a personal relationship with Jesus Christ?"). Provocative discussions in which assumptions are questioned require that instructors become highly involved in the group's problem-solving as gadflies or devil's advocates, working to keep the group on its toes.

Guiding discussion is much more difficult than eliciting it and requires considerable interpersonal sensitivity, enthusiasm, and intellectual sharpness. Students learn most from struggling with a problem or issue, so you should not propose a solution too quickly even if directly asked. It is much more productive for a college teacher to shape the students' ideas and withhold personal comments until the end, if not completely.

When discussing, most students address the instructor, but students occasionally refer to each other's comments or speak to one another directly. Student exchanges more often occur in small seminars and later in the term, when students have become less dependent on the instructor and more invested in each other. Student debate is encouraged if instructors are silent after student comments, giving other students a chance to respond. Using students' names when referring to their argument ("As Eddie was saying") also promotes student-student interaction. The degree to which students talk to each other is mostly a function of class size and the amount of teacher talk during discussion. In extended discussion, experienced instructors encourage the group to develop as an independent unit by being less active from the start, letting students' discomfort with silence pressure them to relate to each other as well as to the instructor.

However discussion is guided, the class's emotional arousal and investment during discussion must be maintained. An instructor can use humor, spontaneity, or a sense of irony or pathos at different times to keep the discourse lively (Barnes-McConnell, 1978). Instructors contribute to good discussion indirectly through subtle control and stimulation of students' thinking processes.

College teachers must also know when to end discussion or guide the discourse in another direction. The way an instructor ends discussion (to return to lecturing or to end class) affects the amount students learn from the exchange of ideas and the eagerness with which they will discuss next time. Instructors sometimes find it difficult to close discussion when students are highly involved, but the skills required to end discussion well are simple.

First, give students some warning that the discussion is about to end. Asking, "Are there any other comments before we tie these ideas together?" lets students with more to say and those who have not yet spoken know that if they wish to speak, they must do so now. It also communicates that you plan to go on to another topic unless students have something else to say. Students will close discussion more decisively and quickly if they are warned that the end is coming.

When you do shift the focus to another discussion point or return to lecturing, begin talking with the forceful voice and strong bodily movements you normally use in beginning classes or when lecturing, to let students know that you have shifted gears and they should now simply listen. This is an excellent time to summarize the major points of the preceding discussion. An instructor's final review of the discussion frequently appears in student notes and is remembered. All discussion, of whatever duration, should end with a summary.

Ending discussion well makes it easier to initiate discussion again. This is because instructor summaries show students that the teacher was listening carefully to what they had to say and also because a firm ending reminds students that the instructor is in charge. Ending discussion before students run out of steam also preserves their eagerness to discuss again; no one enjoys discussion that goes on for too long. Like the seasoned performer, the skilled discussion leader stops while the audience is still eager for more.

Special Discussion Problems

Other than the difficulty of initiating discussion, the most frequent problems associated with discussion occur when the class strays from the intended topic, students become so emotionally involved that they get angry with each other or the teacher, or some students dominate the proceedings while others withdraw. Though a college teacher may only rarely encounter these problems, it helps to know how to deal with them should they occur.

Skilled discussion leaders select their comments and questions to have an intended effect on students and to lead them in a particular direction. But no one can always predict how students will respond. The excitement many instructors feel during discussions probably comes partly from this unpredictability.

When you notice that the discussion is drifting, ask yourself whether the group is leaving important points dangling, perhaps avoiding coming to terms with a difficult issue, and whether the new direction appears to have potential. If the group has not sufficiently fleshed out some important point, you might refocus the discourse ("Let's tie up the point about the economic causes of the revolution before moving into this interesting new hypothesis"). If the original topic is exhausted, offer a concluding comment to tie together what has been said. Do not automatically assume that the new direction is of little value just because it was not planned. When deciding whether to follow the students' lead, ask yourself whether the direction suggested by their comments is as useful as what you had planned to do next. Of course, sometimes the group must be reined in simply because insufficient time is available to go in the new direction.

A second special problem in discussion results from uncontrolled emotion. Some college teachers avoid discussion altogether because they fear angry outbursts from students. First-rate discussion *is* intense, though student anger is unlikely to become unbridled if you are alert for signs of excessive emotion in students' voices and faces. If such signs are noted, reassert control by shifting the focus or get students to achieve distance by asking, "Why do you think you feel so strongly about this topic?" Making the potential or actual outburst an object of study both controls emotions and leads students to understand the power of attitudes and values.

Classroom discussion allows students to display personality characteristics openly, and students at both extremes of talkativeness can present problems. Students who talk too much may dominate a discussion unless the instructor curbs their talking. Constant talkers typically want, above all else, to impress the teacher, and they never notice the way other students look away, roll their eyes, or whisper to each other when the student begins a comment ("There he goes again!"). Whatever the merits of a verbose student's comments, the instructor must end his or her monopoly of the floor to preserve class morale and the overall quality of discussion. Other students expect the teacher to control such a classmate, but they will be disappointed (and frightened) if the instructor treats the student aversively.

How do you control an overly talkative student without bruising other students' sensibilities? First, avoid looking in the talkative student's direction when asking a question. Turn your back to the student slightly, scan others' faces, and wait for another student to respond. However, never to recognize or look at such a student would be going too far. Sometimes call on the student immediately, but at other times, systematically ignore him or her. Let the student know instantly whether you are going to call on him or her this time around. This practice will bring the student's talking under your control more quickly than trying to ignore him or her altogether. Another technique is to slowly walk away from the student when he or she is talking. Do not turn your back on the student entirely, however. Look around the room at the whole class as the student talks, occasionally making eye contact with him or her as well. This reduces the one-to-one nature of the student's communication and makes it more of a comment to the group—something more likely to involve others. (Incidentally, slowly walking away from the speaker makes *all* students speak more loudly when making class comments.) These two techniques usually suffice to control a dominating student. Occasionally, however, you may need to talk with the student privately. If this is necessary, compliment the student for his or her willingness to share ideas before suggesting that others be given a chance to participate as well.

College teachers are less likely to notice the extremely uninvolved or withdrawn student. Of course, students who are silent are not necessarily uninvolved; one of the beauties of engaging in discussion is that the observers can be as involved and intellectually active as the participants. However, some students do withdraw from discussion proceedings. To recognize such students, scan the faces of the class regularly during discussion, noting how interested each person seems to be, as well as which individuals seem ready to make a contribution. Try to make eye contact with any student who consistently seems preoccupied. Lecturing in that student's part of the room or speaking to him or her casually before class may keep the student engaged. Some students are so information- and grade-oriented that they find discussion an unpleasant waste of time. If more than 10 percent of the class seems withdrawn at any time during discussion, consider whether too much time has been spent in discussion, whether the topic is really important enough to justify using class time in this way, or whether students may be concerned about an upcoming assignment deadline or examination.

A Final Note

Classroom discussion can be a waste of time for everyone and as boring as the worst of lectures. However, when focused on appropriate course material and when done with a class that has been trained to participate, discussion can produce unmatched involvement and opportunities for students to practice the critical, independent thinking associated with active learning. Discussion can be planned, though not with as much certainty as lectures or demonstrations. Discussion is the most interpersonal of all classroom teaching methods; thus, it is the first to reflect a rise or drop in class morale or teacher enthusiasm. Because discussion requires so much energy, creativity, and spontaneity, college teachers will work just as hard during discussion as they do during a lecture and should not be surprised if they feel just as emotionally drained afterward.

The next chapter describes how college teachers decide what to include in a course and how to present the chosen content. Guidelines for planning entire courses as well as individual class meetings are offered. As has been clear throughout the preceding chapters, the best-laid plans do not ensure high-quality teaching, but planning does force the instructor to consider as many options as possible when deciding what to present in the limited class time available.

7

Planning Course Content
and Teaching Techniques
to Maximize Interest

*Suppose you wanted to get to know a tract of coun-
try. The worst way to do it would be to jump into a
car, drive straight from one end to the other, then turn
your back on it and walk away. Yet that is what
many teachers do with complex subjects, and that is
why their pupils seem stupider than they really
are. . . . How much better would they learn the
country if, before setting out, they were briefed and
given maps to study; if they were rested and reori-
ented once or twice during the trip; and if they were
shown photographs of the best spots and taken once
more over the map when they reached the end of their
journey?*

—*Highet*[1]

M any college teachers are ambivalent about planning. Though
most would endorse in theory the value of educational planning, few plan their courses creatively and independently, stepping
outside the traditional curriculum to select the concepts they
believe to be most fundamental or adopt innovative methods of

1.   G. Highet. *The Art of Teaching*, 1950, pp. 79–80. Reprinted by permission of
Alfred A. Knopf, Inc.

teaching them. Like compliant students who do only what is asked of them, too many college teachers adopt a prescribed syllabus or follow the chapter headings in a textbook without considering what students should actually learn from their courses. Too many instructors also choose teaching methods by default, continuing to rely in the main on some variation of lecture/discussion. Most excellent instructors, on the other hand, plan very seriously, fully aware that alternative ways of organizing class sessions are available, which go beyond the mere presentation of material to the promotion of active higher-order learning and motivation.

This chapter shows how the planning of college courses—individual class meetings, as well as the whole course—needs to take into account both objectives and methods. The suggestions offered here apply to any course; see Cahn's collection of essays (1978) and Angelo and Cross's handbook (1993) for guidelines and techniques geared toward teaching specific subjects.

Before planning is discussed, it should be emphasized again that although thoughtful selection of objectives, content, and methods contributes significantly to a course, still, as in warfare and athletics, the value of a strategy depends most on how well it is executed and whether it is flexible when surprises occur. No matter how carefully thought-out and detailed, course outlines and lesson plans do not captivate students—college teachers with well-honed classroom skills do that. Nonetheless, teachers who carefully consider what content should be presented and how learning should be organized are more likely to orchestrate virtuoso performances than those who leave much to improvisation.

Before launching into course design, think of the diversity of those for whom the course is being planned. Students in every course have varying abilities, interests, and expectations. Many students are high achievers and wish to be challenged fully. Others merely hope to get by without doing poorly. Some actively question everything they read and hear, and intuitively demonstrate what has come to be called "active learning" and "critical thinking."

Sadly, others continue to behave as if learning is soaking up what the text or instructor presents and squeezing it back out on exams or in papers. Some students are greatly interested in the course's subject, while others—hopefully few—approach the content with dread. Yet all students must be offered the same class meetings, given the same assignments, and evaluated using identical criteria. How can you adjust for student differences when planning a course?

The initial topics chosen for lecture should attempt to engage *all* students, the least as well as the most able, interested, and motivated, and those who think of knowledge in the most absolute terms as well as those who see it in largely contextual terms (Magolda, 1992). Once the course is under way, topics of less obvious interest can be introduced with a greater probability of acceptance. When previewing a course for students, you should describe a wide range of objectives to maximize the probability that every student will be seeing something of personal value in the course and motivated to do his or her best.

Determining Objectives

Objectives are easier to choose when an instructor appreciates the wide range of available options.

Levels of Objectives

Until recent advances in cognitive psychology suggested techniques for teaching critical thinking (Smith, F., 1990; Woditsch and Schmittroth, 1991), Benjamin Bloom's 1956 taxonomy of cognitive educational objectives reigned supreme as a sufficient model of what we can hope to accomplish in college classes. Most teaching does involve some combination of the six different categories or levels of objectives Bloom describes, though some involves only one or two levels. As is clear from the following presentation of Bloom's taxonomy, the levels become increasingly complex and difficult to specify, attain, and evaluate as they rise from one to six.

They do not, however, sufficiently address contemporary ideas about critical thinking (Smith, F., 1990) or the communication and problem-solving skills described in the learning model presented in Chapter One.

Some college teachers are interested primarily in having students (1) *recall and recognize* information. Committing to memory facts, theories, and principles is the essence of level one in Bloom's system. Almost every instructor has some information for students to handle at this level.

Most teachers also desire students to (2) *comprehend* what they have learned—to understand and be able to explain specific concepts using their own words and images rather than parroting definitions provided by others.

Neither recall nor comprehension is sufficient for those who expect students to be able to (3) *apply* what they have learned. For such instructors, a student's mastery of a topic is incomplete unless he or she can apply it correctly to examples. Still others want students to think about what they have learned in an active way. Students should be able both to (4) *analyze* the subject, breaking it down into its constituent parts, and (5) *synthesize* it into a unified whole once again.

Finally, some college teachers are not content unless students (6) *evaluate* their knowledge critically. For such teachers, learning is incomplete unless students have come to grips with underlying value issues and are able to judge the importance of what they have come to know.

By way of illustration, a professor of abnormal psychology desired to achieve objectives at all six of Bloom's levels. For a section on schizophrenia, she wanted students to be able to define in their own words a number of specific concepts and research findings relating to the theory that biological influences are at the root of this disorder. She also wanted them to be able to apply this hypothesis to other disorders and to use it to interpret the results of studies stressing family influences. It was her wish that students be able to critique various kinds of supporting research (neurotransmitter studies in animals, genetic studies in humans, clinical effects of drugs) and also be able to bring them together in an integrated argument showing how all could result from a common source. Finally, this instructor wanted students to form a personal opinion on the persuasiveness of the biological argument—especially in contrast to competing hypotheses stressing the effects of experience—and make some educated guesses about what future studies might demonstrate. Though this professor knew of Bloom's system only generally, the objectives she had for her students fit it nicely.

Advocates of teaching critical thinking elaborate on Bloom's analysis and synthesis levels and go well beyond them in suggesting ways of teaching students how to think. One camp proposes teaching thinking explicitly, arguing that students lack critical skills (Browne and Keeley, 1986). Another view is that critical thinking is "less a set of sure-fire procedures than an attitude of inquiry" (Siegel and Carey, 1989, p. 26), a disposition of "reflective skepticism" (McPeck, 1981, p. 7). Students need not learn to think differently as much as to become "immersed in a social environment that offers interesting ideas to think about, models of critical thinking to emulate, and rewards for (or at least toleration of) their own critical thoughts" (Gray, 1993, p. 68).

Specifying Objectives in Advance

Since Bloom proposed his taxonomy, professional educators have recommended that instructors specify their objectives for a particular course in advance (Barry, 1978). Advocates of this position have added two corollaries to Bloom's taxonomy. The first is that college teachers should be accountable—that they should commit themselves ahead of time to what they are going to accomplish. The second is that teaching should produce observable behavioral changes in students. Unfortunately, behavioral objectives are most easily written for the concrete, factual levels of Bloom's taxonomy. As one moves up the list, it becomes increasingly difficult to specify and assess what students will be able to *do* differently, although some schools (Wisconsin's Alverno College is the prime example) have successfully defined behavioral objectives for such complex skills as speaking and writing (Carpenter and Doig, 1988.)

A third feature of the educational objectives approach is an emphasis on minimal standards of achievement for a class, that is, objectives that should be met by all. This rule fails to recognize the sizable individual differences in talent and motivation present among college students. What is designed as minimal expectations for all can easily become maximal accomplishments for those students who would otherwise be capable of going far beyond what is expected of others.

Some educators advocate that instructors spend the first part of each course helping students formulate their own objectives for the course rather than dictating objectives to the class (Barry, 1978). Though students may initially like being involved in course planning, this approach does not capitalize on the instructor's greater expertise, and it wastes precious class time that might be spent more productively. Class consensus on a set of objectives is also very difficult to achieve. Most students would rather be involved in choosing activities and assignments within objectives formulated by the instructor than go through the exercise of wording objectives and seeking consensus.

Most college teachers espouse higher-level objectives in theory (Angelo and Cross, 1993), but the best college teachers design their classes so as to actually offer a wide range of challenges for students. They expect students to master facts, demonstrate that they can think about what they have learned in a personally meaningful and intellectually complex way, apply their learning to real-world examples, show an array of problem-solving skills as well as a skeptical disposition, and be able to communicate their ideas effectively. Designing a course that has a wide range of goals ensures that students with different interests and abilities will find something that captivates and challenges them. More importantly, a wide range of objectives will stretch students' intellects and pique their imaginations more than will an agenda that stresses only the acquiring of information. The following section suggests ways to plan a course with a range of objectives.

Designing a Course

Although some instructors successfully design courses intuitively, most will benefit from a more systematic approach.

Selecting Topics and Skills

The first step in planning a course is to make a large, tentative list of topics or skills that might be included. From this comprehensive list, eliminate the least desirable using two criteria: how essential the topics or skills are to the course as a whole and how interesting they might be to students. As less essential and less interesting possibilities are eliminated, a mixture of especially important or interesting ones will emerge. Another option is to select the most desirable topics or skills first, rank-ordering each according to these same criteria. A final list can be constructed by alternately selecting items high on each separate ranking, particularly those high on both lists. Regardless of the specific method used, your choice of topics or skills depends ultimately on your subjective judgment about what is most important in your field and what students' interest might be.

Forming Topic Objectives

You must next consider what you would like students to learn about each topic. Sometimes, you will simply want them to define a concept correctly; at other times, you will want them to apply it to an example. You may wish to promote a critical attitude by emphasizing *ideas*—topics about which there is disagreement and that can be tested empirically, as opposed to isolated facts or overly general themes (Gray, 1993). In deciding how to treat each topic, consider what you want students to know, be able to do, or feel following the course. Thinking about objectives is particularly useful in deciding what reading or written assignments to include. Formulating objectives is admittedly a difficult process and, other than the advisability of putting them on paper for inspection and revision, no rigid guidelines are proposed. This stage of course design requires careful instructor judgment and maximum creativity.

Forming Skill Objectives

Many faculty (as well as students and parents) are accustomed to thinking of education as what one knows rather than what one can do. Consequently, it may be hard to anticipate what you will want your students to be able to do (or to do better) as a result of your course, even if you teach a subject such as English composition, foreign language conversation and grammar, laboratory sciences, or engineering, which aim to train students to perform specific activities. If you teach a subject in which skills are not usually taught, taking a broad perspective when selecting your course objectives can suggest appropriate writing, speaking, or problem-solving skills. Formulating skill objectives requires a shift in how faculty often think about their courses and methods of evaluating students, because it is easier to measure what students know than what they can do. Thinking in behavioral terms, however, will make it more likely that instructors will select appropriate formats for teaching skills and for evaluating how well students have mastered them.

Adjusting Goals to Reality

You should remember that stated course objectives are goals to be pursued, not sacred injunctions. They must be fitted to realistic constraints.

Time is the major constraint on what can be accomplished in a college course. A three-credit-hour course that meets for two-and-one-half hours per week in a sixteen-week semester allows for at most forty hours of class time—equivalent to a typical work week.

The first and last classes deal largely with administrative or group maintenance concerns, and one or two additional classes will be taken up by exams, so a better estimate of maximum class time is thirty-seven hours. Given the limited time for class presentations and activities, an instructor has no choice but to carefully temper his or her ideal objectives with a healthy dose of realism.

As experienced college teachers know, the first step in fitting their goals to the available time is to list all class meetings. Fill in this schedule with tentative topics, including at either end the predictable administrative concerns. It is advisable to schedule exams first and to leave open the class just before each exam to allow for catching up or review. The number of available class meetings rapidly shrinks. In fitting lecture topics into the available meetings, begin if possible with high-interest topics and those that must be mastered before others can be introduced. Particularly complex or difficult concepts may take several meetings; on the other hand, several simple ideas may be combined in a single session. Chapter Eight advocates spreading out writing or problem-solving assignments over several class meetings. Because the initial list of topics is almost sure to be longer than what can be accommodated, you will have to eliminate some. Strive for a varied schedule, changing the format every three or four classes and mixing lecture, case study, demonstration, or discussion to maintain high interest and prevent predictability.

When scheduling, remember that several classes are especially important. The first and last classes and the classes just before and after exams have a great impact on class morale. Attempt to make these classes especially interesting or provocative. The last two or three classes are much better suited to integration and evaluation of what has been covered in the whole course than to introduction of new topics.

Other important constraints on planning are class size and the time students have to devote to the course. Objectives requiring extensive discussion are much more difficult to meet in large classes.

Lecture classes with large enrollment require more dramatic methods of presentation and creative uses of discussion and group work.
Planning for small seminars and for very large lecture classes is discussed in a later section of this chapter. You should also remember
that students have other courses and demands; make your requirements reasonable, relative to common practices at your school. Bal-
ancing intellectual objectives and the need to maintain student
interest is difficult, but many college teachers, seeing the difference
that good planning can make in the quality of their courses, have
become convinced that it is worth the effort.

Sharing Objectives with Students

Students are much more likely to meet expectations if course objectives are clearly stated at the outset. During the first class meeting,
present orally (and perhaps also in writing on a handout or your syllabus) the objectives you have formulated. Full details need not be
offered, but a few minutes spent on objectives at the very beginning
gives students an idea of where they are headed and why it is important to go there. Some instructors state objectives as questions that
the students should be able to answer when the semester is over
(Maas, 1980). Others prepare an "enriched syllabus" that goes into
considerable detail about what students can expect (Duffy and
Jones, 1995). Going back to the objectives during the last class
meeting reminds students what they should have gotten out of a
course and makes a good basis for a final discussion.

Selecting Formats

Deciding which specific teaching techniques to use in a course is
much easier once you specify what you want your students to know
or to be able to do at the end of the course. Selecting formats can
also be creative—even fun—if you are aware of the great range
available for organizing today's college classes. This section describes
the major options you might choose from when organizing a course
or specific class. Unlike the next section, which focuses on issues

more confined to special types of classes, such as large lectures, the formats presented here are applicable to most courses.

First, two caveats about course format are in order. My observations of outstanding instructors and reading of the research literature have convinced me that no single format—whether lecture, discussion, active or cooperative learning assignments, or multimedia laboratories—is the *best* way to teach. Exemplary teachers can offer classes of very high quality using any of them; conversely, poor teachers can ruin the potential present in every class format. Second, instructors should beware of thinking that alternative teaching formats are necessarily new or unique. As the following pages demonstrate, there is a great deal of overlap in techniques; they differ mostly in what they emphasize, and each shares much with the fundamental view of college teaching emphasized in this volume. What matters most is the instructor's general communication skills, ability to motivate students, and dedication to teaching. That theoretical position notwithstanding, any college teacher is more likely to become an exemplar by expanding his or her repertoire of teaching formats and learning how to enrich an already excellent course by selecting techniques to meet specific purposes. Learning to use a variety of formats also enables an instructor to adapt to whatever teaching setting and whatever type of student audience he or she may encounter in the future.

What are the formats from which to choose? Lecturing and leading discussions as described in Chapters Five and Six should be considered first, as they are the backbone of instruction in most American colleges and, if done well, will meet many of your course objectives. But a number of alternative techniques are commonly interspersed in traditional lecture/discussion classes, largely to promote motivation and active learning by encouraging students to be more intellectually critical and to take more responsibility for their own and their classmates' learning.

Active learning refers to a number of techniques that aim to encourage students to do more of the coursework during class sessions.

Such techniques, it is believed, are likely to make them active rather than passive participants in class sessions (Bonwell and Eison, 1991; Duffy and Jones, 1995; Meyers and Jones, 1993). Whether students are asked to talk, to listen, to write, to read, or to reflect, the goal is always to promote involvement in their own learning, in a manner that reflects their individual learning styles and preferences. Common techniques involve assigning students to small groups to reflect on readings or instructor presentations, to participate in simulations, to make group presentations or engage in small-group debates (Smith, R. A., 1990), or to work on cooperative projects. But students can also be asked to work individually to solve problems, apply general principles to real-world examples, or record in journals their critical reactions to readings or class presentations. Guest speakers or field trips can also be used to promote student involvement. What appears to be more important than the specific student assignments is the instructor's general teaching role and attitude toward the class. A classroom environment that encourages active learning is one in which the instructor has carefully selected objectives and techniques and shared them with students, actively promoted interpersonal rapport, and been sensitive to the classroom as a teaching space that can be used creatively (Meyers and Jones, 1993). Most of the techniques advocated in this book aim in effect to foster students who are actively involved in their studies.

Classroom assessment refers to a closely related group of techniques that also promote student involvement in classes, but more for the purpose of giving instructors information about what students already know and are learning, or how they are feeling about themselves or the course. Tom Angelo and Patricia Cross spent several years developing and evaluating a long list of classroom assessment techniques, which are presented in a comprehensive handbook (1993). Most of the techniques produce written information to be evaluated by instructors between classes, although some do provide more immediate feedback during class.

Angelo and Cross describe and evaluate fifty techniques, about half of which deal with *course-related knowledge and skills*. Many of the techniques assess students' knowledge at the beginning of a course; for example, a physics instructor asks students to list five words or phrases that define work. Others assess what students are learning during a class; for example, toward the end of a class, a nursing professor lists major topic headings from that day's presentation on the board and asks students to write as many terms as they recall under each heading. Or students can be asked to write a focused minute paper on a topic of interest to the instructor or to name the muddiest point in the day's class. The list of course-related techniques goes on to include methods for assessing critical and creative thinking, problem-solving, and application to specific problems.

The remaining assessment techniques focus on learners' awareness of their *attitudes, values, behavior as students*, and *study skills*. These are particularly useful in courses that emphasize these objectives or with students needing to improve their behavior as learners. Angelo and Cross also offer several alternative means of assessing *students' reactions to the teacher;* these are presented in Chapter Ten, in the section on evaluating teaching.

Classroom assessment offers a wealth of options to the instructor wishing to promote high involvement in classes and to fine-tune his or her presentation to promote learning. More than anything, Angelo and Cross recommend that instructors who follow their suggestions be creative rather than slavish: "adapt; don't adopt" (1993, p. 37). B. F. Skinner once said something to the effect that all teachers will eventually become good teachers if they will simply pay close attention to their students' behavior. Classroom assessment offers ways of also looking into students' minds.

The *case method*, common in management, medicine, and law, aims for the critical, independent thinking and group problem-solving skills of active learning, but is much more focused on practicing professional skills in a safe environment (Boehrer and Linsky, 1990; Christensen, 1991a; Christensen and Hansen, 1987). Students taking a case-based business class, for example, might focus on an elaborate narrative description of an actual (or realistically simulated) business decision. If the case has been selected and written skillfully, students will become "active and animated; offering ideas, raising questions, building on each other's statements, constructing a collective analysis, reframing the discussion, challenging the teachers, and learning with and from each other as much or more than from the teacher" (Boehrer and Linsky, 1990, p. 42).

Modern case studies often involve more than text and require students to analyze quantitative or multimedia data. For example, several years ago, I developed *SuperShrink,* two computer case simulations for use in undergraduate psychology courses (Lowman, 1990c). Students interview the individuals via computer keyboard, make diagnoses and write case formulations of the kind used by mental health professionals, and present their conclusions in animated class discussions. Although empirical research has shown that students preferred to read the *SuperShrink* cases in a more convenient book form than via computer screen (Lowman, 1990a), more recent multimedia displays would likely prove superior to text.

Unlike courses in which general points are presented in lecture followed by specific examples, classes using the case method reverse the order: the general conclusions come at the end of extended discussion and problem-solving and are more likely to be generated by students. In addition, a smaller number of cases are treated, and in greater depth. Management, legal, and clinical medical training have emphasized the case method for many decades; at some schools, the undergraduate engineering and preclinical medical curricula have also been organized on this basis. Wherever it may be applied, the case method is successful at teaching real-world application of ideas because of the strong personal identification students feel with the portrayed decision makers and the problems they encounter. In this sense, the well-constructed case and the well-presented lecture capitalize on the same student responsiveness to dramatic situations as is discussed in previous chapters.

Cooperative learning (and its close cousin, *collaborative learning*) share many objectives with active learning. One recent book on cooperative learning, for example, is entitled, *Active Learning: Cooperation in the College Classroom* (Johnson, Johnson, and Smith, 1991). Students are encouraged to become involved in their own learning by working with other students (sometimes the instructor, too) in small groups. Although the two terms can refer to broad educational movements applicable to lower grades as well as college classes (Johnson and Johnson, 1994), may describe similar classroom activities, and are often used interchangeably, it is my view that each approach attempts to realign traditional power relationships between instructors and students for a somewhat different purpose.

Cooperative learning aims to promote student mastery of traditional content—often in technical subjects such as business, science, mathematics, and engineering—by enlisting students as fellow teachers and learners in small learning groups or pairs. The techniques involve much more than simply having students interact in class or help others with their work. There must also be a combination of *positive interdependence*, whereby each student's learning benefits when the entire group improves, and *individual accountability*, in which each student is held accountable for his or her learning (Johnson, Johnson, and Smith, 1991), usually via traditional individual evaluation. Students may also improve social skills and motivation as a result of working on cooperative tasks. Research has demonstrated that college students learning cooperatively do show increased mastery and motivation and ability to see things from another's perspective (Johnson, Johnson, and Smith, 1991).

Collaborative learning, on the other hand, is more popular in the humanities, perhaps because of its stronger philosophical or political emphasis. Although a visitor might be as likely to see students discussing course content in small groups in a cooperatively run class as in a collaboratively run class, the primary concern here is with realigning traditional power relationships by creating knowledge in different, more egalitarian "communities of learners" (Smith and MacGregor, 1992, p. 9). Student learning groups are often active throughout a course, not just to work toward instructor-defined objectives—which might characterize a cooperative learning situation—but to promote an often unique approach to the curriculum—to what is important to know (Kadel and Keehner, 1994) as well as to how it is to be learned. Collaborative techniques stress student responsibility and interaction, more for what they do for the curriculum and students' self-determination than for how well they help students master course content selected by the instructor. Because cooperative learning includes a broader range of specific techniques than does the collaborative approach, it can be more easily applied outside its philosophical context to fit the aims of most college teachers. In fact, almost any instructor can make effective use of cooperative learning techniques to increase involvement and learning.

Three main types of cooperative techniques have been described (see Johnson, Johnson, and Smith, 1991, for a more complete description of these techniques). *Formal cooperative learning groups* include many variations on the theme of small student groups working together on course content and being evaluated together, at least in part (Cottell and Millis, 1994). For example, an economics instructor might use the "jigsaw" technique to help students master the many technical terms they will be covering in the course. When a new topic is introduced, different lists of terms are assigned to different groups of students, who learn them on their own and teach them to other students during classroom group sessions. "Jigsaw" refers to breaking up the content into pieces, which different students in each group are responsible for mastering and teaching the others. Students are evaluated as individuals, but they may receive bonus points based on the overall performance of their group.

An engineering instructor may assign sets of homework problems to groups of four students, who work on the problems together; every member then comes to class prepared to present the answer or describe the methods used to reach it. As in the economics course, each student takes exams alone but may receive bonus points reflecting how well the entire group does. Coaching groups in English composition offer another variation of formal cooperative groups. Here, students exchange drafts of their weekly essays for shared editing by the rest of the group before final drafts are submitted for grading. Again, the entire group usually benefits in some way when everyone's writing improves. Whether aimed at discipline terminology, specific problem-solving skills, or general communication skills, formal groups can be built in from the very beginning of a course to ensure that students will meet instructors' objectives.

A key technique when using formal groups effectively is to assign students to their groups rather than letting students form groups on their own. Keeping this power for the instructor prevents students clustering according to friendship, gender, or racial cliques and makes it possible to ensure each group has a range of academic ability in its membership. Some cooperative learning devotees rotate group membership several times over the term and use performance on exams or papers as a basis for reassignment.

Informal cooperative learning groups need not be so structured and can be instituted on an impromptu basis to increase intellectual engagement during a lecture. Students can be clustered in groups and asked to discuss topics or solve problems. The most common technique here involves the assignment of focused discussion tasks to pairs of students before, during, or after class. Student pairs can be given a few minutes at the beginning of a class to grade each other's homework and to use what they learn in the process to improve their own work. They can also be asked to exchange questions about the day's reading and to take a minute or two to write down answers to their partner's questions. During a lecture, any discussion probe can be turned into a pairing exercise by asking students to write down their response and exchange it with a neighbor or two. Then ask students to share with the entire class especially interesting comments they have seen. At the end of class, pairs can exchange minute-paper responses before they are turned in to the instructor. Although some cooperative learning advocates argue that small groups or pairing structures are a weak imitation of complex formal structures (Cottell and Millis, 1994), informal groups offer tremendous flexibility, promote interpersonal rapport, and help to break up the routine of instructor-focused class meetings.

All cooperative learning techniques can increase student motivation, but the third type, *cooperative base groups*, aims explicitly to do so. Students are assigned at the beginning of a course to support groups that meet regularly—usually at the beginning of class, even outside class—to discuss anything that might affect a student's learning. Students may ask each other if they understood last night's reading or homework problems, if they are having difficulty finding reference materials, or how they are feeling about themselves as college students. Base groups are formed to be heterogeneous and usually continue over an entire course or academic year, even over four years of college. However they are implemented, the objective of cooperative base groups is to ensure that every student is part of a small support network of the kind students and others under stress often create informally to help one another.

As should be clear from the preceding descriptions, there are many available formats for the college teacher seeking to provide an exemplary course. But planning often involves additional considerations that result from atypical class structures.

Planning for Special Types of Classes

As has been argued throughout this book, all college classes share common features and present common challenges to the instructor. Yet, some formats offer special demands.

Very Large Classes

Few college teachers prefer large sections to smaller ones. But if practical considerations require that a large class be taught, an instructor can adapt effectively by recognizing how the objectives, methods of presentation, interpersonal atmosphere, and administrative problems of a large class differ from those of a small one (McGee, 1986; Weimer, 1987). Instructors should bear in mind that large classes are offered only for convenience; they have no educational advantages over smaller ones. The relevant question is whether large classes are *less* effective than small ones. (To review the research on this question, the variable of "class size" must be quantified. I will define *very small* as 15 students or fewer; *small* as 16–35; *moderate* as 36–60; *large* as 61–120; and *very large* as over 120. Like many quantitative labels, these are approximate and are used for convenience.)

Student achievement and satisfaction have been compared in small and large classes. Research suggests that college teachers can achieve many educational objectives just as well in large classes as in smaller ones. Scores on final exams do not vary with class size, for example (McKeachie, 1986). Large classes cannot, however, realize objectives best facilitated by discussion—for example, retention, critical thinking, or attitude change.

Research on class size indicates that large classes are less effective than small ones for students who need personal attention from teachers in order to do their best (McKeachie, 1986). Highly dependent, less academically able, and poorly motivated students do not do as well in large sections. Thus, large classes are not as effective as small ones for a significant percentage of students.

Though most students and instructors prefer smaller sections, skillful lecturers can offer exciting and meaningful educational experiences and can compensate for the liabilities associated with large class size. In planning for a large or very large section, wise instructors recognize that most objectives must be met using the lecture format and that the lectures must be more dynamic and engaging than they would have to be in small or moderate-sized classes. Active learning techniques such as pairing, brief discussion, or classroom assessment can be used to stimulate involvement by breaking up a lecture momentarily (Benjamin, 1991). Extended discussion can also be effective if formal or informal cooperative techniques are used.

Because large classes are less personal and intimate than small ones, teachers of large classes should offer as many opportunities as possible for individual contact with students outside of class. Some instructors invite small groups to observe their laboratory or field research ("Sign up on the sheet by the door if you would like to visit my laboratory on Wednesday afternoon" or "I have room in my car for four students to accompany me on a two-hour trip to collect botanical specimens this Thursday afternoon"). Regularly inviting students to sign up in groups of four or five to share lunch with the instructor at the school's dining hall has helped many instructors promote a sense of intimacy in large or small classes.

Requiring students to take advantage of such opportunities for personal contact is not a good idea, however. Doing so increases their fears of both intimacy and autocratic teacher control and weakens rapport. It also takes away students' freedom to make their own decision about whether to seek closer contact with an authority figure. Furthermore, requiring student attendance necessitates monitoring which students appear and deciding how to treat those who do not. None of these outcomes is desirable. It is better to offer attractive events that students, even those who are most afraid of teachers, will want to attend, and to ignore the fact that some students will choose not to sign up and that others will forget to show up despite their best intentions. All students appreciate having such opportunities available, and those who take advantage of them will feel more personally involved in the course.

Maximizing opportunities for personal contacts with students during class is also important (Benjamin, 1991). Instructors of large classes can come to class five to ten minutes early, stroll around the room, and chat informally with students. They can walk up and down the aisles frequently when lecturing, to make eye contact with every student several times during each class. Occasional personal disclosures also add intimacy to large lecture classes (Meredith, 1985). Pairing and other techniques for maximizing rapport outlined in Chapter Three are especially needed. Just as lecturing to a large audience requires a more forceful and energetic delivery, fostering rapport with a big group requires more aggressive interpersonal strategies.

College teachers planning large sections should be aware that administrative nuisances increase with class size (McKeachie, 1986). Not only does it take longer to score the exams of a large class, it also takes considerably longer just to distribute them. If handouts are to be used, they may be placed in stacks near classroom entrances before class to save the time that would otherwise be required for distribution. Access to reserve readings may be difficult in large classes unless sufficient copies can be produced. Several problems associated with evaluation also become more troublesome. Students are more likely to cheat in a large class where they feel less personal involvement, and it is more difficult to prevent them from doing so. Teachers can also expect to be disturbed by more phone calls on the night before an exam. All the irritations of teaching are magnified as the number of students increases, and greater instructor patience and tolerance are required.

A traditional method of easing the burden of large sections is to have one or more teaching assistants (TAs). The argument for this practice is that assistants can do much of the "grunt" work—especially grading—and free the professor to teach. TAs can help with the more routine chores, but they cannot promote interpersonal rapport as well as the instructor can unless they are actively involved in classes and also available to students outside class. They also require considerable supervision if their labors are to be satisfactory to all parties. Teachers who delegate all their office hours to TAs fail to recognize that such times are set aside for interpersonal reasons as much as academic ones and that many students seek a relationship with the professor—the group leader and symbolic parent figure—not with an underling. To maximize student choice and flexibility, both professors and TAs should hold regular office hours. If TAs assist *only* with technical matters (running audiovisual equipment, setting up demonstrations), they are unlikely to create problems. If TAs grade students' work, they must be integrated into the class from the beginning. Ideally, TAs should help to plan the course, attend all class meetings so that they know what has been presented, and make occasional presentations of their own, even if only brief comments, to establish relationships with the students. TAs may also model note-taking on overhead transparencies, as described in Chapter Five. Leadership of small discussion groups is an ideal role for teaching assistants and, coupled with a comprehensive TA manual (Lowman and Mathie, 1992), provides a good training ground for their own teaching skills. TAs can boost the instructor's morale and gain useful exposure to college teaching, but they can do only so much to offset the disadvantages associated with large sections.

Very Small Classes

Very small classes (fewer than fifteen students) will be more involved and emotional settings than larger ones, regardless of what the instructor does. Psychological research has demonstrated that group members become increasingly responsive to each other emotionally as the size of the group decreases (Cartwright and Zander, 1960). When class size drops below fifteen, interpersonal involvement among group members, including the leader, becomes noticeably more intense.

Close involvement is not always pleasant, however, as the conflicts that occur within families demonstrate convincingly. In extremely small classes, instructors' leadership role is of great importance, because their attitudes are more obvious and their methods of control more crucial to classroom atmosphere. How should college teachers adjust their teaching techniques and treatment of students to the interpersonal intensity of small classes?

Getting to know students personally is even more important in small classes than in average or large ones. In a class of one hundred, being unknown is not as aversive as it is if there are few other students from whom to be distinguished. Even if an instructor does not ordinarily seek familiarity with students, he or she must at least learn students' names in a small class. Instructors must also adjust their goals and preferred methods of presentation for very small groups. Richard Tiberius (1990) relates hearing what is probably an apocryphal story from students about a professor who was so rigid, he lectured to a class of only one student. The unbending instructor paused to ask if there were any questions and the lone student actually raised his hand. For most instructors, the interpersonal closeness of small classes allows them to increase students' active learning and comfort with independent thinking, as well as the likelihood of attitude change, but it rules out a course geared to learning facts and theories primarily from instructor lectures. When planning small courses, experienced teachers know that students in such courses expect less lecture, more discussion, and more independent work.

College teachers who ordinarily use discussion frequently will find the small class delightful, but they too should adjust the way they use discussion. Many students are comfortable being silent in a large class, but it is the unusual student who will sit through a very small class without speaking. Thus, leading discussion in small classes can take more time, because more students expect to speak. In smaller classes, students often speak without raising their hands and interrupt each other's comments—sometimes even the instructor's—so it is also more difficult to control the discussion and make it possible for quieter students to hold the floor. Especially in smaller classes, leading successful discussions requires a sense of when to let the students go and when to exert even subtle control. It is still important in small classes for the teacher to set the stage for student comments at the beginning and to bring things together at the end.

Small classes have many advantages. It is easy to get to know students in such classes and to evaluate their work closely. It is also easier to stimulate discussion and to use it to promote independent thinking. Less concrete, more complex objectives are easier to achieve in small classes. However, the greater personal contact in small classes can be uncomfortable at first for teachers (or students) who prefer or are accustomed to more distant relationships or content-focused instruction.

Greater flexibility is required in planning for very small and very large classes. A college teacher who tried to use discussion exclusively in a class of over a hundred would be just as unresponsive to the setting as a teacher who lectured for an entire semester to a group of ten.

Some courses require special planning because of their atypical format. Such courses include individual instruction resembling the traditional tutorial and innovative courses based on contemporary technology.

Tutorials

Individual or small-group tutorials are the backbone of graduate education, and every college teacher is likely to encounter such a situation at some time. A student may ask an instructor to direct honors research, independent study, or a program of guided reading. An instructor may even be asked to offer a formal tutorial in the British style, which involves regular group meetings of three or four students, who submit weekly essays. Teaching students individually requires skills different from those needed for traditional group classes.

Individual instruction is commonly given for purposes not easily achieved in typical group formats, especially to help students expand library or laboratory research skills. They usually have the goal of encouraging students to think generally as well as using specific skills and to create and express their ideas independently. Students should be aware of the purpose of the course and be in agreement with it when signing on.

Because students are expected to act differently in tutorials, they should be told at the outset how tutorials differ from ordinary classes. They should be warned that they must work more independently and learn to use the instructor as consultant rather than supervisor. They should also be prepared for the critical nature of tutorials and reassured that comments about their ideas or work should not be taken too personally. Few undergraduates have learned to value criticism as an aid to improving future performance, and they can benefit from discussion of critical methods and intellectual development. If an instructor shares his or her own difficulty with criticism, students are helped to develop a more mature attitude to learning.

When more than one student will be participating in a tutorial, the teacher should instruct them in how to *give* criticism. Most students will copy the teacher's style of offering criticism, but explicit instruction in how to criticize constructively can eliminate beginner's mistakes and get the tutorial group off to a good start.

In tutorials, teachers direct the proceedings less and give students more time to talk. As with regular class discussion, though, a college teacher must structure the dialogue if a tutorial is to be instructive. Regular meetings are one important way to structure independent student work. Even the best-intentioned students will have trouble if they are instructed to appear "whenever they have work to present or questions to pose." A tutorial instructor should schedule weekly meetings and have the student(s) attend even if they have nothing new to report or present. If no one has anything to present at a scheduled meeting, general discussion of research methods or theoretical issues can be profitable. Because college teachers rarely receive teaching credit for individual courses, they too may not treat them as seriously as regular courses and may tend to avoid formal structure. A successful tutorial, however, should meet as regularly as other courses.

Instructors can further structure students' independent work by focusing on the subject and avoiding a drift into casual or social topics. The intimacy of tutorials makes the student-teacher relationship personal, which is generally advantageous. However, this personal quality increases the temptation to engage in conversation that can take the tutorial off track if allowed to occupy too much meeting time. The instructor must monitor the amount of time spent on personal concerns and refocus the discussion when indicated. ("It sounds like you had a particularly interesting trip to New York City, Kathy. What did you learn at the libraries there that you want to focus on today?")

Some tutorials follow the traditional British format, which routinely begins with a student reading his or her essay and the don interrupting at will to make points or ask questions. Individual or group music lessons (especially master classes) also follow this traditional pattern of student performance and instructor critique. Even in such structured cases, the tutor must keep the group on track and resist temptations to avoid serious artistic, intellectual, or scientific inquiry by lapsing into too much social or irrelevant discourse.

The major responsibility of a tutor is to set limits within which students can exercise independence and responsibility. Experienced college teachers know it is tempting to be overly helpful. It requires tremendous patience to watch students struggle with a problem or learn a skill one has long since mastered without doing it for them, rescuing them too quickly from their impasse. Most good teachers are compulsive sharers, and a tutorial requires them to hold back for as long as possible before revealing their own ideas or techniques. For students to learn independence, the instructor must facilitate their thinking and problem-solving by giving them ample opportunity to find solutions on their own. To many teachers, nurturing intellectual growth makes the tutorial more satisfying than lecturing; but tutoring is frustrating to others, because it requires unusual teacher restraint.

More than anything else, tutorials require that college teachers be sensitive to the *process* of their interactions with students. A successful tutor constantly monitors what is happening interpersonally—whether the students are being independent or asking the instructor to do too much for them, whether they are actively involved in the process or seem passive; whether they take criticism well or become defensive. Sometimes, an instructor must keep a student motivated by commenting on his or her behavior ("I get the impression, Mark, that you are finding it hard to do what we agreed you would do at the start of term"). Most of all, tutors must remain flexible and modify their approach when indicated ("I can see how excited you are about the new collection of Douglas's letters you discovered in the library, Maura. Perhaps you'll want to rethink the planned organization of your thesis"). Whether they are formal tutorials, writing workshops, reading courses, or independent research, I believe individual courses require more interpersonal sensitivity and skill than any other instructional format.

When planning a tutorial, the most important consideration is the objectives. Teachers should be sure that they and the students are clear and in agreement on the purpose of the class. Beyond the motivation and abilities of the individual student(s), the success of a tutorial depends most on the teacher's ability to structure an effective consultative relationship.

Computer-Assisted Classes

To many, the most popular and promising contemporary teaching innovations capitalize on current technology to individualize learning. Computer and multimedia approaches are extensions of Skinner (1968) teaching machines and programmed learning techniques of the 1950s and the Keller (1968) Personalized System of Instruction (PSI) that was popular in the 1970s (Sherman, Ruskin, and Semb, 1983). These behavioral systems are based on sound learning principles and require students to master each unit of content on their own (or with the assistance of an undergraduate proctor) before proceeding at their own pace to other topics. Although programmed learning and PSI did not revolutionize higher education as its proponents had originally hoped (Keller, 1980), the emphasis on tailoring instruction to individual students' ability to master all course objectives is now seen in courses based on computer technology.

Early computer-assisted instruction offered little more than a way to use a million-dollar mainframe computer instead of a $25 textbook to present material to students, but the affordable small computers of today far outstrip earlier forms of programmed instruction in their ability to serve as highly engaging and sensitive electronic tutors, which both present information and correct the mistakes of students (Graves, 1989; Herman, 1988). Contemporary computer simulations (such as *Castellon,* a simulator of the politics and economy of a mythical Latin American country [Scott, 1987]) are complex individualized versions of the case method that, when combined with skillful group discussion, give students experience in "as if" problem-solving in preparation for solving real problems later on. In addition to offering individualized approaches to the mastery of content, computer-assisted instruction can help students to think more effectively. (See Hodges and Sasnett, 1993, and McGraw-Hill Primus, 1993, for descriptions of a variety of innovative teaching software.)

What should instructors consider when deciding whether (or how) to use computers as one of their teaching aids? First, distinguish between the use of computers as tools—to help with writing, calculating, or communicating—and the use of computers as teachers. Because of the necessity for computer literacy in the workforce, courses in many disciplines—composition, mathematics, engineering, and accounting, for example—require students to use computers to perform work or to communicate with the instructor via electronic mail. These uses are distinct from teaching.

Second, ask how essential computers are to meeting your objectives. If you need large and engaging displays for a sizable lecture class (as is described in Chapter Five) a computer-driven blackboard program may be superior to overheads or blackboards. On the other hand, if you are teaching a small course, the costs in time, money, and flexibility of regularly using an electronic blackboard may not be justifiable. By all means experiment with a graphing mathematics program if it will help students visualize calculus problems better than diagrams in texts. But look more skeptically at a computer program that essentially presents text on a screen; students may prefer the greater convenience of reading from books.

Third, use computer assignments only as much as you need to meet your objectives. If they are essential, you may build an entire course around them, as in a computer-based writing laboratory in a journalism school or a laboratory course based on computer-simulated experiments in a psychology department. However, as devices introduced to vary the pace of a course, computers may fulfill their function with only one or two uses.

When deciding whether to use any individualized format, remember that no format—neither active or cooperative learning techniques nor computer-assisted instruction—can stand alone and eliminate the need for a creative and committed college teacher who interacts with students in ways the students find satisfying. Students still need living teachers to inspire, to motivate, and to reassure them. As O. P. Kolstoe (1975) notes, "To learn, students must react to the presentation, whether that is a person, place, or thing. The successful teacher is apt to be the one who honestly faces the fact that communication is a very personal thing between each instructor and each student. . . . Universal [alternatives to this] simply are myths pursued by naive teachers and technology hucksters" (p. 72).

Planning for Individual Class Meetings

Though a college teacher will have noted objectives for each class meeting when planning a course, these will be too general to use for specific presentations. College courses are too unpredictable to be planned completely, even by experienced instructors, and they would be lifeless affairs if they *were* so thoroughly planned. To be fresh and involved and closely connected with the previous topic, each class meeting should be organized only a few days to a week beforehand. What should be considered when planning for a specific class?

Selecting specific objectives from available options is the first task. There are a number of ways in which an instructor might want students to understand a topic: the goal might be the development of a historical perspective, or the memorization and comprehension of difficult details presented in readings, or the ability to apply a concept to contemporary events and issues. A teacher might wish to present a theory or piece of literature, or to show how others have tested or criticized an idea. Because the possibilities are almost end-less, instructors should carefully select both what is most important and what is most needed, dramatically and interpersonally, on a given day.

In planning single classes, review the topics last presented and those scheduled immediately afterward. A useful technique for selecting the focus of a given class is to imagine what you want students to tell their friends about the topic over lunch or after class. Thinking about topics from the students' perspective can give you clues as to what you want most to accomplish with a given topic. This in turn can help you decide how to present it.

You should first list three or four major points you wish to make in a class meeting. You must then decide how to make them. Creativity, a sense of drama, and sensitivity to student interests come into play here. If lecture is to be used, remember the guidelines about variety and timing when deciding how to present each point and where in the presentation it should appear. If discussion is appropriate, note potential queries and where in the presentation they can be raised. If a classroom assessment, small group, or cooperative technique is chosen, be sure to allow sufficient class time. Demonstrations or slides must, of course, be prepared well in advance. When constructing a presentational outline for a given class meeting, think of the meeting as an artistic event needing an overall theme, an engaging beginning, and a buildup to a decisive conclusion.

Modifying Plans

This chapter began with the premise that planning is valuable because it helps college teachers anticipate classroom events. But how rigidly should course plans be followed? The answer depends on a number of things.

It depends on the college teacher's experience. Not surprisingly, experienced instructors are better able to plan accurately, but even the experienced may find their plans for a new course or presentation disappointing in application. Anyone teaching a course for the first time should view his or her plans with considerable skepticism and be willing to drop or add topics if too much or too little was planned for the time available. An instructor may also need to adjust the relative amounts of time spent on discussion or lecture. The first set of exams can indicate whether too little or too much was asked of the students.

If an instructor has successfully taught a course at a given school before but is now finding it difficult to stick to the planned schedule, he or she should look for personal reasons for the difficulty. Occasionally, instructors may notice themselves being unnecessarily wordy or tangential when lecturing or too willing to let a class wander from the point or discuss too long. This may be because the teacher is preoccupied with personal concerns, physically tired, or simply bored on that day. Whatever the cause, teachers who have difficulty sticking to their class plans should examine their own attitudes and increase their motivation to teach well, rather than assuming that the plans need changing.

If a college teacher senses on a given day that what was planned is not going well, he or she should definitely consider taking a different tack. The methods of presentation are more likely to need change than the planned topics. Perhaps the class has not gone well because of an unanticipated drop in class morale or a consuming campus issue that has affected the students. Whether the malaise rests with the students or with the instructor, increasing discussion, presenting humorous anecdotes or injecting more energy into lecturing may turn things around. A rule of thumb is to be wary of changing course outlines unless you are new to a course, but to be quick to modify your behavior in a given class when things do not go as expected.

One exception to this policy deals with requirements and evaluation. Students will become upset if requirements (exams, significant readings, or papers) are added after the semester is well under way. All major work expected of students should be announced in the syllabus and on the first day of class. College teachers should also avoid decreasing assigned work unless it is apparent that a serious error of planning has occurred. The teacher should not ask students if they would like requirements changed—of course they would. Asking indicates that the instructor is not confident and raises the possibility that other requirements are negotiable. An unconfident instructor raises students' anxiety about class leadership and reduces their motivation to complete assignments. If an instructor decides to combine two short papers into one long paper, he or she might ask students to vote their preferences and then announce the final decision later. The work expected of students in a college course is a solemn social contract, and modifying it significantly risks reducing student satisfaction and motivation to assume work responsibilities.

Plans, then, generally should be followed once a course is under way. They represent (or should represent) the results of careful thinking about the topics of the course, the objectives to be pursued, and the methods to be used. But planning involves more than classroom presentations. Student course requirements and the means of evaluation must be planned as well. This chapter has dealt with planning generally. Chapter Eight focuses on course requirements, including assignments that students are asked to do outside of class, and Chapter Nine details methods of evaluation and ways to use them to increase motivation and learning.

Integrating Learning
In and Out of the Classroom

Attending class is akin to regular religious observance:
the ritual or sermon is less important for what it
teaches directly than for its motivational impact on
what believers do between services.

Coming to class is essential to mastering the content of a college course, yet most learning actually occurs outside the classroom (Eble, 1988). Recall and recognition of specific information most often results from solitary reading and concentrated study. Independent thinking about course content is also fostered by written assignments that students complete on their own. For some subjects, firsthand observation of the phenomena, research methods, or artistic performances under study provides an essential framework within which to organize learned facts. Most courses can benefit from occasional field trips or observations that students make on their own. Do not let this book's emphasis on college teaching as artistic performance in an interpersonal arena obscure the fact that the ability to read and write critically has long been the fundamental skill of an educated person, and this is developed largely through individual efforts outside the classroom. The real issue is not whether in-class or out-of-class activities are most important but how they can best be integrated for the purpose of meeting an agreed set of ends.

When a few illustrative statistics on a typical college course are calculated, the importance of outside assignments becomes clearer. In harmony with regional accrediting guidelines, most three-credit-hour courses meet for two-and-one-half hours during each of the sixteen weeks in a semester. This means that a total of forty hours (2,400 minutes), or one work week, are available for class sessions. Actually, even fewer hours are available for class instruction, because of exams, the first and last class sessions, and the few minutes usually spent on administrative matters during each class session. Most college teachers are surprised by these data, which reveal how little actual class time is available to meet course objectives. However, when two hours or so per class hour are added for out-of-class assignments, a more comfortable figure is arrived at of 120 hours per course. Effectively integrating those outside hours with class meetings may be challenging, even for experienced college instructors; nevertheless, outside assignments offer the best means of meeting a variety of learning objectives.

What Is Best Accomplished in Class?

To understand how to integrate outside assignments, instructors need to look first at the intellectual (or cognitive) and emotional (or affective) objectives that can be met in class. A primary intellectual objective is to cover course content—the specific facts, theories, or procedures under study. To be sure, students learn some content simply by attending class, but what they can absorb in a few hours of class is extremely limited, and designing class sessions primarily to transfer information wastes precious time as well as opportunities for more complex learning. Given the higher-order intellectual objectives of application, analysis, synthesis, and evaluation, it is more important that instructors use classes (1) to clarify especially difficult concepts or procedures, (2) to illustrate content using engaging examples, and (3) to emphasize the connections between concepts. Research on human cognition during the last few decades has strongly demonstrated the potency of efforts to help students better organize what they are studying (Applebee, 1984; McKeachie, 1986). Students who have learned specific concepts within a meaningful context have many more ways of retrieving information than when they attempt to learn them in a vacuum. In effect, studying the forest in class is the best guarantee that knowledge of individual trees will be retained.

As important as class meetings are in the formation of an organizing intellectual perspective on course content, they promote learning most by stimulating positive emotions in students about the domain of ideas under study and by increasing motivation to master those ideas (Lowman, 1990b). The importance of affective objectives is illustrated well in a 1992 article in the *Chronicle of Higher Education* about Jerry King, a Lehigh University professor who speaks eloquently of his efforts to help students see the beauty and elegance of mathematics (Wheeler, 1992). The best college classes also promote positive emotions about the course as an interpersonal experience; students come to see the instructor as being concerned about their learning and as a fair evaluator of their work. Those who feel positively about the content of a course and the instructor are most likely to be motivated to take book, calculator, or computer keyboard in hand on their own and get down to the often difficult business of solitary study.

A final purpose served by class meetings is the pacing, structure, or discipline that comes from regular reminders that one has considerable work to complete in a finite amount of time. Many students who have difficulty keeping up with their work during a semester report that the daily schedule of summer sessions helps their performance by making it harder for them to forget that they *are* taking a course, that they have obligations and commitments.

Although this pacing effect of class attendance is more mundane than the intellectual and emotional purposes discussed previously, it is strongly connected to the effectiveness of outside assignments. Outside assignments should be spaced out over a course so as to motivate students to work on them steadily rather than to cram them into a few days of frenetic activity at the end. The handling of assignments should also be such as to encourage students to complete them for learning-oriented reasons rather than mainly to avoid punishment for nonperformance.

Key Issues in Assigning Work That Promotes Learning

The two major issues concerning assignments deal, respectively, with (1) the ticklish relationships between the difficulty, the enjoyment, and the educational value of the work that instructors ask students to do outside class and (2) the methods used to motivate students to complete it. Research has consistently suggested that these general issues contribute a great deal to how much learning actually results from specific types of outside assignments (Baird, 1987).

The degree of motivation and enjoyment associated with an assignment is greatly affected by its educational value and the way it is integrated with what happens in class. Unfortunately, some instructors seem to equate educational value with the amount of effort or time assignments require. It is much easier to assign work that is overly time-consuming or frustratingly difficult than work designed to accomplish clear course objectives. It is also easier simply to issue assignments without giving them much further mention in class than regularly to draw connections between assignments and class presentations. If college teachers design assignments that are closely aligned with their overall course objectives and integrate them with what is happening in class sessions at the time, students are much more likely to find the required effort worthwhile, the final product satisfying, and the motivation to tackle the next assignment easily summoned.

Motivation is such a critical issue to the effectiveness of outside assignments because students need internal discipline to complete them. Class meetings are social, externally structured events in students' lives that require minimal self-discipline: students need only arrive on time, stay awake, and take notes to give them the illusion that they are meeting their academic responsibilities. In contrast, outside assignments usually require students to choose among competing activities (many of them inherently more pleasurable for the typical student than schoolwork), to schedule periods for solitary concentration and effort, and to maintain concentration in the face of distractions. Because reading challenging text, solving complex problems, practicing a foreign language or artistic technique, or crafting one's words on paper or computer screen are demanding solitary activities, the choice of methods used to motivate students is critical to the learning outcome.

The motivational strategies used to promote student completion of assignments vary along two broad and related dimensions: (1) structured versus unstructured leadership (Baba and Ace, 1989) and (2) grading versus learning orientation. (Milton, Pollio, and Eison, 1986). When planning their courses, many instructors simply adopt the leadership techniques they experienced as students, without ever thinking about the effects of those and possible alternative techniques on the motivation stimulated in students or on what students may be learning. Research suggests different leadership styles do make a difference in student learning (Baba and Ace, 1989).

The structured-unstructured dimension is illustrated at the laissez-faire end by instructors who simply announce assigned chapters, problem sets, or papers in the syllabus and rarely mention them again. They assume that college students are or should be mature enough to take responsibility for doing the suggested work and seeing how it relates to what is happening in class. This approach may work well with the independent and academically able students in every class, who are internally motivated enough to keep up with their work without much external encouragement and to see the connections between assignments and class topics on their own. However, such an unstructured regime ensures that many students will inevitably fall behind in their work as competing social and academic pressures build up over a semester and that they will consequently do less well than they might have done on assignments and exams. Even highly motivated students may have difficulty keeping up without any acknowledgment of the reading or problems in class. The laissez-faire approach, though requiring less effort and responsibility on the part of the instructor, sets up many students to achieve far less in a class than they would have done under more engaging and sophisticated instructor leadership.

At the other extreme of structure are instructors who have daily quizzes—or unannounced "pop" quizzes—on assigned reading or who grade homework problems only on the basis of right and wrong answers. Although these procedures are likely to produce more short-term compliance among students than are unstructured methods, they also often create student anxiety and an adversary relationship with instructors that color the orientation students bring to their learning (Lowman, 1990b). Many instructors use structured control strategies because of the belief, now questioned by many (McKeachie, 1986; Milton, Pollio, and Eison, 1986), that they are the only way to ensure that students will actually do the assigned work. In fact, students can be motivated to do outside work using a variety of creative structured techniques that minimize the use of grades for behavior control. The cooperative learning techniques discussed in Chapter Seven can motivate students to prepare for class carefully, even enthusiastically. In addition, the specific sections of this chapter on reading, problem solving, and writing assignments offer a number of motivational techniques that involve giving ungraded feedback on students' initial performance to prepare them for subsequent graded work.

The homework problem sets universally assigned in mathematics, physics, or engineering courses provide an illustrative example here. A common objective for assigning such problems is to teach students to use higher-order cognitive skills to decide (1) how to formulate problems initially and (2) when to try other approaches when initial attempts fail, as they usually do for most students

(Woods, 1987). To solve such problems, students must learn to be flexible in their thinking and to remain confident that they can, with persistence and an openness to creative "Aha!" insights, eventually succeed. Instructors typically assign a series of increasingly difficult problems, which give students practice in using the problem-solving processes described in class and prepare them for subsequent exams.

What are some of the likely effects on learning when students' homework sets are graded solely on the basis of whether the correct solutions were found? Some, if not most, students are understandably more likely to focus on getting the correct answer than on experimenting with the problem-solving procedures under study. Their anxiety about receiving a low grade for unsolved problems or incorrect answers is sure to interfere with their confidence and persistence and with the relaxed mental attitude needed to be open to creative insight. The section of this chapter dealing with problem-solving assignments describes alternative ways of motivating students to complete and to learn from such assignments.

The second leadership dimension, grading versus learning orientation, speaks to the complex relationship between grades and learning and is closely related to the structured-unstructured dimension. For any course, using grades to motivate compliance with routine homework or reading assignments has the unintended side effect of orienting students more toward the external grades they receive than toward internal intellectual satisfactions (Lowman, 1990b; Milton, Pollio, and Eison, 1986). Students' intrinsic curiosity and pleasure in learning can be diminished considerably by excessive emphasis on grades as an exclusive motivational technique. Instructors who assume that students are interested only in the grade they receive and design their leadership strategies accordingly help produce, ironically, the very grade-oriented behavior they disdain. Fortunately, there are effective motivational options occupying a middle ground between laissez-faire and grade-oriented strategies.

For example, as described in Chapters Two and Three, something as subtle as the language instructors use when talking about assignments in class communicates powerful expectations about the kind of attitude they expect students to show when completing their assignments. Rarely mentioning assignments, as in a laissez-faire approach, may give students an unintended message that instructors do not consider them worth talking about and may lead to students' not taking them seriously. On the other hand, talking about assignments frequently and using phrases such as "I require," "I demand," and "You must" foster an image of instructors as powerful authorities and students as underlings who cannot be expected to do anything they are not forced to do. In contrast, phrases such as "I think you will find," "I hope you will see," and "I will be interested in what you think" imply a less vertical power relationship between students and instructor and raise the possibility that students may sometimes want to complete assignments for their own reasons.

The keys to motivating students to complete assignments with more of a learning than a grading attitude are (1) to avoid using overly structured carrot-and-stick inducements, (2) to talk about assignments in ways that communicate the assumption that students will want to do them and will find them interesting, and (3) to provide feedback on assignments that will help students learn the information and skills they will need on later evaluated work.

Reading Assignments

Reading remains the primary means by which educated people gain information, and it is difficult to imagine a college course without reading assignments—most of them based on the printed word. Even in today's computer-rich environment, when every college student must achieve a modicum of skill and comfort with computers as aids to writing or calculating, the importance of books in their many contemporary forms is undiminished. As Wilbert

McKeachie (1986) writes, "But each of the new media has settled into its niche in the educational arsenal without dislodging the textbook. In fact, the greatest revolution in education has come not from teaching machines or computers, but from the greater availability of a wide variety of printed materials" (p. 148). He goes on to illustrate this greater access by noting the open library stacks, the large number of paperback editions and reprint series, and most importantly, the ubiquitous photocopy machines now scattered around every college campus and neighboring commercial area. Without doubt, it is easier than ever for teachers to make assigned readings available to students.

When selecting readings, instructors should begin by asking themselves how readings contribute to the intellectual and emotional objectives around which they are organizing their course. Does a reading present desired content? Does it stimulate students to apply general course concepts to an engaging example? Does it prompt them to think critically about an issue? Instructors should also ask how much students are likely to enjoy the reading. To be sure, some classical texts and technical materials should be assigned even though they are difficult at first, even a little forbidding. But not all readings need be that demanding. When available, readings should be selected that engage students easily as well as serve instructors' intellectual ends.

An initial decision that must be made is whether to use a prepared text or something put together for the specific purposes of the course. Some instructors may avoid texts, believing that students will learn more from reading original sources. Actually, research indicates that the structural organization (for example, headings, summaries, key questions, figures or graphs) characteristic of modern texts aids learning, especially for less able students (Wilhite, 1983). But instructors should not avoid putting something together on their own if they do not find a suitable text. The extra time required initially may be more than offset by a better fit with specific course objectives, especially if the instructor envisions using the materials for more than one term. In introductory courses, where helping students master a large basic vocabulary for the discipline is a major objective, prepared texts are usually preferable. In more advanced courses aimed at promoting critical thinking and independent analysis, reading in original sources may fit better. Even though few texts or customized sets of readings are likely to fit one's needs perfectly, instructors who ask themselves how they will integrate readings with their course will be able to decide more easily which readings to select or adopt. This will also help avoid assigning any readings that will not be used.

Unread assignments are unlikely to contribute to student learning, and two practical considerations affect the probability that students will actually do the reading that is assigned: access to the material and cost. An initial question is whether instructors should ask each student to buy a personal copy of a reading or should put it on reserve for shared use. If the reading material is going to be used by every student and is too long to be easily and legally photocopied, it is usually preferable to order personal copies in addition to placing copies on reserve. If students own personal copies, they can do their reading when and where they wish and it is more likely that they will actively grapple with the text, underlining key points and writing in the margins, which promotes understanding and retention (McKeachie, 1986). Unfortunately, some students may be unwilling (or unable) to buy readings they see as excessively expensive—$75–100 texts are not uncommon—and their learning may suffer from their having to borrow others' texts or do all their reading in library or instructor copies of texts placed on reserve. Because instructors receive complimentary copies of books, it is easy for them to be ignorant of how much texts cost. Before making final decisions on which readings to assign and how to make them accessible to students, instructors should ascertain the prices of texts or course packs; this may help them choose between equal or near-equal alternatives. At the very least, it may help them empathize with the challenge faced by students and their parents in paying for college education.

Once readings are assigned and available to students, how can they be integrated into what is covered in class and, most importantly, how can students be motivated to do the readings when they are assigned? Frequently referring to readings in class is probably the best single option. For example, when an instructor comments, "Your text gives a number of reasons for the decline of the British Empire, let's look at only the two most compelling," students who have read the assigned chapter beforehand will hear an organizing reminder and those who have not will get a brief foundation for what they will learn when reading later. Another option is to use discussion to encourage students to think critically about a topic discussed in the text. Giving a brief summary beforehand reminds those who have read it and prevents others from being left out of the discussion completely. Critical questioning in class promotes student understanding and retention and also models the mature attitude we want students to bring to all the reading they do (Browne and Keeley, 1986). Integrating readings into class presentations and discussions is the best means of motivating students to read beforehand—not out of anxiety at the prospect of receiving a low grade on a pop quiz, but in response to the encouragement of an instructor who gives them both an intellectual reason and the freedom to fulfill the assignment.

A very effective instructor I once observed began her freshman course with a discussion of the teaching and learning process. She asked students to construct metaphors that captured their views of teachers, students, and learning. The resulting discussion produced a wide range of images, which became the basis of a short presentation on her vision of learning. She described learning as an active process that was highly dependent on students' taking personal responsibility; this began with their doing assigned work beforehand. She went so far as to make the following proposition to her class: if they would commit themselves to reading each of their assignments before coming to class, she promised to organize the classes so as to reinforce them for having done so. And if students noticed any class in which she failed to incorporate assigned readings, she promised to bring them doughnut holes for the next class. I now use this technique myself and, like the instructor who shared it with me, usually bring the students a snack near the end of the term anyway.

Problem-Solving Assignments[1]

Instructors of technical courses in engineering, mathematics, and other sciences usually make frequent use of problem-solving homework assignments. A study by Donald Woods (1987) of a four-year engineering curriculum, for example, found that students observe faculty solving over one thousand problems of various types on the board and work on over three thousand themselves out of class. Woods's study also found that solving many problems does not in itself ensure that students will learn problem-solving skills they can apply in new situations. For students to make the most of these assignments, the problems must be selected carefully and integrated closely with classroom activities.

What kinds of objectives can problem-solving assignments meet? First, students are much more likely to learn the general principles or structure of a scientific discipline if they have close contact with specific examples, and solving problems can give them such intimacy. Second, problems can also help students learn a number of explicit thinking skills associated with problem solving: analyzing a problem conceptually, formulating and evaluating various ways of seeking solutions, and putting potential solutions into operation and evaluating their effectiveness. Third, students can learn a number of

1. Campbell Lowman, my engineer son, contributed many insightful suggestions to this section.

implicit attitudinal components to problem solving: confidence in their problem-solving abilities and lack of fear about making mistakes; willingness to postpone judgments and to be open to insight; and most importantly, persistence in the face of ambiguity and frustration. Fourth, students can study problem solving as an explicit topic in itself, to help them solve problems they have not encountered before. Research suggests, however, that most of the problems instructors assign serve to illustrate discipline concepts and that few are aimed at problem solving per se (Woods, 1987).

Woods, a chemical engineering professor who has written extensively on problem-solving instruction, suggests that instructors take the following steps to create assignments that are likely to teach discipline problem solving as well as illustrate concepts. First, ensure that students gain a fundamental understanding of their disciplines. As Woods notes, "Research in problem solving has shown that 'good learning' is vital to effective problem solving" (p. 66). Second, require students to memorize the tacit knowledge of the sort that usually comes from years of experience and that is required to make decisions about how well a given solution will work. Third, sensitize students to the cognitive processes they use when solving problems and to the importance of learning general problem-solving skills as well as how to solve specific types of problems. Fourth, begin by teaching students how to solve particular kinds of problems, but gradually shift toward a focus on higher-order problem-solving skills, especially with more advanced students. Woods's suggestions illustrate well that the way problems are treated in class and the techniques used to motivate students greatly influence student learning.

For example, it is essential that problems be discussed in class before and after students tackle them. Some instructors believe it is so important that students learn how to approach and set up problems from scratch that they rarely go over them in class beforehand, but more effective teachers of technical subjects aim for a better balance of frustration and helpful hints on homework and go over at least an abbreviated example or two beforehand. This enables more students to gain from homework the cognitive skills and the confidence that they need when asked to solve exam problems on their own.

After problems are handed in, however, it is always important to go over them, in ways that emphasize the critical steps in setting them up and solving them. Not only does this reinforce students who solved problems correctly, but it makes it more likely that they will learn *why* they arrived at the correct answer. Some may fail to understand the problem but get it right nonetheless. More importantly, it gives students who were not successful initially a second or third chance to experience the flash of insight so essential in problem solving. Every student also needs a completed example of each problem in his or her notes for study before exams; going over the homework in class is the best way of ensuring that they have it. Homework review in class clearly contributes to students' intellectual understanding of principles and problem-solving procedures.

This type of review also meets a number of emotional objectives. The concentration and mental effort required for most students to master technical material are extremely vulnerable to interference from their emotions. Although too much frustration can produce debilitating anxiety that may lead some students to avoid courses requiring calculation, some degree of frustration is inevitable in these subjects, and students must learn how to handle it. As much as anything, students need to remain confident in their abilities if they are to persist in the face of difficulty and be open to solutions that can come even after significant setbacks. Sometimes, the insight does not occur until after their instructor has shown them how to set up and solve the particular problem that has caused difficulty. If students know that their instructor will take the time to go over homework and to answer their questions in class, as well as welcoming them genuinely during office hours if they still do not understand, they are far less likely to feel overwhelmed when working on problems on their own. The teacher's handling of problem-solving assignments is a prototype of how acknowledgement of students' emotional needs has a major impact on learning.

Motivating students to complete homework problems before class is easier than with reading assignments because the work is so clearly connected to class content and what students know they will be asked to do on exams. Reviewing homework early in class emphasizes to students the importance of what they were asked to do outside. In contrast, waiting until the end of a class and asking casually, "Does anyone have any questions about the homework?" makes it unlikely that very many questions will be asked and may lead individual students to assume that the instructor did not expect anyone to have had difficulty or that they are the only ones who did not understand. Instructors who are able to define their homework role with students as a coach who is trying to get them prepared to meet difficult problems on exams have tremendous power to motivate their students to work hard on assigned problems. As was mentioned earlier, grading homework mainly on the basis of whether correct answers were obtained unduly raises students' anxiety and narrows their focus on the end product rather than the problem-solving process. Furthermore, this practice makes it unlikely that students will have their homework in hand when problems are discussed and lowers the probability that they will experience much personal satisfaction in successfully mastering the kinds of problems under study.

Writing Assignments

When most college students and instructors think of written assignments, they imagine the traditional library or research term paper that was once an almost universal fixture in college courses. In students and teachers alike, such papers often produce much frustration and little satisfaction, because independent thinking and clear writing are difficult for most students and because many instructors eventually conclude that the low quality of student papers fails to justify the time required to grade them. Fortunately, we now know a lot more about how to use writing assignments in college classes than we did two decades ago. For example, several focused writing assignments in the course of a term may promote more active reading, critical thinking, and regular study than traditional term papers. The options for assigning written work presented in this section are much broader than the limited range of objectives possible with the traditional term paper. From these more varied assignments comes written work that promotes more learning and is more satisfying for everyone. As Kenneth Eble (1988) notes, "Good assignments elicit good work; bad assignments, bad work" (p. 132).

Objectives for Formal Written Assignments

Too often, college teachers have overly broad objectives when they assign formal written work and assume that an interesting and informative paper will result if students are simply asked to search library resources for information on a topic and write up what they have found. In addition, instructors often assume that students will both know what is wanted when they are asked to "discuss" or "compare and contrast" and be able to execute it well. Some students, to be sure, are able to produce well-defined work from vague assignments, but the key to getting good work from an entire class is to focus the assignment sufficiently so that students know what the instructor wants them to gain intellectually from the experience and to give them practice in the skills that will be involved. Making writing assignments more specific greatly increases the probability that students will hit the mark and that instructors will be able to judge easily when they have done so.

A selection of specific objectives and writing assignments designed to meet them are as follows:

Objective: Students will develop skill in searching library collections and data bases for articles or books on a subject. *Assignment:* Distribute a list of topics relevant to current research or scholarly topics in your course and ask students to write up a two-to-three-page description of relevant references they find in your school's library and data bases. Because the objective is to learn to use the local resources, avoid asking them to summarize or critique what they find. That would be a good assignment for a different objective.

Objective: Students will see how course concepts are illustrated in specific works of art, literature, or research studies. *Assignment:* Distribute lists of key concepts and the works that are to be examined. Ask students to write a paper of four-to-five pages showing how the concepts are illustrated in one or two of the works.

Objective: Students will reflect intellectually and emotionally on what they are reading in a course and on what occurs to them during class sessions. *Assignment:* Ask them to keep a log or journal of personal reactions to course readings, meetings, or outside events (for example, films, concerts, or lectures) that you suggest to them. Ask them to use their log to write a short essay near the end of the course that gives an overview of how their thinking or aesthetic sensitivity has progressed over the term.

Objective: Students will question the validity of theories or concepts under study and formulate an argument presenting their position. *Assignment:* Distribute descriptions (or original text) of several studies, critical essays, magazine articles, newspaper editorials, and so on. Ask students to write a one-sentence argument about some controversy or limitation in any one of these pieces and to illustrate their argument with two or three illustrations from the text (see Cuddy's 1985 description of this one-sentence technique).

Objective: Students will see the similarities and differences between two literary works, compositions, elections, scientific studies, or other comparable items. *Assignment:* As in the previous example, give them descriptions or copies but this time ask them to write a short paper presenting similarities and differences.

Objective: Students will discover the joy of using their imagination and creativity to understand better the human side of the events under study. *Assignment:* Give students a list of several brief fantasy scenes or news stories relating to your course and ask them to write a narrative of three-to-five pages in which one of the characters relates what he or she is thinking or feeling about the events described. The student will also speculate about what might happen next. For example, a vignette in a political science course might deal with an unsuccessful political candidate who ponders whether to run again or how to win next time.

These examples vary in length from very short to moderate, and in substance from the concrete to the imaginative; each of them illustrates how specific objectives shape focused writing assignments. These examples could, of course, be given sequentially or combined to form a single ambitious project. See Durkin's *Writing in the Disciplines* (1986) and Connolly and Vilardi's *Writing to Learn Mathematics and Science* (1989) for descriptions of many focused writing assignments for use in the humanities, mathematics, and social and natural sciences.

Objectives for Informal Written Work

One of the most valuable developments of recent years has been the introduction of informal, non-graded writing assignments that are often done during class. These exercises are conducted in ways similar to those used for the classroom assessment techniques pioneered by Angelo and Cross (1993) and described in Chapter Seven. For example, instead of stopping during a lecture and asking students to discuss some aspect of what has been covered, an instructor can ask them to take a few minutes to write their reactions, suggestions, comparisons, or other critical comments. A few students can then be asked to read their comments or you can ask everyone to pass them in for you to read. A popular group variation described several times in this volume is to ask students to pair, to exchange comments with a neighbor, and to discuss them briefly together. Brief writing like this—including the popular minute papers—takes only a few minutes of class or instructor time, even if it is collected, reviewed, commented on, and returned later. If informal writing is returned to students, a short comment or two should be added, but no grade. Students could be asked to complete brief, informal writing assignments outside class, but this usually fails to capture the informal, spontaneous quality of in-class writing and to provide immediate feedback to instructors that can help them modify their presentations.

Using Writing Assignments

The most important consideration in using written assignments is to be sure everyone is clear about an assignment's purpose. Giving students the objectives in writing as well as discussing them in class makes it more likely that everyone will write the kind of paper envisioned rather than the kind they believe (perhaps on the basis of what high school teachers or other students have told them) college professors want. Unfortunately, even if an instructor carefully designs a focused assignment, explicitly asks students to demonstrate their own thinking, distributes a written description, and spends part of a class session answering questions about the papers, a few students will still write the immature cut-and-paste paper they learned to write in high school. To make it more likely that every student will understand what is expected, give examples in class of what to avoid as well as what to aim for and put exemplary papers from previous classes on reserve as models.

Instructors must also decide how many written assignments to use in a course, how long they should be, and when they should be due. The objectives for using writing assignments in a course guide how long they should be; experienced instructors usually give a range rather than a specific number of expected pages. Assigning a single broad paper without giving students practice with shorter papers aimed at focused objectives runs the risk that students will not meet the specific objectives instructors have for them. Although research (Meyers, 1986) suggests that two smaller papers create less anxiety among students than a single longer one (perhaps because the stakes are not as high on any one piece of writing), multiple assignments will create more administrative work for teachers than a single one. Instructors' objectives will also influence when they want papers submitted. It can be safely said that rather than requesting papers at the very end of term, an instructor will do well to call them in early enough so that they can be read carefully and returned to students with an invitation to revise and resubmit their work if they so desire. Unfortunately, no simple answers exist to these scheduling dilemmas.

Instructors most often assign written work for their course alone, but increasingly many schools offer programs that integrate or link writing assignments in composition and general education courses. These so-called "writing across the curriculum" programs typically bring together composition and other discipline faculty to design writing assignments jointly. These assignments are intended to increase content mastery as well as expose students to the kind of writing desired in that discipline (McGovern and Hogshead, 1990; Zinsser, 1988). Although evaluation studies suggest that it has been difficult to demonstrate an improvement in writing or content mastery as a result of such programs (Madigan and Brosamer, 1990), students and faculty who participate in them generally report success and satisfaction.

Evaluating Written Assignments

The substantial liability of writing assignments is the difficulty of grading them fairly and in ways that improve students' course knowledge, writing skill, and confidence. Differences among students in the complexity of their thinking and the clarity, smoothness, and artfulness of their writing make comparative evaluation a subjective task that is highly vulnerable to a variety of distortions (Cronbach, 1984). Even though there are no widely accepted formulas or guidelines for the assigning of grades or numbers to written work, there is a growing literature on how to assign grades in ways that promote better writing and that are accepted by students as fair.

Fair grading is usually defined as being objective, valid, and reliable. Objective grading is based on qualities of the writing, not of the writer. The best way to be objective is to be blind to authorship. Valid grading occurs when the criteria used in assigning grades fit the objectives students thought they were seeking. Even if students are given a clear statement of an instructor's objectives, evaluation of their papers will be invalid if grades are based on criteria unconnected to the objective. For example, grading papers on the basis of stylistic features such as economy or maturity of expression would be considered invalid if these features were not connected to the original objectives as communicated and taught to students (Zinsser, 1988).

Reliable grading refers to the probability that we would always give the same grade to a given paper. Experienced teachers know all too well that their concentration and grading standards can tend to drift up or down over time, especially when they are tired. Research conducted over a fifty-year span has repeatedly demonstrated that the grade a specific paper receives can be influenced by the context in which it is read (see Jacobs and Chase, 1992). For example, the quality of papers read immediately preceding a given paper can influence evaluation, such that if a paper of average quality comes after two or three poor ones it can seem better than it is (McKeachie, 1986). Students usually feel very strongly about how their work is evaluated and have every right to expect instructors to strive for the reliability everyone would equate with fairness.

Several well-established techniques can ensure that instructors' evaluation of students' writing is objective, valid, and reliable. Reading students' papers without knowing their names is an easy way to remain objective. Use the last four digits of students' Social Security or school identification numbers or some other system in lieu of names. Grading work blind to authorship also impresses on students that it is their work and not their relationship with the instructor that is being evaluated.

Valid grading comes from constructing criteria for different grades that are tied to instructors' specific objectives for the assignment and that are communicated clearly to students beforehand. Early in the writing process, some instructors take class time to ask students meeting in small groups to apply the scoring criteria to sample papers, thereby ensuring that students are familiar with the criteria that will later be applied to their work. Such so-called holistic scoring of papers has been found to increase grading reliability, because scoring criteria are made explicit, as well as validity, because students are intimately acquainted with what is expected (Madigan and Brosamer, 1991).

Reliable grading comes from reading papers in small batches and being alert for shifts in grading standards over time. Reliability is also promoted by grading five or so model papers jointly with a TA or colleague—ideally one assigning a similar paper—and discussing your tentative grades and criteria before tackling the papers on your own. These techniques for fair grading do take a bit more planning and effort, but the improved accuracy of instructors' grading and satisfaction among students with the evaluation process make them worth using.

An objective for every writing assignment should be to help students increase their skill at using writing to clarify and communicate their thinking. Returning a paper with only a letter grade jotted on the title or last page has far less power to shape a student's thinking or writing than returning one with notes or reactions scribbled throughout and a brief overview written near the grade that shows how well the paper was judged to have met the various evaluation criteria that were being applied. Comments that are a good balance between encouragement and criticism are most likely to motivate students to try their best next time (McKeachie, 1986). Learning to write well is a never-ending process, and just as professional writing is improved by editors' notes and suggestions, students' writing is likely to improve as a result of seeing written comments from a careful and concerned reader.

Observational and Hands-On Assignments

Because science is based on empirical investigations and the application of general principles to real-world examples, science lectures are universally accompanied by laboratory experiences. Similarly, studio courses in the visual and performing arts and applied professional courses in health, business-related fields, and journalism always give students direct contact with projects or activities outside the classroom. But other disciplines can also benefit from assignments that ask students to work on projects or make systematic observations outside of class and then integrate their experience into class discussion or written work. The final section of this chapter deals with these nonlaboratory and nonstudio uses of observational and hands-on assignments.

Instructors teaching a variety of college courses occasionally ask students to observe activities or phenomena outside of regular class meetings. For example, history courses take students on field trips to local sites or ask them to conduct oral history interviews with elderly or influential citizens. Students in abnormal psychology courses may visit mental hospitals and those taking sociology or criminology courses may visit prisons. Fine arts courses routinely expect students to attend exhibitions or concerts. Government or political science courses may ask students to visit municipal council meetings or attend court proceedings. (Spending a Monday morning observing local criminal court proceedings is guaranteed to be a civic eye-opener for almost anyone!) Finally, business or engineering courses often encourage students to visit local offices or manufacturing plants. Observational assignments are not uncommon in many lecture-discussion courses.

Other observational assignments are more unusual and may not occur to instructors whose objectives could be met by them. For example, students studying controversial issues in a religion or philosophy course might be asked to attend a local meeting of a group with whose aims they strongly disagree and to use their observations in a subsequent class presentation or writing assignment. Depending on students' personal views, meetings of either an abortion rights or right-to-life group (alternatively, of a local handgun control committee or gun club) will give almost any student an opportunity to meet people holding strong philosophical positions different from their own. Students taking statistics, business, or accounting courses can be asked to collect observational data on students frequenting popular campus nightspots; these can be used in various quantitative analyses under study. Students taking foreign language courses can be asked to volunteer as language tutors or to visit local support groups or festivals for immigrants whose native language students are studying. These examples illustrate the many possibilities for using outside visits, which are limited only by instructors' imaginations.

Options for giving students hands-on experiences with relevant course materials or concepts outside class are greater than ever, thanks largely to the use of computer and video-recording technology. Since 1985 or so, the explosion of small computers on campuses has opened up a wide range of engaging computer-based assignments that can be undertaken outside of classes to meet a variety of objectives in almost any discipline (Graves, 1989; Herman, 1988; McGraw-Hill Primus, 1993). As Chapter Seven describes, most of these are (1) tutorials designed to help students with repetition and drill of basic information, especially in foreign languages, or (2) simulations in which students apply general principles to interactive case examples. Almost all existing computer-assisted instruction and projected instructional uses of the Internet represent supplements to what is happening in the classroom.

Another type of hands-on assignment involves the use of modern videotape technology, which is now so convenient that objects or activities can be videotaped more easily than photographed with a still camera. Students can, of course, be asked to view conventional videotaped materials, such as films or documentaries, that are on reserve in the library or media center. But instructors can also put together their own short tapes to illustrate course concepts or for students to analyze as case studies. For example, an ecology professor can videotape a favorite forest stream at several different times of the year and during different weather conditions to illustrate a variety of phenomena. Similarly, an animal behavior course can be enriched by homemade videos of neighborhood dogs at play or by animal behavior clips recorded during visits to a local zoo. In effect, instructors whose goal is that students simply see the phenomenon under study, without either manipulating it or learning field research methods, may find video recordings to be more cost-effective than traditional field trips.

Another use of video technology is to ask students to make their own recordings for classroom showings or for submission to the instructor as part of a written assignment. For example, a sociology class can have students make their own short documentaries to illustrate the conditions of the homeless, conspicuous consumption at a local shopping center, or the class markers that distinguish neighborhoods. Similarly, political science students can be sent out with video recorders on election day to conduct exit interviews at polling sites, to illustrate demographic or attitudinal variables that are related to how individuals say they voted. Whether students are asked to watch or make video recordings, this technology builds on the traditional use of the written word for presenting information to students and obtaining a reliable picture of what students have learned.

At the very least, observational and hands-on assignments can enrich students' interaction with regular course content and help them to see the course's relevance to real-world issues and human experiences. But if students are encouraged to attempt an intellectual integration of their out-of-class experiences with course content, such assignments can also help them analyze, synthesize, and evaluate the concepts to which they have been introduced. As is true with the many other types of assignments discussed in this chapter, observational and hands-on activities will have more educational value if they are planned so as to be integrated with overall course objectives and actively connected to what is happening in class. Taking the educational value of outside experiences for granted is a danger in any subject, even in the sciences, where students sometimes complain that their laboratory work is often ignored in lecture sections. Instructors who discuss the purposes of observational assignments beforehand and give students an opportunity to discuss them afterward, in class or in writing, recognize what research has consistently demonstrated (Meyers, 1986; Meyers and Jones, 1993): that active processing of educational experiences increases the number of students who incorporate them into what they are learning.

Except for studio art classes and laboratory courses, outside observational or hands-on experiences are likely to be only a small part of most college courses. But even when these activities represent only a small part of a course, they can, like spices in food, greatly enrich the whole if they are blended thoroughly. (Many of the outside assignments described in this chapter can be organized as group rather than as individual projects; see the section on cooperative learning in Chapter Seven.)

The next chapter makes the logical progression from the planning and making of assignments to their evaluation. General assessment issues and specific methods of testing and grading are discussed.

Evaluating
Student Performance

A basic source of the misunderstandings that sur-
round evaluations of student work lies in the fact that
normally such evaluation has vital consequences for
the one being evaluated, whereas it has no such con-
sequences for the one who does the evaluating. The
grades a student receives not only determine whether
he graduates with honors or flunks out of school; they
may also guide him in choosing his field of specializa-
tion, affect his plans for graduate study, and ulti-
mately influence his choice of career. On the other
hand, the grades a teacher gives do not affect his pro-
fessional stature, his commitment to a field of study,
or his future success as a scholar. A student may for a
long time harbor a deep resentment against a teacher
who grades him harshly, but were he to confront that
teacher years later, the teacher might not even
remember the student and would almost surely not
remember the grade. Indeed, the teacher would most
probably be astounded to learn the student cared so
deeply about the grade.

—Cahn[1]

1.   Cahn, S. M., Scholars Who Teach (Chicago: Nelson-Hall, 1978, p. 218).

For most students and many college teachers, tests and grades are an unpleasant but unavoidable reality. Most schools require instructors to assign letter grades for student work, and society, rightly or wrongly, judges as important these distinctions between high, passing, and failing performance. For everyone personally associated with higher education—students, faculty, and parents—evaluation is an emotionally charged topic.

All students are concerned about exams and grades. Anxious-dependent or failing students dread them, and any student may become unduly grade-oriented. In contrast, the more independent, capable, and learning-oriented students look forward to the challenge and the potential success they offer. For most students, being evaluated provokes a mixture of anxiety and positive anticipation.

College teachers also exhibit a range of attitudes toward grading but, not surprisingly, the attitudes are slightly different from those of students (Runco, Okuda, and Thurston, 1991). Some, especially those new to teaching, identify with their students' dread of exams, deny their evaluative role, let students grade themselves, give undemanding exams or uniformly high marks, or admonish students not to worry about exams and grades. Others enjoy evaluation and view arduous exams and stingy grading as necessary to student achievement and maturity. Both overly lenient and excessively stringent grading can overemphasize grades and fail to strengthen students' learning orientation.

Exams and other evaluations introduce the possibility of cheating, which induces guilt in students who succumb to the temptation, anger in classmates who observe or learn of the infraction, and displeasure in instructors who become aware of it. Fortunately, cheating is less likely to occur in the kind of engaging and personable classes advocated here.

Almost as unpleasant as dealing with cheating is the necessity of assigning a failing grade to a student whose work was unacceptable. Even in courses taught by exemplary college teachers, some students may fail. Regardless of whether a student earns a failing grade because of poor ability or lack of motivation, the teacher usually assigns such a grade with reluctance and regret.

In this chapter, evaluation is examined on several levels. First, specific suggestions are offered for constructing and scoring multiple-choice, short-answer, and essay examinations. The suggestions are keyed to the type of learning each kind of examination promotes. They also assess the amount of instructor time each exam requires. (Evaluation of writing assignments is covered in Chapter Eight.) Procedures for assigning end-of-course grades and dealing with cheating—including ways to prevent it—are outlined as well. Because evaluation is the most critical interpersonal issue in college classrooms, suggestions are also given for maximizing the positive effects of exams (increases in learning orientation as well as in confidence, motivation, and effective coping skills) and minimizing the negative ones that reflect an excessive grading orientation and interfere with performance (feelings of anxiety, unfairness, anger, and hopelessness). Before specific evaluation methods are discussed, several introductory topics need to be examined.

Evaluation in Context

Like everything else associated with college teaching, evaluation needs to be considered within the context of instructors' and students' objectives.

Purposes of Evaluation

Examining must first be differentiated from grading (Milton, 1978). Examining or testing refers to constructing and scoring test questions (or assigning papers) to produce comparisons between students. The specific evaluative comments written on exams are taken very seriously by students and can have a powerful effect on student motivation for the remainder of the course. Since more than one exam is usually given during a course, early tests can motivate students to try harder, study more efficiently, or give up and withdraw emotional investment in the course. Examining has a powerful effect on students' attitudes toward their courses, on the way they study, and on what they learn.

Unlike examinations, grades come only at the end of a course; they indicate how well a student has done on all work in the course. Even when accompanied by narrative evaluations, grades are the final evaluative message and can have little impact on learning: it is too late for a student to behave differently in that course by the time the grade is assigned. End-term grading is a global evaluation, not a series of reports on specific successes and failures. The thought of grades does motivate students, many of whom study all term because of the grade they hope (or fear) they will receive at the end. End-term grading does have an influence on students' future course selection, but it does not motivate students and focus their learning as directly and immediately as do tests and papers.

The purposes of evaluation are many. Tests are given, students say, "to see what we don't know" or "to give the teacher something on which to base a grade." Instructors believe that evaluation aids learning through feedback and motivation. Testing gives students a gauge of the scope and depth of their knowledge, much as athletes learn their strengths and weaknesses through active competition. Similarly, just as coaches learn from observing their athletes in competition, college teachers learn from tests how effective their teaching has been. A thoughtfully constructed exam can actually teach by stimulating students to think about concepts in a new way, notice new relationships, and come to different insights. Tests aid learning most by motivating students to study for them (Cahn, 1978) and, if specific guidance and practice is provided by the instructor, focusing their efforts. Though term papers can achieve objectives unattainable through exams, few things can be counted on to prompt students to really master a content area as much as a rigorous examination.

On some campuses, "comprehensive evaluations"—or "assessments"—are used to assess how much students have learned, especially in their majors and in support of their general speaking and writing skills. Although such broad assessment ventures are undertaken to increase accountability and ultimately the amount that students learn, in effect, they reflect a lack of confidence in the grades assigned by classroom instructors.

Testing and Student Motivation

How can testing and grading practices be understood in terms of what we know about the psychological needs students bring to the classroom? The need to meet challenges and overcome obstacles is a basic and deeply rooted psychological motive (Lowman, 1990b). Examinations, like athletic contests or artistic competition, satisfy this need in many students. Without either unduly emphasizing the competitiveness of exams or ignoring the individual differences in ability and motivation that occupy a central place in the learning model presented in Chapter One, a skillful instructor can create exams that meet both the security needs of students and their need to be challenged. College teachers, like good athletic coaches, bring out the best performance from their charges by promoting strong internal motivation to meet personal goals, which go beyond mere triumph over competitors. (College teachers can learn much from observing skilled athletic and artistic coaches.) The absence of a real challenge in exams leaves students as dissatisfied as they would be if tests were unduly harsh or unfair.

Ohmer Milton, Howard Pollio, and James Eison's book, *Making Sense of College Grades* (1986) offers, in my opinion, the best perspective available in print on the interaction of student motivation and college tests. It is based on Eison's research on two different orientations that college students show toward their studies. Students with a strong *learning orientation* see classes as a place to satisfy their curiosity about the subject and to meet some of their own objectives ("I hope I'll get to understand how Hitler got so much control over Germany"). Learning-oriented students are usually independent and tend to be motivated from within. By contrast, students with a strong *grading orientation* think of classes in terms of require-ments ("Do we have to write a paper?"), the instructor's externally imposed expectations ("What is it you want from us?"), and the necessity of getting degree credits out of the way. For grading-oriented students, the class is an obstacle to be overcome with the least possible cost in terms of time, energy, and the almighty grade point average.

The Milton, Pollio, and Eison volume (1986) includes Eison's LOGO questionnaire that students can use to assess their strengths on these two dimensions. Research suggests that they are relatively independent—that is, a student can be high or low on both. Eison has more recently published a LOGO F scale for college teachers, which assesses the degree to which their teaching practices encour-age students to have a learning or a grading orientation toward a class (Eison, Janzow, and Pollio, 1989).

The suggestions in this chapter are designed to produce exams that both challenge and reassure students, that encourage a learn-ing orientation and allow students to show an appropriate attitude toward grades, and above all else, that are seen as fair. Testing and grading are not treated as distasteful inevitabilities but as experi-ences that can be beneficial and satisfying to students and instruc-tors alike. More than anything, the suggestions presented here aim to shift the perceived role of the teacher from that of the distant evaluator who designs forbidding obstacles (even traps) for students to that of the approachable coach who provides plenty of practice and support in preparing students to meet clearly defined challenges.

Myths Concerning Evaluation

A few myths about evaluation must be mentioned and dispelled first. The following common beliefs are *simply untrue:*

1.   *The quality of education that students receive is commensurate with the difficulty of earning high marks.* Colleges, academic depart-ments, or instructors who imply that their students learn more because average grades are lower delude themselves. Students can

learn just as much in a relatively easy course as in a hard one. If high average grades are accurate, they reflect greater rather than less learning. Because tough grading is so commonly endorsed, many instructors fear being reputed to offer "slides" or "gut courses." However, as Chapter One's learning model argues, the quality of a college education is more a function of the quality of the faculty, the teaching, and the overall student population than of grading stringency.

2. *Differences in grade point average (GPA) reflect differences in student quality.* Whatever historical forces led most American schools to use the grade point average as the single metric with which to compare students' achievement, problems with the GPA abound. First of all, there is a technical issue of measurement: a scale with five broad categories (A, B, C, D, F) is converted into a continuous variable that gives the illusion of precision to two or three decimal places. In addition, differences between colleges, departments, or schools within the same college, as well as over the four years of a student's career, make rigid comparisons between students on the basis of a single grade index untenable. Most importantly, in spite of the modest relationship consistently demonstrated between college grades and adult achievement, especially in liberal arts subjects, many employers and professional schools use class ranks based on GPAs as inflexible selection criteria. Some state legislatures have even gone so far as to set rigid GPA criteria for the awarding and the continuance of scholarships. Perhaps society's obsession with the GPA results from both the illusion it gives that individual merit is fixed and the convenient means it offers to differentiate individuals on the basis of a presumedly valid index of merit.

3. *Hard grading and student satisfaction are inversely correlated.* Research on the relation between grading and satisfaction (Abrami, D'Apollonia, and Cohen, 1990; Abrami and others, 1980; Howard and Maxwell, 1980) does not support this contention. Students report liking quality presentations and good rapport, not easy grades. Students like hard graders as often as easy ones, and they have been shown to seek out difficult courses rated positively over easier ones

rated poorly (Coleman and McKeachie, 1981). Teachers seen as *unfair* evaluators receive low ratings, but course difficulty does not predict student satisfaction.

4.   *Strict grading is necessary to motivate students to study.* Though student motivation is enhanced by testing, unduly harsh grading may simply promote a grading orientation. On the other hand, if exams are at a level of difficulty where most students feel challenged but few feel overwhelmed, and if students are given adequate practice beforehand, motivation can arise from a learning orientation. Fostering positive personal relationships and activating students' desire for competence are also more likely to promote motivation based on a learning orientation than intimidating them with unduly negative evaluations.

5.   *Tough grading encourages memorization, while a nonjudgmental classroom atmosphere is necessary for higher-level learning or for independent or creative thinking to occur.* Anxious-dependent students do respond to difficult exams by dwelling on details and memorization, but not all students restrict what they study to this level. Evaluation stringency does not guarantee attainment of educational objectives, and although objectives may call for particular evaluation procedures, they do not prescribe their level of difficulty.

It is inaccurate to equate a college teacher's grading practices with the quality of his or her teaching, but skill in using challenging examinations to promote motivation and learning does reflect teacher quality. A skillful instructor uses examinations in ways that motivate rather than discourage students, and this influences student achievement more than anything inherent in testing methods or standards.

Social Functions of Evaluation

Whether they like it or not, college teachers serve an important selective function in contemporary society. Powerful, well-paid, and responsible jobs are open mainly to those who successfully run the gauntlet of formal education, who through academic ability, persistence, and/or conformity earn baccalaureate or advanced degrees. Higher education is a prerequisite for success for most citizens in a technological society, even though the credential is often of more importance than the knowledge or skill the graduate is assumed to possess.

How do professors view their role in this social selection process? Some view individual differences in ability and persistence as enduring, and they may prefer the task of identifying and encouraging students showing developed academic skill and motivation to nurturing potential in others. They may also believe that the role of college instructors is to encourage all students to compete, so that those with greater talent and self-discipline can be channeled to jobs requiring such qualities.

Other instructors may desire that more students have the chance to select their occupations and that all live less competitive lives. Those with this philosophy are more likely to favor evaluation methods that reflect mastery at the recall and recognition level— the kind of knowledge easiest to acquire from effort alone—rather than more intellectual attainments that tend to reflect individual differences. College teachers holding these beliefs may also see it as reasonable to offer some students opportunities to do extra-credit work to raise their averages. Mastery learning touted in the Personalized System of Instruction (Keller, 1968), for example, rewards students for attaining objectives that are reasonable for all and bases these rewards more on persistence than on ability.

Midway between these two philosophies is a developmental perspective that acknowledges both individual differences in ability and the potential of motivated students to grow as thinkers and learners. No student is fully formed when he or she begins a course, and the instructor's job is more to help develop each student's work habits, specific study skills, and overall view of himself or herself as a competent person than to separate the weak from the strong. As Chapter One argues, even though college teachers have limited power to modify the individual differences that affect student learning, they have tremendous power to influence that learning—directly through exemplary teaching and indirectly through enhanced student motivation.

The suggestions on testing and grading offered in this chapter are more consistent with a developmental than either a selection or a mastery philosophy. They are designed not so much to endorse the social function grades serve as to recognize the universality of individual differences and the plasticity of motivation. This chapter proposes methods of evaluation aimed at motivating all students to do their best. The methods reflect a guarded optimism about what that level of optimum performance may turn out to be.

Examination Strategies

Selecting the types of examinations to be used in a course and considering the ways examinations will be used to motivate learning are among the most important decisions a college teacher makes.

Preparing for Examinations

Examination procedures should be determined when the course is first planned. Because students differ in their preferences for styles of exam (most student polls are split equally between multiple-choice and short-answer or essay) and because different methods fit different objectives, instructors should use a variety of testing methods. There is no reason for college teachers (or students) to put all their eggs in one basket by having only one type of exam during a semester. In fact, empirical evidence shows that self-assessment can also be used validly, especially in advanced classes (Falchikov and Boud, 1989).

Similarly, there are very few good reasons to use only a single testing session, a final exam. There are no rules about frequency of testing, but one exam in an undergraduate course is surely too few and more than five too many. The number of testing sessions should be determined by the difficulty and amount of material covered. As to pacing, exams should occur at regular intervals in the term. To test only once denies students and instructor feedback on the students' progress and wastes an opportunity to promote and guide motivated study. A single final exam makes grading and testing synonymous. Periodic testing during a term has been shown to improve performance on final exams (Gaynor and Millham, 1976). On the other hand, too frequent testing is costly in class time and in teacher time spent on grading; it also leads to an overemphasis on external motivators at the expense of internal student motivation.

Remember that not all assigned work has to be graded. Many of the classroom assessment techniques described in Chapter Seven are based on ungraded written work. Practice exams and thought-provoking essays not only prepare students for actual exams, but they also encourage a learning orientation.

Before writing tests for a course, formulate the objectives for the evaluation (Jacobs and Chase, 1992). Use recognition multiple-choice or recall identification items if you want to see whether students learned specific concepts or names; use conceptually complex multiple-choice items or compare-and-contrast essays if you want to assess their critical thinking. Always ask yourself *what* you wish to measure with a given question or exam. Having a colleague take the exam is a good way to see whether the instructions and questions are clear. In the case of short-answer or essay questions, writing answers yourself also provides benchmarks to help with scoring.

When selecting specific topics around which to write test questions, avoid both trickery and triviality. There are always important, subtle, and complex points that can be assessed on an exam, and there is no good reason to surprise students with questions about unexpected topics or about minutiae (Milton, Pollio, and Eison, 1986). Making tests difficult by focusing on unimportant details induces anxiety, gamesmanship, and a sense of unfairness. It is better to design tests that will motivate students to learn critical content than to reward them for memorizing trivia. Neither student motivation nor learning is fostered by putting surprises on exams.

Topics included on exams should be representative of the content assigned. Items should be selected from all major chapters, articles, or books covered. They should also vary in difficulty. Include a few relatively easy items to keep the less able or less prepared students from feeling devastated after an exam. Similarly, include a few difficult items to keep the most prepared students from feeling let down—from thinking as they leave the room, "I sure didn't get a chance to show what I knew on that test!" An exam with varied items—one or two of them, perhaps, even funny—is more interesting for students to take and instructors to grade. Varied items also produce greater spread in distribution of total scores.

Avoid using the same examinations every time you teach a course. Students are likely to have seen old exams in test files, and repeat exams will not reflect recent changes in what you present or emphasize. Like old lecture notes, old exams can help an instructor prepare, but exams are unlikely to be timely unless they are constructed a week or two before they are given.

There are several ways to prepare students intellectually before an exam. Share your objectives so that students will not feel that they "didn't know beforehand what the prof wanted," and make copies of old exams available, as concrete examples of what can be expected. Short practice exams that are graded and returned but not recorded also are helpful in guiding study and instructor presentations. Give tips on answering multiple-choice or essay questions, especially if the students are freshmen or the course is introductory. Tell students beforehand the total number of test items of each type and, if possible, the number of recall, analysis, or evaluation items that will appear on the test. All these techniques will steer students into appropriate areas of study and help maximize what they learn.

Like a coach speaking to the team on the night before a contest, you should also help your students prepare emotionally for a test. Speak to them as adults ("The test will require you to know the most important concepts thoroughly, and you should review them carefully. But the test is not designed to trick you or make you fail"). Do not joke about the exam, especially with irony likely to feed their anxiety ("Don't worry about the exam. After all, nothing rides on it except your future careers!"). Also avoid speaking either as a judgmental parent ("If you don't study hard, you're likely to do poorly") or as a reassuring peer ("Hey, this test isn't the most important thing in your life!"). Help the class to take the test seriously without their spending the whole night in ineffective study or needless anxiety.

Some college teachers spend the class just before an exam reviewing material and answering questions; others hold optional review sessions for the same purpose. Many students appreciate such opportunities, but others will not attend a class (or outside sessions) with that agenda. Open-ended review sessions can be frustrating when students do not have questions, and they waste precious time when done during class. Frequently, only the most compliant students come to such sessions, more to avoid missing something than to participate or contribute. A better means of helping students prepare effectively is structured review sessions where they answer practice questions and then compare answers with their neighbors or with selected answers projected from overhead transparencies. Another valuable approach is to encourage students to telephone you (even at home) with last-minute questions before the exam; this will take relatively little of your time (rarely will more than 10 percent of the class call), but will benefit those who really are confused or need special support. Instructors who encourage e-mail communications with students often receive questions from individual students, and then distribute answers to the entire class by e-mail.

Administering Examinations

Even if a school has an effective honor system or does not require proctoring, college teachers should administer tests themselves and be available from time to time during the session to answer questions and offer reassurance. A test is a major event in the interpersonal life of a class, and instructors who routinely send assistants or secretaries to administer exams miss a golden opportunity to motivate and reassure students personally. Tell students that you will arrive early on the exam day to answer questions and ensure that they will have as much time as possible to work. Most students are concerned about not having enough time, and they will appreciate this consideration. Distribute exams as soon as early-arriving students are ready, then stay around to answer questions for latecomers. Students appreciate instructors who stop by frequently during exams to answer questions and keep them posted on the remaining time.

Getting students to turn in their papers can be troublesome. Return to the classroom ten to fifteen minutes before the next class period and say, "It's time to pull your answers together. You have only five minutes or so to go." If you remain in the classroom, many students will turn in their papers, and others will make last-minute additions. Avoid coming back at the very last minute and announcing, "Time's up! Stop. Give me your exams." Though this practice is traditional in some schools (for example, the service academies), it raises student anxiety, forces you to decide what to do when students exceed the time limit, and encourages a grading orientation. If one or two anxious-dependents still have not stopped when only a few minutes remain before the next class, simply invite the students waiting in the hall to come in; then your students will stop. College teachers have an important responsibility to ensure that all students are given roughly similar time to complete exams and that they are out of the classroom before the next class is scheduled to begin, but excessive concern about equal time encourages a competitive grading orientation. So move them along—but gently.

Evaluating Examinations

Exams should be graded and returned quickly—by the next class meeting if possible, and within one week at the latest. Prompt return of exams is appreciated by students anxious to know their grades, and it encourages relearning or corrective learning of the material that appeared on the exam. Avoid simply giving papers to TAs for grading. Students want papers graded by their instructor, even when assistants help. In large classes where assistants are necessary for scoring exams, develop specific scoring criteria and model papers for your TAs and double-check selected papers to ensure that all graders adhered to similar guidelines. The professor is responsible for the way others grade his or her students' exams, and this responsibility cannot be delegated completely, even when it is convenient to do so.

Like term papers, tests should be graded blind. Blind grading of essay papers is especially important. Even when multiple-choice exams are given, it is good practice to have students use only school identification numbers.

Write detailed comments on exams to demonstrate that the papers were read carefully and to show students how they could have done better. Even short comments such as "Yes," "No," "Insightful," "Not quite," or "Good guess" tell students that their work was taken seriously. To tell each student how every discussion item could be improved would take too much time, but try to make one or two corrective comments, especially about longer essays. Specific feedback of this kind maximizes student learning from exams (McKeachie, 1986).

Instructors' written comments are powerful communications that affect subsequent motivation. A student doing unacceptable work might receive a note saying, "I'm sorry you did poorly, Laurie. Please stop by to speak with me to see if we can find a way for you to do better next time." Students who respond to such an invitation usually indicate that they know they did not study enough, but some will be perplexed by their poor performance and will welcome suggestions on studying and test-taking. Personal notes are also an excellent way to reward superior work. Comments such as "Good work, Jamie" or "Excellent ideas, Amy" very positively affect students who receive them. Such notes reinforce past effort and strengthen students' desire to do well in the future. Write something like "Much improved, Sarah" for students who have improved their performance by at least a letter grade and "Your usual superb work, Ashley," for consistently outstanding students. Such comments make the evaluation process more personal for instructor and students alike, especially in larger classes (Lowman, 1987).

Returning Examinations

For almost all students and teachers, the return of exams is a time of anxiety. Students want to know how they did and how the instructor feels about their performance. Instructors may be fearful that students will be angry, they may themselves be angry that students have not performed well, or they may feel guilty about giving low grades. The first set of exam papers is particularly emotional, reminding instructor and students of the evaluative aspect of their relationship. Novice teachers' first sets of papers can be particularly disheartening and can lead them to question both their competence and their motivation for an academic career.

How should you return exams? First, remain calm and relaxed. Emotional instructors only stimulate emotionality in students. Avoid defensiveness or apology. Be reasonable but firm in discussing the exams. Second, exhibit distributions of scores so that students can see exactly how their performance compared with that of others—even though, in theory, comparative data are likely to encourage a grading orientation. I continue this practice because even my learning-oriented students say it gives them a yardstick against which to measure their performance. Third, ask whether students have general questions about the exam, but do *not* spend the entire class going over specific items. Offer to go over individual papers in detail outside of class. Circulate the correct answers to multiple-choice items and pass around photocopies of the best two or three discussion papers, with students' names removed. Many students have an unrealistic estimate of their own knowledge and abilities as compared with those of other students; seeing samples of peers' work provides a more objective basis for comparison. It also provides further reinforcement for the exemplary students whose papers were selected for display. Returning papers well is essential to making sure that the evaluation process accomplishes desired intellectual and interpersonal objectives.

The final stage of evaluation is often neglected by instructors. Before being filed away, exams should be critiqued and revised. College teachers can best improve an exam immediately after grading it and hearing student reactions. If the teacher waits too long, such information will be forgotten (Milton, 1978).

The preceding strategies apply to examinations of any form. In the next section, various types of examination are discussed, with suggestions for maximizing the advantages and minimizing the disadvantages of each.

Types of Examinations

The traditional classification of examinations as objective and subjective can be misleading. Multiple-choice items are thought to be objective because they can be scored easily and reliably using templates or computer scanning devices, but subjectivity is involved in item construction and in decisions on which multiple-choice option is most correct. Similarly, "subjective" discussion questions can be scored rigorously using specific criteria and a point system.

A more useful distinction is between *selection* (multiple-choice) and *supply* (short-answer or essay) examinations. Research suggests that selection exams are easier (Gronlund, 1982). Multiple-choice items require knowledge of specifics, and students have adapted their studies accordingly, concentrating on details when preparing for such exams (Milton, 1978). However, college teachers can construct multiple-choice items that require students to think, critique, and evaluate what they know; selection exams need not deal only with details.

Supply questions are more variable. Short-answer or identification items may be as specific as multiple-choice items. More commonly, in supply items, students are asked to write broad, integrative summaries (essays); thus, in studying for essay exams, students focus on broader issues (Milton, 1978). The construction of items determines the level of knowledge measured more than does the item type.

Exam items of any type must be clear and unambiguous; students should have no doubt about what they mean. Imprecision and ambiguity are the greatest failings of exam items, even on mathematics exams (Crouse and Jacobson, 1975). Teachers who write clear, precise exam questions can more accurately and fairly assess what students know than those who compose tests carelessly.

True-False and Matching Exams

True-false questions and matching tasks do not work well at the college level. The cognitive complexity of college content makes constructing "never true" or "always" items exceedingly difficult. True-false items are also poor because of the high probability that students will get them correct by chance alone. Matching lists of names or concepts promotes memorization and cannot be used easily to assess understanding.

Multiple-Choice Exams

Multiple-choice items are derided by many college teachers, who think that they tap only memory for isolated facts. For most teachers of the humanities, the notion of a student passing a test without demonstrating understanding or thinking processes in writing is an educational absurdity (Highet, 1950). Yet multiple-choice exams have become a mainstay in many disciplines and schools, especially when many students must be evaluated simultaneously. Multiple-choice items certainly can assess levels of knowledge other than memorized facts. Almost all group psychological tests of intelligence, academic aptitude, and achievement are multiple-choice, for example. With thought and practice, a clever instructor can construct multiple-choice items that assess competence at any level of educational objectives.

College teachers must be careful to make sure, however, that items test knowledge of the subject rather than general intelligence. For example, economics students asked on a multiple-choice item to compare and contrast "maximizing utility by consumers" and "maximizing profits by companies" must weight several possible comparisons as well as know the individual concepts. Picking the most important difference may reflect their ability to make abstract generalizations or to notice subtle differences in wording more than their knowledge of the two course concepts. Even though content, too, will be better understood by the more intelligent students (assuming comparable amounts of study), college teachers should focus exam questions on content and not mainly on students' thinking skills. Unless they construct multiple-choice exams carefully, teachers risk measuring differences in academic aptitude rather than knowledge acquired of the course material.

Multiple-choice exams are ideal for a large class that the teacher expects to teach for several terms. Experienced multiple-choice users typically put items on index cards (or computer disks), with statistical data concerning previous use; they select items from this pool for current exams. To make cheating more difficult, a computer pool of potential multiple-choice items can also be used to generate alternative exam forms that vary item and option placement and that are distributed evenly around the classroom. Many fundamental concepts will be taught without fail every semester, and these are best assessed with proven items when possible. Revising items and adding new ones to the pool is easier than writing a whole new exam and frees the instructor to grade written work.

Potential multiple-choice items come from several sources. One way to create items is to ask students to write and submit them. Letting students do this has a positive interpersonal value: it shares with them some of the control of evaluation and may make them more sympathetic to the instructor's role in it. This practice also suggests concepts for teacher-written items. Teacher's manuals issued by textbook publishers also contain items, though they have seldom been pretested and refined. Like student items, published items may suggest concepts for which questions can be written by teachers.

Experience indicates (McKeachie, 1986; Milton, 1978) that the college teacher constructing a multiple-choice examination should do the following:

1. Begin with a single concept, definition, or research finding that has been covered thoroughly in the text or in lecture. Be clear on what you want to measure with the item; students will then be more likely to understand the question and—if they know the material—answer correctly.

2. To reduce the role of chance, include five options rather than four; the probability that a student will get an item correct from guessing alone drops from 25 percent to 20 percent when five items are used.

3. State the main stem of the item in positive language; avoid "not," "no," and especially, double negatives.

4. Place all qualifications in the section of the item that precedes the options; keep the answer options short and clear-cut.

5. Avoid irrelevant sources of difficulty, such as uncommon vocabulary or unnecessary details.

6. For areas of opinion, qualify the stem with "according to. . ."

7. Avoid giving clues to the correct answer, avoid "never" and "always" in the stem, and make all options grammatically consistent with the stem.

8. Vary the position of the correct answer by keeping running totals of the options that have been used.

9. Include options of varying difficulty: one fairly obvious incorrect answer, another the opposite of the correct answer, and one or two that are only slightly different from the correct one. The correct option must clearly be the *best*, the one reflecting the fullest understanding of the concept(s) referred to in the stem.

10. Never use "all (or none) of the above" as options; such answers are easy to construct but require little student thinking or subtlety and do not discriminate well between students with differing degrees of knowledge.

Once items are written, the teacher should select as many as students will have time to answer. Students can complete between 1 and 2 items per minute; 1.5 per minute is a good average.

Even if a computer will score the exam later and generate item statistics, the instructor should make a hand-scoring template to figure tentative scores for students desiring an immediate estimate of their achievement. Usually, no more than about 50 percent of a class will ask for hand scoring. The teacher will anyway need a hand-scoring system if any students take the exam late or if there are too few students to justify computer scoring (less than twenty). Hand scoring also lets you mark the correct answers on the answer sheet, which students will need to see.

Two variations on multiple-choice exams have become popular with students and instructors in recent years. To keep students from missing questions that were unclear or that involved concepts the students understood at a higher level than the instructor anticipated, add an "explain" option (Dodd and Leal, 1988). Tell students they may write a brief explanation of why they selected the option they did if they believe the item can be interpreted in different ways. For a well-constructed and polished exam, few students— about 25 percent in one study (Nield and Wintre, 1986)—will include explanations, and instructors will need to award additional points for even fewer. The opportunity to explain answers to frustrating multiple-choice items reassures both students and faculty that this impersonal method of assessing learning will not place students at an undue disadvantage. A second variation invites students to prepare and bring in small "crib sheets" for the exam (Janick, 1990). Tell your students they may put anything they wish—definitions, formulae, examples—on both sides of a single three-by five-inch index card. Warn them that a well-constructed crib sheet should contain only the basic terms and will take time to make. This technique recognizes that students will learn a great deal by preparing a crib sheet, which is, after all, a primary purpose of the exam. Teachers who ask their students to turn in their crib sheets afterward also learn a great deal about what their students think is important. Regardless of how multiple-choice exams are given, they should be studied afterward to ensure that differences on the exam really reflect different amounts of knowledge.

Most colleges have computer packages for scoring and analyzing multiple-choice exams. Such analysis relates the probability of a student's correctly answering each item given his or her total score. Instructors should inspect computer printouts for item difficulty (percentage of students answering the item correctly) and item discrimination (statistical index reflecting the differences between the numbers of students in the top and bottom fifths of the class who passed the item). An instructor can have reasonable confidence in the results of analyses done on classes of forty or more students. Even then, however, item analysis data must be interpreted if items are to be improved.

What are good difficulty and discrimination scores? Optimally, difficult items are those that about 75 percent of the class answer correctly. Exams should contain only a few items that more than 90 percent or less than 60 percent pass. Discrimination scores are more difficult to interpret, because they can be computed in more than one way and because it is impossible to have high discrimination scores for easy items. Items of moderate difficulty (difficulty scores of 70–85 percent) should be correctly answered more frequently by students in the top fifth of the class on total score than by those in the bottom fifth. Teachers should seek advice from those running the item analysis service at their school for appropriately interpreting the kind of discrimination indices used. Instructors should examine very closely any items missed by more than half of the class. Items of appropriate difficulty and discrimination can be saved, while an inspection of less successful items may suggest how they could be improved. Over successive semesters, college teachers can compile a sizable pool of tested items that address fundamental concepts, and these can be used in subsequent examinations.

The instructor should have the results of the item analysis handy when talking with students about their exams. Students are usually interested in knowing how many others missed an item. Also, it is easier to argue against an incorrect answer if data show that only a few students chose it.

Short-Answer or Identification Exams

Short-answer questions require as much knowledge of details as do multiple-choice items. In such questions, students are given a concept or term and asked to define it or "tell what is important to know" about it in a few sentences. Short-answer items can also assess thinking if students are asked to compare concepts. More space is usually required for such questions than for definitions. Multiple-choice and short-answer items are similar in what they can assess.

Short-answer exams differ significantly from multiple-choice tests, primarily in the amount of time they take to construct and score and how thoroughly students will prepare for them. Short-answer items are quick and easy to write but much more time-consuming to score. Twenty identifications commonly take the average student over an hour to complete, and an instructor will need between ten and thirty minutes to score each paper.

But identification tests have advantages as well. Unlike multiple-choice exams, they are seldom seen as unfair by students, although students may recognize that they will be unable to guess and must study harder for them. Students can express their thoughts exactly in such tests, and instructors can see directly how well they have understood. Student verbal facility does not contribute to the quality of answers as much as it does with longer essays, and instructors need not worry so much about having unwittingly constructed an intelligence test. There are usually specific answers to short questions, so they can be scored reliably and objectively. The time required to score short answers may be excessive for very large classes, but for many others, short-answer exams are an ideal compromise between assembly-line multiple-choice exams and literary-free-for-all essays.

How should short-answer exams be constructed and scored? As with any item, the teacher should begin with a specific purpose for each question. He or she must then decide how much space to allow for the answer. Students should be given between four and five minutes per item. To assist in scoring, the teacher should write out the best answer possible, based on the information supplied by the course. (Having a colleague or more advanced student take the exam also helps.) The instructor should then decide how many points to give to each item and how many of the specific facts or ideas in the exemplary answers will be required to earn full or partial credit.

Before scoring any items, the teacher should read through five to ten questions to see if most of the ideas students are including have been correctly anticipated and to revise scoring criteria if indicated. It is not advisable to score all answers on each paper before going on to the next one; items will be scored more consistently if they are done one at a time or one page at a time. If an answer is especially good, much better than required to earn full credit, the instructor might consider giving extra credit (one-half point or so). Writing "good" or "excellent" beside the answer also reinforces students who went well beyond what was expected.

When all papers have been scored, the teacher adds up the points (or computes percentages) and plots the distribution, deciding which groups of scores to convert to which grades. If the class has few students and the teacher wants to check scoring, he or she can look at some items twice, keeping a record of the initial marks separately. Team teachers frequently score a few exams jointly to ensure agreement on the final grades awarded. Though less objective than multiple-choice exams, identification exams can be scored with acceptable reliability. The scoring criteria should be made available to students (along with copies of superior papers) to provide detailed feedback about the way questions might have been answered.

Though they take more time to grade than multiple-choice items, identification or short-answer items are ideal when a class is small. Many college teachers include both multiple-choice and short-answer items on an exam in an attempt to satisfy students' differing preferences and capitalize on the merits of both formats.

Essay Exams

Examinations consisting of broad, integrative essays or discussion questions are common in the humanities and in much course work at the graduate level. In long essays, students can display detailed knowledge as well as reveal their understanding of overall contextual issues. Essay questions are particularly apt for evaluating students' abilities to think critically, independently, and originally. For integrating concepts and comparing theories, they easily surpass multiple-choice and short-answer questions. Essays are ideal for measuring higher-level analysis, synthesis, or evaluation and for increasing writing skill. When the impact of general education requirements on various academic and personal variables was evaluated across a comprehensive array of colleges and universities, two of the top predictors of a quality education were the opportunity to take essay exams and to receive feedback on papers (Astin, 1992).

Essays, however, are difficult to grade reliably and objectively. Even in a class of ten students, the range of ideas in answers to a broad discussion question will be large. Differences in how clearly, correctly, and expressively students communicate their ideas will also influence the way their knowledge of content and ideas is evaluated. Even handwriting can influence the grade an essay exam receives; it also makes the preservation of student anonymity difficult in small classes. Essay exams take considerably more time to grade than multiple-choice exams, though not necessarily longer than identification exams. The most troublesome drawback of essays is unreliable grading resulting from teacher fatigue, lack of concentration, or other subjective factors.

A one-hour exam of three essay questions will take at least as long to grade as a ten-to-fifteen-page term paper—fifteen to forty-five minutes per student. Because all students write about the same questions, maintaining concentration when reading essay exams is more difficult than when reading varied term papers. Though essays seem much fairer to many students than less personal multiple-choice questions, some will be graded unfairly if the instructor allows his or her concentration to fade.

To minimize the liabilities of essay exams, instructors should do the following (based in part on McKeachie, 1986, and Milton, 1978):

1. Focus essay questions by specifying parameters, so that students will be less tempted to "bullshit" ("Discuss the economic reasons why United States government leaders feared expanding Japanese power in the Pacific between 1935 and 1939," rather than "Why did America fear the Japanese expansion of influence in the Pacific?"). Ask for critical evaluation with supporting evidence rather than personal feelings.

2. Limit the space available by providing paper for the essay questions. Asking students to use blue books encourages them to fill up the available pages with unimportant verbiage.

3. Beware of giving take-home essay exams; some students will spend an inordinate amount of time on them, and most will

not study (and learn) as much in preparation. The teacher should tell students the general topics of the questions ahead of time and have them write answers in class ("We have discussed five theories of human learning in this section. I will ask you to compare and contrast two of them on the exam").

4. Before scoring, read all answers to the first question in a preliminary way, noting the overall quality and deciding which grades to give the best and worst papers; select a model paper or two at each grade for later comparison.

5. Read papers for detail in groups of five to ten at a sitting. Underline key phrases or words to maintain concentration. Refer frequently to the model papers when deciding which specific grade to assign. Take frequent breaks or time your reading to keep attention on each paper.

6. Go through all answers to each question before moving to the next question.

7. Write specific comments throughout, as well as an overall evaluation of each question, complimenting the student on what he or she did well and showing how the answer could have been improved.

Essay exams have advantages and disadvantages. Constructing and scoring them as advocated here ensure that students will demonstrate their best thinking on essay tests and that the instructor will be able to give each student's work the same concentrated attention.

Oral Exams

Though students can answer both detailed questions and broad, integrative ones orally, such exams are extremely rare at the undergraduate level. They have the liability that students cannot revise their responses, and the instructor has nothing to refer back to when grading, unless the answer is taped. However, an oral exam is sometimes necessary when a physical disability prevents a student from writing. Also, students bound for graduate or professional school might find taking an oral exam useful preparation.

Selecting Types of Exams

College teachers base their choice of exam type on personal preferences, philosophical beliefs, time available, and/or habit. It is obviously more efficient to pick the testing format that best assesses the desired educational objectives. Most instructors have varied objectives and use several different testing methods: multiple-choice or short-answer for detail and essays for comprehension and thinking. Practical considerations such as class size and availability of test-scoring service or teaching assistants will also influence the choice of testing format, but these should be secondary.

Grading

College grades deserve neither the criticism nor the adulation given them. High grades are not synonymous with a good education, nor do they necessarily interfere with one. Americans are ambivalent about grades and grading practices, because they bring into focus the clash between egalitarian ideals and the reality of unequal intellectual abilities and opportunities (Milton, Pollio, and Eison, 1986). No doubt some college teachers abuse their power to assign grades; the final section in this chapter lists several common abuses. Grading-oriented students also abuse grading in a sense, by focusing so narrowly on grades that they learn neither in-depth content nor the importance of independent thought. Students also abuse grading who handle their frustration or lack of preparation by cheating. College teachers should strive to take grading seriously but should also remember that it is of less consequence than what students learn. "And only by demonstrating that grading is not always necessary and that other kinds of feedback and evaluation are both possible and useful can one honestly minimize the importance of grades" (Eble, 1988, p. 160).

The following suggestions will keep grading in perspective for students and instructors. How a teacher chooses to combine scores on exams and papers over a semester reveals his or her attitude about effort, success, and failure. For example, weighting final examinations as more than 50 percent of the total grade encourages students to cram at the end rather than work throughout a course. Even if they have studied all along, this practice forces them to stake much of their fate on one throw of the dice. Allowing students to drop their lowest grade is popular, but doing so may encourage them to be irresponsible. College teachers who base final grades on how hard the student appears to have worked, on relative improvement, or on simply completing extra-credit work make clear that they value effort more than performance. Grading policies should be determined thoughtfully, to be certain that they are consistent with the instructor's philosophical beliefs about ability, effort, the motivational role of evaluative feedback, and the degree to which he or she desires to select or develop student talent.

The following general suggestions on assigning final grades have seemed reasonable and useful to many teachers:

1. Let students know throughout the term how they are doing. Awarding cumulative points after each exam or paper without indicating what letter grade has been earned does not give students a firm idea of the grade they are likely to receive at the end of the course, and assigning grades only on the final point distribution can produce unexpected results for individual students. The simplest way to help students predict their grades and thus to encourage their studying is to assign a letter grade (or numerical equivalent) for each exam and compute the average at the end of the course.

2. Construct a system for combining exam and paper scores that rewards effort all along, not just at the end. Describe the system to students at the beginning of the course. Students will learn and remember more if they apply themselves steadily rather than sprinting

in the final weeks. The weights given to different assignments help to determine appropriate levels of effort for each one.

3. If a student does extremely poorly on an initial exam, it may be mathematically impossible for him or her to achieve an acceptable grade of C, even with significant improvement. Personally encourage such a student to do well on subsequent exams, and be generous when averaging that initial score with later, higher ones. Do not tell the student that you will ignore the low score, only that you will increase it somewhat when computing the average if he or she improves subsequently. More than anything, encourage students to keep trying and not to give up.

4. When computing final grades, perform each calculation twice and consider all marginal cases together, taking into account subjective factors such as your perception of class attendance, demonstrated involvement, and improvement over the semester. No evaluation procedures are precise enough to be used automatically. At the borderline, college teachers must show wisdom in assigning grades that are fair to the individual students and the rest of the class.

5. Do not explicitly assign points for class participation. As Chapter Five on discussion argues, it is almost impossible to assess participation fairly, and allowing a significant part of a student's grade to be determined by such a subjective measure opens the door to a perception of personal bias.

6. Avoid encouraging a grading orientation by assigning credit for activities many students would have done on their own. Practice exams, journals, and reaction papers need not be entered into students' final grades; simply read them, comment, and return them to students. Using an external carrot simply as a motivational tool demeans the students who would have worked for intrinsic reasons and discourages a learning orientation.

7. Most grades are distributed somewhat normally, but never force grades to fit quotas or theoretical expectations. Administrators who declare that "no more than 15 percent of a class should receive A's" are employing a poor method to curb grade inflation.

8.   If posting grades is traditional at your school, post them in a way that protects student identities.

9.   Do not change a grade after it has been turned in, unless you were clearly in error. Once students have successfully begged a grade change after the fact, this can become a habitual way of handling academic pressure. Offer to write a letter explaining why a student earned a certain grade, but resist the temptation to rescue the student by changing in a stroke a grade that he or she spent an entire semester earning. Some instructors announce at the beginning of courses that students who, for whatever reason, "need" a certain grade in a course should let them know then rather than at the end when it is too late to help. An instructor can then know to schedule a conference with a student who needs a B to stay in school when his or her performance falls below that level.

Above all, college teachers should remember the importance of grades to students and treat grades seriously, though without undue anxiety. "Giving" a student a grade significantly higher than he or she deserves may provide momentary pleasure or relief to the student but is unlikely to engender respect for educational institutions or to help him or her accept responsibility or appreciate learning. The lessons students learn about responsibility and evaluation are important to their success as adults. Since the adult world is often less fair and predictable than school, college teachers have an obligation to teach students two things that will help them succeed: to take responsibility for themselves, and to carefully choose how to spend their time.

Cheating

"The wise teacher takes ordinary precautions against cheating, but equally important, uses the kinds of tests, assignments, and teaching practices that provide few rationalizations for cheating" (Eble, 1988, p. 165).

Though cheating among college students cannot be justified or condoned, the motivations that lead to it are too universal and understandable to allow instructors to treat perpetrators harshly. A teacher should not view cheating in simple terms of right-wrong, honorable-dishonorable; almost anyone is capable of cheating, given opportunity and sufficient motivation. Conversely, even the habitual offender is less likely to cheat in some courses than in others. Experienced teachers know that it is better to prevent cheating than to try to catch students in the act.

How can cheating be prevented? Students are far less likely to cheat if they are excited by a subject and if they have a personal relationship with the instructor. Cheating is most common in impersonal, adversarial relationships in which "beating the system" is expected. In a hospitable classroom, students are less likely to want to cheat or to give in to the temptation.

Specifically, students are less likely to cheat if these things are true:

1. Students know why exams are being given, because the instructor has shared objectives with them.
2. Students know and like the college teacher as a person and believe that he or she knows and likes them as well.
3. Students are excited by the material and internally motivated to learn it.
4. Students believe that they will be graded fairly and will receive detailed feedback on their work.
5. Students know it will be hard to cheat.

These preventive suggestions apply to plagiarism as well as to in-class examinations, but plagiarism is more difficult to identify than cheating on exams. The best prevention for this kind of cheating is detailed instructions on the sources that can be used for papers and the way they must be referenced. Some students deliberately misrepresent the sources of their work, but many more plagiarize unwittingly out of ignorance or inexperience with different instructor policies. On any work students do outside class, the instructor should be exceedingly certain that they understand what material they can and cannot use. Plagiarism is a difficult issue even for professional and scholarly writers. College teachers can make this issue easier for students to understand by specifying the rules under which they should work and, whenever possible, encouraging students to help each other.

Every college teacher will eventually encounter what appears to be a clear instance of cheating. What should you do if this happens to you? Confront the student in class only if the offense is flagrant (notes on the lap during an exam, paragraphs in a paper lifted from books, with no reference notation), and if you are so sure that cheating occurred that you can risk irreparably damaging your relationship with the student by mentioning your suspicions. When confronting a student, adopt an air of concern about the reason for the cheating rather than of punishment or criticism. If possible, discuss cheating in private. The student will feel unhappy enough about being caught; there is no need to add shame to his or her misery. Indicate the seriousness of the offense and try to get the student to participate in deciding what to do about it. Students who admit cheating and turn themselves in to the honor council or whatever other administrative body is indicated are better treated and learn a greater lesson than those turned in by instructors or other students. Speak with the student first and the authorities last. However, be sure to follow your school's procedures; do not take justice into your own hands and impose a private sentence such as a lower grade or an F—even with the student's collusion. This might seem kinder than official proceedings, but it can teach students to disregard established laws and procedures and will demonstrate that you prefer vigilante justice to due process.

A Dozen "Nevers"

Though teaching by negative example is risky, it is instructive to conclude this chapter with some illustrations of extremely poor testing and grading practices that have actually been observed. The following list has been adapted and expanded from one offered by McKeachie (1986, pages 118–119).

1. Never announce that one type of exam will be given, change your mind, and distribute something different.

2. Never say some sections will (or will not) be covered and then do the opposite of what you announced.

3. Never ask students to solve problems or write types of essays on an exam that have been given no exposure in class.

4. Never spend the first fifteen minutes of a one-hour exam making oral changes in the printed questions or instructions.

5. Never include two right answers on multiple-choice items.

6. Never fail to finish reading essays and cover up your failure by making a brief comment on the last page of each paper to make it appear to have been read.

7. Never give everyone the same grade because you have not read the essays, and avoid giving the same grade when you have read the essays.

8. Never decide after the first exam (or paper) which students are A students, B students, or C students and never sort subsequent work into corresponding piles before reading it to confirm that initial impression.

9. Never fail to give an indication during a course of the grade that a student is likely to receive.

10. When a student asks about a grade, never say that he or she actually earned a grade higher than the one given but that the grade was lowered because the supervisor's, the department's, or the school's guidelines indicated that there were too many A's, B's, or whatever.

11. Never tell students that the grade distribution was really quite arbitrary and that you could have just as easily called the C's "B's" or the B's "A's."

12. Never give a student suspected of cheating a lower grade or an F without telling the student or the honor council.

The final chapter of this book takes another look at the question put forth in Chapter One: What are the essential ingredients of outstanding college teaching? It gives special attention to these secondary questions: (1) To what extent is virtuoso classroom skill the result of talent and to what extent is it the result of a supportive environment? (2) How can teaching excellence be evaluated and fostered? (3) Given the emphasis on research productivity and service to the institution, why should any college teacher make the continued effort to hone his or her teaching skills to the finest edge?

The Art, Craft, and Techniques of Exemplary Teaching

We have classified teacher prototypes in two major categories. The first includes those teaching modes in which inquiry on the part of the student is not required or encouraged for the successful completion of the learning set by the professor. We call these teaching styles the didactic modes. The other category includes those teaching modes in which inquiry on the part of the student is required if he is to complete successfully the tasks set by the teacher. We call these teaching styles the evocative modes. Those teachers who achieve excellence in the didactic modes we shall call craftsmen; those teachers who achieve excellence in the evocative modes we shall call artists.

—Axelrod (1973, pp. 9–10)

As Joseph Axelrod suggests, excellent college teachers differ in their style and intellectual values. Even the evocative teachers he studied varied considerably. Some emphasized their subject ("I teach what I know"), some focused on themselves ("I teach what I am: an educated person"), and others were student-centered ("I train minds" or "I work with students as persons"). In the observations and interviews that generated the models and teaching suggestions offered in this book, considerable variation was also observed. Some professors were animated and enthusiastic, others intense and aloof; but all had an energetic presence when working before groups of students. Compared with completely competent instructors, the exceptionally skilled are in thorough command of classrooms as either dramatic or interpersonal arenas.

The final chapter returns to the seminal question: What constitutes exemplary college teaching? A number of styles of outstanding teaching presented in the two-dimensional model in Table 1.4 could serve as goals for college teachers. The specific techniques for achieving teaching excellence presented in this book are consistent with that model and are based on the view (discussed in Chapters Two and Four) that classrooms are dramatic and interpersonal arenas. Of concern here are several related questions:

1. Does outstanding instruction result more from individual talent or from a supportive academic environment?

2. How can college teaching best be evaluated to reflect the full range of teaching effectiveness?

3. How can graduate instructors and junior faculty be taught to teach well?

4. Given the rewards and requirements for survival in academia, why should any instructor attempt to strive for excellence in the classroom, especially in teaching undergraduates?

Talent or Effort?

To what extent are exemplary teachers born or made? This question underlies every discussion of college teaching. It is difficult to answer confidently, as there is evidence to support both arguments.

As the learning model in Chapter One shows, a student's performance in a course is a function of both individual ability and the motivating effects of classroom climate. College teachers' effectiveness is also a function of both personal and environmental characteristics. Some teachers are more naturally skilled than others, but conditions affect the way any instructor's skill is applied. The key issue is, of course, the *relative* contributions to the quality of teaching of individual skill and institutional support, either of which may strengthen or frustrate an instructor's commitment to teach well.

When considering an individual's teaching ability, innate talent for teaching comes to mind first. An instructor's intelligence and academic preparation also are essential to good teaching; dull or shallow college teachers are not likely to be effective. However, within a given faculty, those who are most effective in the classroom will not necessarily be the brightest or most outstanding researchers. Other skills and personal qualities most distinguish the outstanding classroom artists or craftsmen from the merely adequate.

Foremost among personal characteristics contributing to teaching of the highest quality is an intelligent, clear, and thorough understanding of content. But the ability to present ideas in an engaging manner is also required. Some individuals are initially more comfortable in front of groups and more able to give fresh and involving presentations. They have a natural talent for public speaking that enables them to learn the lecturer's art quickly. It goes without saying that an eloquent speaker is more likely to become an exemplary instructor than a fearful, stiff, and halting one. However, regardless of degree of talent, no person will learn the art of lecturing without practice; and conversely, most who have no gift can learn to speak adequately.

Another quality important in teaching is the ability to explain abstract concepts clearly and simply. Natural talent is less evident here. Whether the ability to explain ideas easily to the uninitiated results from high empathy, a capacity to focus on fundamental assumptions, or a facility for thinking of creative or concrete examples quickly is unclear. Almost any instructor can develop sufficient clarity to be a good college teacher by seeking and using student feedback.

Similarly, some instructors are naturally more sensitive and insightful than other people. Reading the meaning of interpersonal communications and empathizing with the varieties of human experience is second nature to some individuals. People of this type who become college teachers are more naturally comfortable with students than are those who find it difficult to understand or like undergraduates and remain tense and distant despite attempts to promote positive relationships. However, any instructor can increase his or her knowledge of classroom dynamics and learn to create a pleasant and work-conducive atmosphere. With effort and support from others, most new college teachers eventually overcome any initial discomfort or difficulty with the interpersonal requirements of teaching.

Talent clearly plays a role in determining how easily instructors succeed in the classroom. But persistent effort can offset low or moderate initial performance and is required for anyone to develop his or her assets to the fullest. It has been highly gratifying to see how graduate instructors following the lessons presented here improve their student ratings from well below to well above departmental averages over successive semesters. These favorable results were more often due to effort than to innate talent.

It would be fair to ask: after applying the lessons in this book, could any college instructor attain the highest levels of teaching proficiency? The answer: probably not. Considerable experience over several years is normally required to become one of the exemplary types described in the first chapter. Also likely to be necessary are flair for spontaneous oral exposition, a gift for the production of creative examples, the capacity to apply innovative pedagogical approaches, an intuitive empathic sense, and the ability to interpret the subtle messages of students.

Whether a teacher settles for being merely competent or strives to become outstanding is significantly affected by the environment in which he or she labors. We now turn to the characteristics of an academic culture that influence instructor motivation, that encourage or discourage outstanding teaching.

Supportive Teaching Environments

It might often seem to faculty that colleges and universities, with their excessive emphasis on research and committee work, are subtly designed to promote *poor* classroom instruction (Sykes, 1988). "I could be a much better teacher if only I had the time" is a common sentiment. Is the absence of competing demands a characteristic of a supportive teaching environment?

Not necessarily. Faculty can be overworked, but they rarely are. More commonly, they *feel* overwhelmed by the variety of things expected of them—keeping up-to-date on the content of various courses, publishing good scholarship, becoming nationally conspicuous, preparing for and conducting classes, meeting with students individually, supervising individual research projects, serving on committees. This is inherent in the job: college teaching offers tremendous freedom to structure time and channel energy, but it requires commensurate levels of internal motivation, personal organization, self-discipline, and ability to pursue multiple goals. Because the obligation to teach in the classroom is the most structured demand placed on college teachers, it is not surprising that many new faculty have difficulty deciding how much energy to direct toward the immediate demands of teaching and how much to invest in the more intangible, distant goals of scholarship. Graduate instructors suffer from similar conflicts between their own studies and their teaching responsibilities. It is not work load per se that most creates discomfort among college instructors but the necessity of deciding how to spend time. To borrow a thought from Erich

Fromm (1941), anxiety is caused more by the freedom of college teaching than by its demands.

"Not enough time" can become a convenient rationalization for not becoming a better teacher or scholar. Some new instructors who are anxious about their teaching (especially if it is not initially easy or satisfying) denigrate its importance: "Why should I break my neck for the students? They don't give me tenure!" Others throw themselves into teaching to sidestep the pressure to conduct important research or bring in a big grant. They can then explain their failure to complete dissertations, produce publications, or obtain tenure as arising from their choice to pursue teaching excellence. Such "champions of good teaching" often fail to notice that some colleagues *can* balance the competing demands on their time and do well at both teaching and scholarship.

Fortunately, the kinds of scholarship that a novice professor might now pursue are broader than they were in recent years. In *Scholarship Reconsidered*, Ernest Boyer (1990) identifies a narrowing focus on original research in American colleges since World War II, which has produced an imbalance between the roles of teaching and publishing. He argues convincingly that colleges and individual departments should adopt a broader definition of what is considered legitimate scholarly activity—one that is consistent with the diversity of their individual faculty members, their disciplines, and their institutional missions. The following quotations capture the expanded vision he recommends.

> We believe the time has come to move beyond the tired old "teaching versus research" debate and give the familiar and honorable term "scholarship" a broader, more capacious meaning, one that brings legitimacy to the full scope of academic work. Surely, scholarship means engaging in original research. But the work of the scholar also means stepping back from one's investigation, looking for connections, building bridges between

theory and practice, and communicating one's knowledge effectively to students. Specifically, we conclude that the work of the professoriate might be thought of as having four separate, yet overlapping functions. These are: the scholarship of *discovery*; the scholarship of *integration*; the scholarship of *application*; and the scholarship of *teaching* [p. 16].

What we are calling for is *diversity with dignity* in American higher education—a national network of higher learning institutions in which each college and university takes pride in its own distinctive mission and seeks to complement rather than imitate the others. While the full range of scholarship can flourish on a single campus, every college and university should find its own special niche. Why should one model dominate the system [p. 64]?

Institutions adopting Boyer's broader definition of scholarly achievement are also more likely to be *genuinely* supportive of outstanding classroom teaching. Almost every teaching culture pays lip service to the importance of classroom instruction. Information sent to prospective students, parents, and alumni or released to the press (especially near budget time for public institutions) commonly stresses the value that the institution places on quality teaching. Speeches by deans and departmental chairs may also contain ritualistic homage to this basic academic duty. However, informal and implicit messages and the actual behavior of administrators and other faculty tell a novice more accurately the extent to which classroom teaching is valued in a given institution.

What does one find in an academic community that supports excellent classroom teaching? First, teaching effectiveness of all faculty is routinely assessed, and such information is used in personnel decisions about junior faculty. At such schools, teaching effectiveness may not be the primary factor in tenure decisions, but it *is* entered into the equation and can make the difference—up or down—in borderline cases. Schools that grant tenure to outstanding scholars without polling students about their teaching give a clear message that the quality of teaching is not valued there. Similarly, when poor instructors are hired, reappointed, or promoted, it is clear to all members of the faculty that failure in the classroom will not affect professional survival. Universities and research colleges should not give tenure to excellent instructors who are unproductive scholars, but they should select and reward those who excel in both areas.

Supportive environments are also those secure enough in mission and reputation to avoid a narrow definition of scholarship and, following Boyer's recommendations, to allow faculty the freedom to pursue a wide range of publishing options. Feeling secure about one's school lets faculty and administrators emphasize both teaching and research.

A university's national reputation is a function of its graduate programs, but its financial survival comes from its undergraduate alumni, who remember most the quality of instruction they received. How universities handle graduate students who participate in the school's teaching mission is a sensitive indicator of the school's support for undergraduate teaching. Assigning TAs to classes primarily to do the grunt work of setting up audiovisual equipment or grading papers fails to develop either teaching skill or positive attitudes in these future professors. On the other hand, if they are assigned as instructors to large introductory classes, it is a clear indication of how little the school values skilled teaching— and its undergraduates. Another telling measure of the respect in which teaching is held is the way a school offers a stipend that carries some undergraduate teaching duties. The supportive school does not say: "Sorry, Lynn, but your performance last year was not good enough for us to be able to give you a fellowship or research assistantship. You'll have to teach." Supportive environments treat graduate student involvement in undergraduate teaching both as a developmental experience for the graduate students and a coordinated team effort to provide undergraduates with a high-quality education.

Also reflective of a supportive teaching environment or the lack of it are the faculty's attitudes toward students and classroom performance. These are communicated in informal conversation and jokes during faculty meetings, as well as in official memoranda. A new instructor hearing colleagues refer routinely to "immature," "lazy," "stupid," "untrustworthy," or "inconsiderate" students risks becoming socialized into a culture that does not value students or have rapport with them. If colleagues never comment on the process of teaching except to complain, an instructor runs the risk of adopting the beliefs that there is nothing important to learn about teaching, that it does not matter how well one teaches, or that teaching is a necessary evil associated with an academic appointment. Departments or schools in which faculty discuss teaching methods they have tried and speak positively about students are much more likely to motivate new instructors to take the classroom seriously.

Supportive teaching environments also recognize high-level teaching. Awards are a common method of giving public recognition to outstanding teachers, and they can be respected if the procedures used to grant them are systematic and open (Meredith, 1990). But teaching awards are too scarce to go to everyone who deserves them. Their usefulness is further limited by the tendency for political considerations to affect the choice of recipients. Practices such as departmental claques swamping the nomination process by meeting beforehand and agreeing to commend the same colleague, administrators informally rotating awards among administrative units, or reserving awards for senior faculty nearing retirement create more ill will than good among classroom instructors. If an awards program is to be motivating, student input should play a primary role in the processes of nomination and final selection, the monetary reward should be significant, and the criteria should stress work with students, not research productivity or service to the institution. The latter activities can be evaluated independently (Kremer, 1990) and awards offered for outstanding performance. Given the cost and limitations of a good teaching awards program, teaching skills may be recognized more effectively by letters from departmental heads or deans to *all* instructors receiving particularly high teaching evaluations from students. Inviting those receiving poor ratings to seek consultation about their teaching is also advisable.

Whether or not it actively rewards outstanding instructors, a supportive culture at least does not punish individuals for successful classroom performance. College teachers, like anyone else, are vulnerable to petty jealousies, and in some settings junior faculty find themselves fearful of being too successful or popular with students. Even if a teaching award is not a kiss of death for an untenured faculty member, as the lore at some institutions suggests, college teachers risk a reputation as an unintellectual "prostitute" or "clown" among some colleagues if students seek out their classes or publicly praise their teaching. In supportive environments, however, outstanding teachers are not criticized for their popularity with students or their high ratings. Faculty feel pride rather than resentment when a colleague's teaching is recognized.

Teachers who excel in the classroom for personal reasons are the most likely to be happy teaching over a number of years. Those who are motivated primarily by the hope of winning teaching awards are certain to be dissatisfied in the long run. Still, more instructors will choose to apply their energies to developing outstanding classroom skills in a supportive environment than in a negligent or punitive one.

Evaluating Teaching Effectiveness

The truth is that one cannot adequately evaluate a teacher until years after one has sat in his classroom. Proper evaluation can perhaps only be made after the spell of the powerful teacher has worn off, in the former

> student's maturity, when in tranquillity he can recollect
> influence. Influence is subtle, sometimes accidental,
> often mysterious. It cannot generally be analyzed on a
> computer form in the last ten minutes of the last class of
> a course [Epstein, 1981, p. xiii].

There is both wisdom and fallacy in Epstein's position on teacher evaluation. College teaching is most often evaluated at the easiest time, at the end of a course when impressions are fresh and the students available. Though the long-term significance of particular instructors and courses in a student's life is, as Epstein says, best evaluated in maturity, his contention that ratings given while "under a teacher's spell" will differ substantially from those made later has not been supported by empirical research (see Chapter One). Epstein also assumes that people can accurately identify which of their adult qualities resulted from various earlier influences. To assess the clarity and interest value of a college teacher's presentations and his or her short-term inspirational or motivational impact on students, overall evaluations should be made at the end of the term. But useful data can also be collected during the course, when there is still time to make changes in methods or style (Abbott, Wulff, Nyquist, and Ropp, 1990).

Several of the classroom assessment techniques presented by Angelo and Cross (1993) provide useful information about an instructor's teaching—information that is collected during the term and that is related more directly to learning than to satisfaction with the teaching. For example, instructors can give students focused opportunities to comment on specific teaching techniques (such as cooperative group activities), assignments, or readings via suggestion envelopes, electronic mail, short questionnaires, or open-ended minute papers. Another technique is to ask a colleague to lead a small-group discussion about your teacher behaviors, giving students the opportunity to state which have been most helpful to their learning and which least. Feedback assessment techniques used during or at the end of a term must include summarization of students' responses as a group to identify consistent trends.

When to evaluate teaching is relatively clear. *How* to measure effectiveness and how to use the evaluations are most troublesome issues. Student ratings of instruction are the most common method of teacher evaluation and the focus of much of the controversy surrounding it. Social science faculties are generally most sympathetic to rating-scale questionnaires, because this evaluation method is common in their discipline. Interestingly, rating scales commonly draw fire both from humanities faculty, who feel that they reduce teachers to numbers, and from natural science faculty, who view the application of measurement theory to people as a bastardization of scientific methodology. What both groups fail to appreciate is that students' ratings must be interpreted in order to be useful and that such ratings, when properly understood, can be considerably more objective than any alternatives. Common alternatives are unsolicited praise or criticism, interviews with selected students, or one-time visits by other faculty. Each of these is vulnerable to distortion due to sampling. Giving well-scaled rating forms to a group of students who have been exposed to an instructor repeatedly is much more objective than these options.

To be sure, teacher evaluation should include methods other than multiple-choice ratings: narrative descriptions by students, observations by faculty colleagues, interviews with randomly selected students, and self-ratings (Drews, Burrough, and Nokovitch, 1987). *Teaching portfolios* include a variety of materials and are discussed later in this chapter as a way to develop effective instructors as well as to document their effectiveness during personnel evaluations (Centra, 1993; Seldin, 1991). However, collecting an array of data is time-consuming and the method is unlikely to be used routinely. Student questionnaires are a good compromise between the ideal and the possible.

At whatever point evaluation data are collected, and whether questionnaires provide statistical information, written descriptions, or both, college teachers must interpret them wisely in order to benefit from them. This section deals with ways in which instructors can use student ratings to improve their teaching. Specific objectives for asking students to evaluate teaching are discussed first, followed by reasons why some teachers object to ratings. After this general discussion, specific suggestions on using student ratings are offered. The broader topics of faculty research evaluation and faculty development are not addressed (see Boyer, 1990; Braskamp and Ory, 1994; Miller, 1987).

The primary purpose for gathering student ratings is to improve the instructor's future performance. Specific feedback is analogous to specific comments on student papers: it offers directions for future work. Overall ratings of teacher performance are comparable to student grades: they reinforce instructors for a job well done and allow comparisons with others. As with students, the more specific the feedback, the more likely it is to guide future changes. Overall grades in teaching are most useful for their motivational value for instructors and their record-keeping function for administrators.

Students are asked to grade instructors because it also improves student morale. College teachers evaluate students all semester, and most instructors consider it fair to turn the tables and allow students to do likewise. Sharing power in this way also leads students to think seriously about the education they are receiving. One school goes so far as to offer undergraduates a course on college teaching (Zechmeister and Reich, 1994). Teacher evaluation acknowledges students as important participants in the school's instructional program and in their own education.

If student evaluations were employed only for these first two purposes, their use would be much less controversial. When student ratings are made public, however, they are opposed by many instructors. For example, student organizers sometimes administer course and instructor evaluation programs that result in published guides to aid students in course selection. These guides have been shown to influence the courses and instructors that students select (Coleman and McKeachie, 1981). Not surprisingly, college teachers who receive low ratings uniformly disapprove of such guides, but even some highly rated individuals see this use of student ratings as inappropriate.

Similarly, using student ratings to compare departments on teaching effectiveness creates controversy. Even private use of course evaluation data by school officials, for the purpose of making informal comparisons, is opposed by some. Other faculty members support comparisons based on student ratings (Gross and Small, 1979), arguing that systematically collected data are preferable to rumor.

There are other bases for faculty opposition to student ratings of teaching. The inclusion of such ratings in faculty evaluation procedures provokes the most opposition. Some professors defend the practice, but others believe that the use of student opinion in this way threatens faculty freedom and academic excellence. Other instructors oppose ratings for personal reasons. For those who fear any evaluation, student ratings will certainly arouse anxiety and anger. Some college teachers—like some students—do not take criticism well. Others dislike ratings because they remind them of what they already know but wish to deny: that they are ineffective in the classroom. Still other professors dislike sharing power with students, and ratings reduce a little of the status difference between them and their students. Some teachers oppose ratings because they assume that their use leads to pandering to student interests or to a softening of academic demands in exchange for high ratings. Finally, some college teachers oppose such ratings because they assume that the ratings reflect the way their research or scholarly expertise is evaluated. Though the last two reasons have not been supported by empirical research (see Chapter One), many faculty members cling to these beliefs.

In responding to colleagues who object to student evaluations, one should discern first which use of them is felt to be objectionable. There can be little argument against providing instructors with feedback on teaching. Any college teacher not interested in learning how satisfied his or her students have been, especially if they make specific suggestions for improvement, is indifferent to his obligations, or is cowardly, complacent, or even arrogant. On the other hand, opposition to the publication of evaluation data or to their substantial use in personnel decisions is more understandable—even though these practices are supported by many.

Using Student Ratings of Instruction

The first and most critical issue is whether a college teacher chooses to participate freely in the use of student ratings. Ideally, no instructor should be pressured to use student evaluations. Those who seek feedback on their own can be expected to value it most and use it constructively. Unfortunately, the consequence of completely voluntary participation is that the college teachers most in need of improvement are unlikely to take part. Voluntary participation is also a potential source of measurement error, because only the better teachers may volunteer to be rated (Howard and Bray, 1979; L'Hommedieu, Menges, and Brinko, 1990).

If student evaluation data are seen only by faculty, the matter is simple. Instructors can be encouraged to gather evaluation data of some kind periodically and allowed a choice of method (rating forms, narrative descriptions from students, observation of a class by a colleague). Packets of forms can even be sent to teachers at the end of each term and private consultation provided for anyone desiring help in interpreting data and improving his or her performance. If faculty are involved in the decision to encourage voluntary self-evaluation and this is all that is done, there is likely to be little objection (Thorne, 1980).

Teachers should be educated about the benefits of student evaluations, especially about what can be gained from reviewing their teaching evaluations with an experienced instructor. Feedback from students by itself is not as likely to lead to improvement as feedback interpreted by an experienced guide who can show an instructor how to improve. Such consultation will make it less likely that ratings will simply be glanced at and tossed in the trash (L'Hommedieu, Menges, and Brinko, 1990; McKeachie, 1986; Wilson, 1986). Instructors object less to student feedback if it is to be used as an instrument of self-evaluation, as opposed to supervision, but they benefit from it more if they discuss it with someone else. Given the importance of voluntary participation by tenured staff, educating them about the advantages of using teaching consultation is the most effective way of motivating them to seek it (Cohen, 1980; McKeachie and others, 1980). As John Centra (1993) argues, evaluations are most likely to improve subsequent teaching when instructors learn something new from a source in whom (or in which) they have confidence, understand what they can do differently to improve, and are motivated to make the effort to do so.

A great deal is known about the technical process of constructing student rating forms. We also know that evaluation data that are specific as well as global are more likely to be received well and used, and that data should be collected during as well as at the end of a course. Even though we know that teaching consultation helps, we know little about the way instructors actually use data from student evaluations and how they can be helped to use the information in the evaluations to improve.

Use of student ratings is typically required of graduate instructors and junior faculty. Novices most clearly need the fine tuning that evaluation can supply, and schools are responsible for ensuring that the performance of new faculty is adequate. Graduate instructors and recently hired staff should be involved as much as possible in selecting the kinds of data to be collected (Braskamp and Ory, 1994). Not only does the opportunity to propose alternative questions or supplemental data increase their sense of control—just as students' morale is increased when they are asked to make some decisions about class proceedings—but it also allows for better, more individualized evaluations.

Even when college teachers are required to submit student evaluations as part of supervision or personnel review, it should be stressed that the *primary* purpose of the evaluations is to aid attempts at self-improvement.

A number of instructor evaluation forms and alternative formats for evaluation have been developed and studied. In spite of much research (Champion, Green, and Sauser, 1988; Cranton and Smith, 1990; Newstead and Arnold, 1989), no single rating scale has been found to be clearly superior. For information on available forms, see Benton's review (1982) or contact the Educational Testing Service[1], which distributes and scores a well-researched student rating scale.

When considering which scale to use, an instructor should look for the presence of specific as well as general items. A few items will suffice for general comparisons ("On a one-to-five scale, what was the overall level of this instructor's classroom effectiveness?"), but ten to fifteen items will be needed to provide feedback on specific instructor behaviors ("How clear was the organization of the instructor's lectures?"). To be most useful, a standard scale of pretested items should be used with a number of classes in a given school to obtain stable norms for comparison. If enough data are available, norms can allow instructors to compare their ratings with those received by other instructors teaching the same course, by members of their department or academic division, and by those at their experience level (graduate instructors, first-year or tenured faculty).

The Enhanced Two-Dimensional Model of Effective Teaching presented in Chapter One can be used to evaluate teaching. I have constructed two formats for this purpose. A checklist version lists the thirty-nine adjectives presented in Table 1.3 in alphabetical order and asks students to check any that describe their teacher. Preliminary evaluation of the research using Marsh's applicability paradigm mentioned in Chapter One shows that students mark

1. Information about the Student Instructional Report (S.I.R.) can be obtained from Educational Testing Service, Princeton, N.J., 08541–0001.

anywhere from none to all of the adjectives and that the specific scores on intellectual excitement, interpersonal concern, effective motivation, and commitment to teaching significantly differentiate "very good," "average," and "very poor" instructors (Lowman, 1994b). Looking just at the average *total* number of adjectives checked produces impressive differences as well: very poor instructors are checked on only four qualities, average instructors on twelve, and very good instructors on twenty-six.

Exhibit 10.1 presents a ten-question traditional rating form that produces scores for the four model dimensions and summary ratings for the instructor and the course. Analyses of the comparability and effectiveness of these two formats are not yet available. However, what is clear is that the same theoretical dimensions of teaching can be assessed using different formats.

The most useful rating forms ask students to complete one or two open-ended questions in addition to rating the instructors quantitatively. For example, students might be asked to evaluate unique course features or to indicate what they would tell another student about the course or instructor, what the best and worst features of the course were, and how the course or teaching could be improved. Research shows that customized questions allow instructors to evaluate how well students believed the class met higher-order objectives (Fernald, 1990), and many college teachers find students' replies to these questions more helpful than summary statistics from multiple-choice items. Each type of rating has advantages, and both should be used.

Administering a centralized program of student evaluations of teaching is a large responsibility. Whoever handles it (dean's office, computer center, instructional support office, student government) should routinely check that data are being computed accurately. Data should also be processed quickly and faculty given feedback within a few weeks after the end of the course. The way student evaluations of teaching are conducted and the manner in which the data are handled are the strongest determinants of whether such

Exhibit 10.1. Teaching Evaluation Questions Based on
Enhanced Two-Dimensional Model.

For each answer, write the appropriate number in the blank:

1	2	3	4	5
		Neither disagree		
Strongly disagree	*Disagree*	*nor agree*	*Agree*	*Strongly agree*

1. My instructor seemed knowlegeable about the course. _____
2. My instructor explained things clearly. _____
3. My instructor was prepared and organized. _____
4. My instructor showed enthusiasm when teaching. _____
5. My instructor was dedicated to teaching. _____
6. My instructor challenged me to give my best effort. _____
7. My instructor's grading procedures seemed fair. _____
8. My instructor demonstrated concern for students. _____
9. Overall, my instructor has been an effective teacher. _____
10. Overall, this has been a high-quality class. _____

Note: Intellectual Excitement is reflected by items 1, 2, 3, and 4; Interpersonal
Concern by item 8; Effective Motivation by items 6 and 7; Commitment to Teaching by item 5.

evaluations will promote improved classroom effectiveness, be seen
as infringing on academic freedom, or be ignored. Student evaluations of teachers are like teacher evaluations of students: if made
with respect and sensitivity, they can benefit both motivation and
performance.

Training College Instructors

College instructors are rarely taught to teach. Meeting Ph.D.
requirements has been counted as sufficient qualification to teach
others, and it is true that many instructors develop excellent skills
on the job without formal training or consultation. Many others,
however, come to dislike classroom instruction or never develop

the competence they could achieve with appropriate instruction and support. Graduate schools are not likely to select as students those individuals with the greatest aptitude for and interest in teaching, as some have advocated (Eble, 1988), but more schools now provide explicit teaching training (Lowman and Mathie, 1992) or mentoring programs (Daloz, 1987) for graduate students. Over fifty journals dealing with general or discipline-specific teaching matters are now being published (Weimer, 1993). In addition, teaching improvement centers now offer a variety of training and consultation services to *all* faculty on most American campuses. Finally, departmental chairpersons have given increased attention to what they can do to promote quality teaching (Centra, 1993). The quality of college instruction is most likely to be improved if training is targeted to those who are most motivated to acquire the skills—graduate instructors and junior faculty—but made available to anyone.

The teaching portfolios referred to in the previous section on teaching evaluation can also play an important role in teacher training (Seldin, 1991). Soon after they take up their posts, instructors can begin working with a mentor (or consultant) to plan the contents of a portfolio that they will use later on when they are being reviewed for reappointment or promotion. Yearly updating of materials can document the actions taken to improve teaching skills, as well as the progress made as a result. (Whether constructing an evaluative portfolio or not, all college teachers can benefit from periodically jotting down what they have done recently to improve their courses.) When used in this ongoing way, more as a reflective journal of self-improvement than a one-time review, a teaching portfolio can contribute to an instructor's professional growth.

Training for college teachers is largely offered via workshops or consultation rather than formal credit courses. Consultation programs (Carroll, 1977; Erickson and Erickson, 1979; L'Hommedieu, Menges, and Brinko, 1990; Wilson, 1986) and workshops have been shown to increase teaching effectiveness (Grasha, 1978; Lattal,

1978; Levinson-Rose and Menges, 1981). Such services are usually offered by faculty development or instructional support centers rather than by individual departments, although a seminar for training sociology graduate instructors has been described in detail (Goldsmid and Wilson, 1980). Some faculty have even reported creating their own support group, in which they discuss specific teaching techniques and general issues (Giordano and others, in press).

Offering interested graduate students a practicum involving both formal coursework and supervised teaching is more conducive to good teaching than the traditional practice of turning novice instructors loose on undergraduates. Such a program should contain preparatory experiences followed by consultation during the initial semesters of teaching. An easily administered preparatory experience is a teaching apprenticeship in which an accomplished instructor teaches the same course that the graduate instructor will later be teaching. Such an individual tutorial in college teaching contrasts sharply with the traditional system in which the TA merely helps with grading and minor tasks. The apprentice is expected to help plan the course, attend all classes, and meet regularly with the professor to discuss such matters as the reason why topics were presented as they were or the way the instructor handled delicate evaluation issues and particular students. A teaching apprenticeship gives novices close-range experience with the course they will be teaching in the future (Center for Teaching and Learning, 1992).

A seminar in college teaching offered before graduate students begin teaching is a more effective use of faculty time than the apprenticeship model, although it does require considerably more organization and must overcome the resistance many graduate students feel to taking additional courses. Students can meet regularly to discuss readings on college teaching and to practice skills such as those described in this volume. Small groups are ideal settings for gaining experience in giving short lectures and leading discussion. Group discussion is useful for helping students examine their attitudes about teaching, learning, and the social functions of grading. My experience suggests that a seminar group can also benefit from two or three follow-up meetings after its members have begun to teach.

Regardless of the kinds and amount of preparation given, new instructors will need regular supportive consultation during their first semester in the classroom. As Braskamp and Ory (1994) note, the word *assessment* is derived from a Latin root meaning "to sit beside." Novices will have questions to ask, emotions to vent, and positive and negative experiences to relate. Receiving regular consultation also helps them take their teaching seriously. No amount of guidance or briefing will be sufficient, however, unless complemented by classroom observation and the use of videotape analysis.

The metaphor of "teaching as performance," which has been invoked throughout this book, supports the need for novices to be observed and to learn to critique their own performances. New instructors learn very quickly, simply as a result of planning and delivering classes and of talking with others about common experiences. Once teachers have begun to feel more comfortable with themselves and their students, however, they are ready to benefit from having someone else visit a class session. Though being observed may initially arouse anxiety, the experience tends to become less intimidating after the first or second such session. Whether observers are supervisors, consultants, or peers, they should all be trained to look for the same kinds of behaviors and to give feedback in helpful ways (Center for Teaching and Learning, 1994). Observing a colleague's teaching helps expand the observer's perspective on his or her own teaching (Austin, Sweet, and Overholt, 1991). Because the monitor can observe students easily and sense the group's degree of involvement, live observation offers the richest and most comprehensive kind of feedback, but it does not go as far toward promoting self-criticism as does the use of videotape.

The widespread availability of compact video recording equipment has greatly stimulated teachers' efforts to improve their classroom performance. Ideally, classes should be taped by staff from a teaching support center, who will be sensitive to the flow of a presentation and know what needs to be highlighted. They will zoom in or pull back to capture significant details, and occasionally pan to include the students as well. If instructors must set up portable equipment on their own, they should ask a friend (or student) to operate the camera, rather than keeping it in a stationary position with a single focus; this will produce a more detailed—and more interesting—record. Although *every* teacher being taped is a little nervous at first, the general process of making a video recording is a relatively painless affair if modern equipment is readily available and if several classes are recorded.

Learning to use video recordings to improve teaching is a much more delicate business, however. As is true for any teaching consultation, the developmental purpose of a consultation dealing with a videotape must be clear to the instructor. (I believe video recordings are too frightening and limited to be used for evaluation purposes.) In addition, it is important to give teachers as much control as is possible and to help them focus on what they *see* and *hear* in lieu of thinking in evaluative terms. Whether used in individual teaching consultation or in small group training, video recordings offer unmatched power to increase self-awareness and to stimulate constructive discussion about teaching (Lowman, 1994a). I have found videotape analysis so useful in efforts to train college teachers at all levels that I would no more work with an instructor without using video at some point than I would attempt to teach biology without a microscope.

Why Strive for Excellence in the Classroom?

Harold McCurdy, one of my graduate professors, asked us at an initial class meeting to write down why we had decided to study psychology. Most of us took the bait of this juicy question and filled up several pages with reasons that we thought were likely to impress our professor. One student in the front row, however, was conspicuous in the small amount he wrote—only a single sentence or so—before he put down his pencil. When we had handed in our papers, Professor McCurdy turned immediately to that short paper and read it aloud. All the student had said was, "So I'll have something to teach."

Few college teachers choose their academic disciplines only to have something to teach, and few regret their choice of an academic career. Sooner or later, every instructor is likely to question whether it is worth the time and energy to become a really effective classroom teacher. It is appropriate to conclude this book by asking: Why should a college teacher strive to teach well, to assiduously go beyond minimal expectations? First, there are the reasons that do *not* provide sufficient justification. Instructors should not attempt to become outstanding classroom teachers for the purpose of making tenure. Moving-company records contain the names of numerous assistant professors who avoided their research and put their energies into teaching, hoping success in the classroom would win the day. Assistant professors at most schools must become minimally competent teachers in order to be promoted, but outstanding teaching will not offset a poor publication record. A better way to attain tenure would be to avoid being a poor teacher and do all you can to excel in the kinds of scholarship valued by your institution.

Once a professor has tenure, should he or she try to become an exemplary teacher in order to gain recognition from colleagues? Probably not. The small amount of recognition offered is not commensurate with the effort required. Administrative service and scholarly productivity are more the coin of the academic realm than is teaching excellence.

Why, then, should college teachers bother? In part, they should seek excellence in the classroom in order to attract the best students to their field. Students' choice of major and career can be influenced greatly by an early encounter with an outstanding professor. Exciting and intellectually imaginative introductory courses can help to attract the top talent to a department. Introductory courses taught by graduate students or uninspired faculty are less likely to draw in the best students for subsequent coursework.

In his memoir of the teaching of Frederick Teggart, Robert Nisbet (1981) notes, "At Berkeley in the early 1930s . . . undergraduate teaching was taken seriously. No matter how illustrious one might be as scholar or scientist, the reputation for giving a good course, above all for being a stimulating lecturer, meant a great deal to the faculty and therefore to the students. . . . Even, and especially, the introductory courses were taught by mature, often distinguished, scholars and scientists" (p. 69). Students were relatively scarce during the Depression, and introductory courses were the battleground on which departments competed for the best.

There is always a scarcity of exceptionally talented students, and faculty members should recognize that superior classroom instruction is one way of investing in the future of their disciplines. Whenever undergraduate enrollments shrink because of economic or population downturns, instructors should appreciate that classroom virtuosity is one way of stemming the tide.

Instructors should also aim for excellent classroom teaching because it is always more rewarding to try to do something well than to settle for mediocrity. College teachers generally have high needs to achieve, to excel at whatever they undertake; otherwise they would not have made it through so much schooling. The classroom is a legitimate arena for satisfying achievement needs, though the prestige and monetary rewards are insubstantial compared with those of publishing, consulting, or administration. Faculty members should include undergraduate teaching excellence among the goals they strive for to satisfy their needs for achievement but should recognize that the rewards will be largely internal, much as they are for learning-oriented students. Conversely, if instructors do not try to do their best at teaching, they are likely to find it drudgery. A very successful colleague of mine once remarked, "You know, Joe, I don't really get a lot of satisfaction out of teaching. But in all fairness, I must admit I don't put a whole lot into it either."

The best reason for taking classroom teaching seriously is that the kinds of college teaching held up as models in this book are personally very rewarding. To captivate a student audience for an hour or more, to stimulate them intellectually and move them emotionally, to instill in them a love for one's subject and a desire to learn more about it, to motivate them to work on their own, to watch them wrestle productively with philosophical and methodological dilemmas, and to see them mature in their motivational orientation and wisdom—these experiences provide an exceptional satisfaction.

Learning to understand students well, to relate effectively to them, and to help them grow into mature and responsible adults is equally satisfying. It is more meaningful (and more fun) to teach persons we genuinely respect and care for than those we barely notice or see as hostile and lazy. Seeing students in a positive light comes more easily to some teachers than to others, but any teacher can cultivate a curious and positive attitude about students as people and thus open the door to many personal rewards.

In this chapter, I have tried to weigh the relative contributions of individual and environmental factors to the creation of outstanding college teaching. Teaching among colleagues who value excellence in the classroom is surely more rewarding than teaching in a school where no one cares about classroom performance or criticizes those sought after by students. However, environment alone cannot inspire college teachers to expend the effort required to become exemplary classroom instructors. My interviews convinced me that *ultimately*, all great teachers decide to work at mastering this art for the very personal reason that being a virtuoso in the classroom is so inherently gratifying. They continue to excel because, as Aristotle noted, excellence is not an act but a habit.

References

Abbott, R. D., and Perkins, D. "Development and Construct Validation of a Set of Student Rating-of-Instruction Items." *Educational and Psychological Measurement*, 1978, 38, 1069–1075.

Abbott, R. D., Wulff, D. H., Nyquist, J. D., and Ropp, V. A. "Satisfaction with Processes of Collecting Student Opinions About Instruction: The Student Perspective." *Journal of Educational Psychology*, 1990, 82, 201–206.

Abrami, P. C., D'Apollonia, S., and Cohen, P. A. "Validity of Student Ratings of Instruction: What We Know and What We Do Not." *Journal of Educational Psychology*, 1990, 82, 219–231.

Abrami, P. C., and others. "Do Teacher Standards for Assigning Grades Affect Student Evaluations of Instructors?" *Journal of Educational Psychology*, 1980, 72, 107–118.

Alcock, J. *Animal Behavior: An Evolutionary Approach.* (2nd ed.) Sunderland, Mass.: Sinauer Associates, 1979.

Aleamoni, L. M. "Development and Factorial Validation of the Arizona Course/Instructor Evaluation Questionnaire." *Educational and Psychological Measurement*, 1978, 38, 1063–1067.

Altman, I., and Taylor, D. A. *Social Penetration: The Development of Interpersonal Relationships.* Troy, Mo.: Holt, Rinehart & Winston, 1973.

Angelo, T. A., and Cross, K. P. *Classroom Assessment Techniques: A Handbook for College Teachers.* (2nd ed.) San Francisco: Jossey-Bass, 1993.

Applebee, A. N. "Writing and Reasoning." *Review of Educational Research*, 1984, 45(4) 577–596.

Astin, A. M. *What Matters in College? Four Critical Years Revisited.* San Francisco: Jossey-Bass, 1992.

Astleitner, H. "Student Ratings: The Problem of Implicit Theories." *Psychologie in Erziehung und Unterricht*, 1991, *38*, 116–122.

Austin, J., Sweet, A., and Overholt, C. "To See Ourselves as Others See Us: The Rewards of Classroom Observation." In C. R. Christensen, D. A. Garvin, and A. Sweet (eds.), *Education for Judgment: The Artistry of Discussion Leadership*. Boston, Mass.: Harvard Business School Press, 1991.

Axelrod, J. *The University Teacher as Artist*. San Francisco: Jossey-Bass, 1973.

Baba, V. V., and Ace, M. E. "Serendipity in Leadership: Initiating Structure and Consideration in the Classroom." *Human Relations*, 1989, *42*, 509–525.

Baird, J. S. "Perceived Learning in Relation to Student Evaluation of University Instruction." *Journal of Educational Psychology*, 1987, *79*, 90–91.

Bales, R. F. *Interaction Process Analysis: A Method for the Study of Small Groups*. Reading, Mass.: Addison-Wesley, 1950.

Bales, R. F., and Slater, P. E. "Role Differentiation in Small Decision-Making Groups." In T. Parsons and others (eds.), *Family, Socialization and Interaction Process*. New York: Free Press, 1955.

Ballard, M., Rearden, J., and Nelson, L. "Student and Peer Rating of Faculty." *Teaching of Psychology*, 1976, *3*, 88–90.

Balthrop, V. W. "Communication Skills for College Teachers." Workshop presented by the Center for Teaching and Learning, University of North Carolina, Chapel Hill, May 1993.

Bandler, R., and Grinder, J. *The Structure of Magic I: A Book About Language and Therapy*. Palo Alto, Calif.: Science and Behavior Books, 1975.

Bandura, A. "Human Agency in Social Cognitive Theory." *American Psychologist*, 1989, *44*, 1175–1184.

Barnes-McConnell, P. W. "Leading Discussions." In O. Milton and others, *On College Teaching: A Guide to Contemporary Practices*. San Francisco: Jossey-Bass, 1978.

Barry, R. "Clarifying Objectives." In O. Milton and others, *On College Teaching: A Guide to Contemporary Practices*. San Francisco: Jossey-Bass, 1978.

Basow, S. A., and Silberg, N. T. "Student Evaluations of College Professors: Are Female and Male Professors Rated Differently?" *Journal of Educational Psychology*, 1987, *79*, 308–314.

Benjamin, L. T. "Personalization and Active Learning in the Large Introductory Psychology Class." *Teaching of Psychology*, 1991, *18*, 68–80.

Benton, S. E. *Rating College Teaching: Criterion Validity Studies of Student Evaluation-of-Instruction Instruments*. AAHE/ERIC/Higher Education Research Report No. 1, American Association for Higher Education, 1982.

Bloom, B. S. (ed.). *Taxonomy of Educational Objectives: Cognitive Domain*. White Plains, N.Y.: Longman, 1956.

Bloom, B. S., Madaus, G. F., and Hastings, J. T. *Evaluation to Improve Learning*. New York: McGraw-Hill, 1981.

Boehrer, J., and Linsky, M. "Teaching with Cases: Learning to Question." In M. D. Svinicki (ed.), *The Changing Face of College Teaching*. San Francisco: Jossey-Bass, 1990.

Bonham, L. A. "Using Learning Style Information, Too." In E. Hayes (ed.), *Effective Teaching Styles*. New Directions for Continuing Education, no. 43. San Francisco: Jossey-Bass, 1989.

Bonwell, C. C., and Eison, J. A. *Active Learning: Creating Excitement in the Classroom*. ASHE-ERIC Higher Education Report No. 1. Washington, D.C.: George Washington University, School of Education and Human Development, 1991.

Bowman, J. S. "Lecture-Discussion Format Revisited." *Improving College and University Teaching*, 1979, *27*, 25–27.

Boyer, E. L. *Scholarship Reconsidered: Priorities of the Professoriate*. Lawrenceville, N.J.: Princeton University Press, 1990.

Braskamp, L. A., and Ory, J. C. *Assessing Faculty Work: Enhancing Individual and Institutional Performance*. San Francisco: Jossey-Bass, 1994.

Bronowski, J. *The Ascent of Man*. Boston: Little, Brown, 1974.

Browne, M. N., and Keeley, S. M. *Asking the Right Questions: A Guide to Critical Thinking*. Englewood Cliffs, N.J.: Prentice-Hall, 1986.

Brownfield, C. *Humanizing College Learning: A Taste of Hemlock*. New York: Exposition Press, 1973.

Bugelski, B. R. *The Psychology of Learning Applied to Teaching*. Indianapolis: Bobbs-Merrill, 1964.

Burns, K. *News and Observer* (Raleigh, N.C.), Aug. 6, 1994, p. 7E.

Cahn, S. M. "The Uses and Abuses of Grades and Examinations." In S. M. Cahn (ed.), *Scholars Who Teach: The Art of College Teaching*. Chicago: Nelson-Hall, 1978.

Carpenter, C. B, and Doig, J. C. "Assessing Critical Thinking Across the Curriculum." In J. H. McMillian (ed.), *Assessing Students' Learning*. San Francisco: Jossey-Bass, 1988.

Carroll, J. G. "Assessing the Effectiveness of a Training Program for the University Teaching Assistant." *Teaching of Psychology*, 1977, *4*, 135–138.

Cartwright, D., and Zander, A. *Group Dynamics: Research and Theory*. (2nd ed.) New York: HarperCollins, 1960.

Cartwright, L. J., "Practical Techniques for Integrating Humor in the Classroom." *The Teaching Professor*, Aug.-Sep., 1993, pp. 7–8.

Center for Teaching and Learning. *TAs and Professors as a Teaching Team*. Chapel Hill: University of North Carolina Center for Teaching and Learning, 1992.

Center for Teaching and Learning. "Peer Observation of Classroom Teaching." *For Your Consideration,* no. 15. Chapel Hill: University of North Carolina Center for Teaching and Learning, 1994.

Centra, J. A. *Reflective Faculty Evaluation: Enhancing Teaching and Determining Faculty Effectiveness.* San Francisco: Jossey-Bass, 1993.

Champion, C. H., Green, S. B., and Sauser, W. I. "Development and Evaluation of Shortcut-Derived Behaviorally Anchored Rating Scales." *Educational and Psychological Measurement,* 1988, *48,* 29–41.

Chandler, T. A. "The Questionable Status of Student Evaluations of Teaching." *Teaching of Psychology,* 1978, *5,* 150–152.

Christensen, C. R., and Hansen, A. J. *Teaching and the Case Method.* Boston: Harvard Business School, 1987.

Christensen, C. R. "The Discussion Leader in Action: Questioning, Listening, and Response." In C. R. Christensen, D. A. Garvin, and A. Sweet (eds.), *Education for Judgment: The Artistry of Discussion Leadership.* Boston: Harvard Business School Press, 1991a.

Christensen, C. R. "Every Student Teaches and Every Teacher Learns: The Reciprocal Gift of Discussion Teaching." In C. R. Christensen, D. A. Garvin, and A. Sweet, *Education for Judgment: The Artistry of Discussion Leadership.* Boston: Harvard Business School Press, 1991b.

Cohen, P. A. "Effectiveness of Student-Rating Feedback for Improving College Instruction: A Meta-Analysis of Findings." *Research in Higher Education,* 1980, *13,* 321–341.

Coleman, J., and McKeachie, W. J. "Effects of Instructor/Course Evaluations on Student Course Selection." *Journal of Educational Psychology,* 1981, *73,* 224–226.

Connolly, P., and Vilardi, T. (eds.). *Writing to Learn Mathematics and Science.* New York: Teachers College Press, 1989.

Cottell, P. G., and Millis, B. J. "Complex Cooperative Learning Structures for College and University Courses." In E. C. Wadsworth (ed.), *To Improve the Academy: Resources for Student, Faculty, and Institutional Development.* Stillwater, Okla.: New Forums Press, Professional and Organizational Development Network in Higher Education, 1994

Cousins, M. *Michel Foucault.* New York: St. Martin's Press, 1984.

Cranton, P. A., and Smith, R. A. "Reconsidering the Unit of Analysis: A Model of Student Ratings of Instruction." *Journal of Educational Psychology,* 1990, *82,* 207–212.

Cronbach, L. J. *Essentials of Psychological Testing.* (4th ed.) New York: Harper-Collins, 1984.

Crouse, R., and Jacobson, C. "Testing in Mathematics—What Are We Really Measuring?" *Mathematics Teacher,* 1975, *68,* 564–570.

Cuddy, L. "One Sentence is Worth a Thousand: A Strategy for Improving Reading, Writing, and Thinking Skills." In J. R. Jeffrey and G. R. Erickson (eds.), *To Improve the Academy: Resources for Student, Faculty, and Institutional Development.* Stillwater, Okla.: New Forums Press, Professional and Organizational Development Network in Higher Education, 1985.

Daloz, L. A. *Effective Teaching and Mentoring.* San Francisco: Jossey-Bass, 1987.

Davis, B. G. *Tools for Teaching.* San Francisco: Jossey-Bass, 1993.

Dodd, D. K., and Leal, L. "Answer Justification: Removing the 'Trick' from Multiple-Choice Questions." *Teaching of Psychology,* 1988, *15,* 37–38.

Drews, D. R., Burrough, W. J., and Nokovitch, D. "Teacher Self-Ratings as a Validity Criterion for Student Evaluations." *Teaching of Psychology,* 1987, *14,* 23–25.

Duffy, D. K., and Jones, J. W., *Teaching Within the Rhythms of the Semester.* San Francisco: Jossey-Bass, 1995.

Durkin, D. B. *Writing in the Disciplines.* New York: Random House, 1986.

Eble, K. *The Craft of Teaching: A Guide to Mastering the Professor's Art.* (2nd ed.) San Francisco: Jossey-Bass, 1988.

Eison, J., Janzow, F., and Pollio, H. *LOGO F.* Tampa: University of South Florida, Center for Teaching Enhancement, 1989.

Epstein, J. *Masters: Portraits of Great Teachers.* New York: Basic Books, 1981.

Erickson, G. R., and Erickson, B. L. "Improving College Teaching: An Evaluation of a Teaching Consultation Procedure." *Journal of Higher Education,* 1979, *50,* 670–683.

Falchikov, N., and Boud, D. "Student Self-Assessment in Higher Education: A Meta-Analysis." *Review of Educational Research,* 1989, *59,* 395–430.

Feldman, K. A. "Grades and College Students' Evaluations of their Courses and Teachers." *Research in Higher Education,* 1976, *4,* 69–111.

Feldman, K. A. "Course Characteristics and College Students' Ratings of their Teacher." *Research in Higher Education,* 1978, *9,* 199–242.

Feldman, K. A. "The Association Between Student Ratings on Specific Instructional Dimensions and Student Achievement: Refining and Extending the Synthesis of Data from Multisection Validity Studies." *Research in Higher Education,* 1989, *30,* 137–104.

Fernald, P. S. "Students' Ratings of Instruction: Standardized and Customized." *Teaching of Psychology,* 1990, *17,* 105–109.

Firth, M. "Impact of Work Experience on the Validity of Student Evaluations of Teaching Effectiveness." *Journal of Educational Psychology,* 1979, *71,* 726–730.

Fromm, E. *Escape from Freedom*. New York: Avon Books, 1941.

Gardner, L. E., and Leak, G. K. "The Characteristics and Correlates of Teaching Anxiety Among College Psychology Teachers". *Teaching of Psychology*, 1994, *21*, 28–32.

Gaynor, J., and Millham, J. "Student Performance and Evaluation Under Variant Teaching and Testing Methods in a Large College Course." *Journal of Educational Psychology*, 1976, *68*, 312–317.

Gibbard, G., Hartman, J., and Mann, R. (eds.) *Analysis of Groups: Contributions to Theory, Research, and Practice*. San Francisco: Jossey-Bass, 1973.

Gigliotti, R. J., and Buchtel, F. S. "Attributional Bias and Course Evaluations." *Journal of Educational Psychology*, 1990, *82*, 341–351.

Giordano, P. J., and others. "Improving Teaching by Participation in an Interdisciplinary Faculty Improvement Group." *Teaching of Psychology*, in press.

Goldsmid, C. A., and Wilson, E. K. *Passing on Sociology: The Teaching of a Discipline*. Belmont, Calif.: Wadsworth, 1980.

Goldstein, G. S., and Benassi, V. A. "The relation between teacher self-disclosure and student classroom participation." *Teaching of Psychology*, in press.

Grasha, A. F. "The Teaching of Teaching: A Seminar on College Teaching." *Teaching of Psychology*, 1978, *5*, 21–23.

Grasha, A. F. "The Naturalistic Approach to Learning Styles." *College Teaching*, 1990, *38*, 106–113.

Graves, W. H. *Computing Across the Curriculum: Academic Perspectives*. McKinney, Texas: Academic Computing Publications, 1989.

Gray, P. "Engaging Students' Intellects: The Immersion Approach to Critical Thinking in Psychology Instruction." *Teaching of Psychology*, 1993, *20*, 68–74.

Gronlund, N. E. *Constructing Achievement Tests*. (3rd ed.) Englewood Cliffs, N.J.: Prentice-Hall, 1982.

Gross, R. B., and Small, A. C. "A Survey of Faculty Opinions About Student Evaluations of Instructors." *Teaching of Psychology*, 1979, *6*, 216–219.

Guilford, J. P. *Intelligence, Creativity, and Their Educational Implications*. San Diego: Calif.: Knapp, 1968.

Haemmerlie, F. M., and Highfill, L. A. "Bias by Male Engineering Undergraduates in their Evaluation of Teaching. *Psychological Reports*, 1991, *68*, 151–160.

Hansen, A. J. "Establishing a Teaching/Learning Contract." In C. R. Christensen, D. A. Garvin, and A. Sweet (eds.), *Education for Judgment: The Artistry of Discussion Leadership*. Boston: Harvard Business School Press, 1991.

Harris, M. B. "Sex Role Stereotypes and Teacher Evaluations." *Journal of Educational Psychology*, 1975, *67*, 751–756.

Harris, R. J. "The Teacher as Actor." *Teaching of Psychology*, 1977, *4*, 185–187.

Herman, B. *Teaching and Learning with Computers: A Guide for College Faculty and Administrators*. San Francisco: Jossey-Bass, 1988.

Herrnstein, J. J., and Murray, C. *The Bell Curve: Intelligence and Class Structure in American Life*. New York: Free Press, 1994.

Highet, G. *The Art of Teaching*. New York: Knopf, 1950.

Hodges, M. E., and Sasnett, R. M. *Multimedia Computing: Case Studies from MIT Project Athena*. Reading, Mass.: Addison-Wesley, 1993.

Hoffman, C. D. "Students Learn More from Better Teachers." *Teaching of Psychology*, 1979, *6*, 186.

Howard, G. S., and Bray, J. H. "Use of Norm Groups to Adjust Student Ratings of Instruction: A Warning." *Journal of Educational Psychology*, 1979, *71*, 58–73.

Howard, G. S., and Maxwell, S. E. "Correlation Between Student Satisfaction and Grades: A Case of Mistaken Causation." *Journal of Educational Psychology*, 1980, *72*, 810–820.

Howe, M.J.A. "Conventional Methods." In J. Radford and D. Rose (eds.), *The Teaching of Psychology: Method, Content, and Context*. New York: Wiley, 1980.

Ikponmwosa-Owie, S. H. "Knowledge of Grades and Students' Rating of the Instructor." *Indian Journal of Psychometry and Education*, 1986, *17*, 47–52.

Iuppa, N. V. *The Multimedia Adventure*. White Plains, N.Y.: KIPI Bookshelf, 1993.

Jacobs, L. C., and Chase, C. I. *Developing and Using Tests Effectively*. San Francisco: Jossey-Bass, 1992.

Janick, J. "Crib Sheets." *Teaching Professor*, 1990. *5*, 2.

Johnson, D. W., and Johnson, R. T. *Learning Together and Alone: Cooperative, Competitive, and Individualistic Learning*. (4th ed.). Needham Heights, Mass.: Allyn & Bacon, 1994.

Johnson, D. W., Johnson, R. T., and Smith, K. A. *Active Learning: Cooperation in the College Classroom*. Edina, Minn.: Interaction Book Company, 1991.

Johnson, R. L., and Christian, V. K. "Relation of Perceived Learning and Expected Grade to Rated Effectiveness of Teaching." *Perceptual and Motor Skills*, 1990, *70*, 479–482.

Jones, E. E., and others. *Attribution: Perceiving the Causes of Behavior*. Morristown N.J.: General Learning Press, 1972.

Jöreskog, K. G., and Sörbom, D. *LISREL 7*. Chicago: SPSS, 1988.

Kadel, S., and Keehner, J. A. *Collaborative Learning: A Sourcebook for Higher Education (Vol. II)*. University Park, Pa.: National Center on Postsecondary Teaching, Learning, and Assessment, 1994.

Keith-Spiegel, P., and others. *The Ethics of Teaching: A Casebook*. Muncie, Ind.: Ball State University, 1993.

Keller, F. S. "Goodbye, Teacher . . ." *Journal of Applied Behavior Analysis*, 1968, *1*, 79–89.

Keller, F. S. Psychology Colloquium. Chapel Hill: University of North Carolina, 1980.

King, P. M., and Kitchener, K. S. *Developing Reflective Judgment: Understanding and Promoting Intellectual Growth and Critical Thinking in Adolescents and Adults*. San Francisco: Jossey-Bass, 1994.

Kinichi, A. J., and Schriesheim, C. A. "Teachers as Leaders: A Moderator Variable Approach." *Journal of Educational Psychology*, 1978, *70*, 928–935.

Kolstoe, O. P. *College Professoring: Or, Through Academia with Gun and Camera*. Carbondale: Southern Illinois University Press, 1975.

Korth, B. "Relationship of Extraneous Variables to Student Ratings of Instructors." *Journal of Educational Measurement*, 1979, *16*, 27–37.

Kremer, J. F. "Construct Validity of Multiple Measures in Teaching, Research, and Service and Reliability of Peer Ratings." *Journal of Educational Psychology*, 1990, *82*, 213–218.

Kyle, B. "In Defense of the Lecture." *Improving College and University Teaching*, 1972, *20*, 325.

Lahr, J. *Astonish Me: Adventures in Contemporary Theater*. New York: Viking Penguin, 1973.

Lattal, K. A. "Workshop for New Graduate Student Teachers of Undergraduate Psychology Courses." *Teaching of Psychology*, 1978, *5*, 208–209.

Levinson-Rose, J., and Menges, R. "Improving College Teaching: A Critical Review of Research." *Review of Educational Research*, 1981, *51*, 403–434.

L'Hommedieu, R., Menges, R. J., and Brinko, K. "Methodological Explanations for the Modest Effects of Feedback from Student Ratings." *Journal of Educational Psychology*, 1990, *82*, 232–241.

Linklater, K. *Freeing the Natural Voice*. New York: Drama Book Specialists, 1976.

Lowman, J. "Giving Students Feedback." In M. G. Weiner (ed.), *Teaching Large Classes Well*. New Directions for Teaching and Learning, no. 32. San Francisco: Jossey-Bass, 1987.

Lowman, J. "Failure of Laboratory Evaluation of CAI to Generalize to Classroom Settings: The *SuperShrink* Interview Simulation." *Behavior Research Methods, Instruments, and Computers*, 1990a, *22*, 429–432.

Lowman, J. "Promoting Motivation and Learning." *College Teaching*, 1990b, *38*, 136–140.

Lowman, J. *SuperShrink II* [Educational software]. San Diego, Cal.: Harcourt Brace Jovanovich College Division, 1990c.

Lowman, J. "Getting Ready: Preparing Faculty to Observe and Be Observed from a Developmental Perspective." *Proceedings: Self-Evaluate or Self-Destruct: A Working Conference on Peer Review*. College Station, TX: Texas A & M University Center for Teaching Excellence, 1994a.

Lowman, J. "Teachers as Performers and Motivators." *College Teaching*, 1994b, *42*, 137–141.

Lowman, J., and Mathie, V. A. "What Should Graduate Teaching Assistants Know About Teaching?" *Teaching of Psychology*, 1992, *20*, 84–88.

Maas, J. Psychology Colloquium. Chapel Hill: University of North Carolina, 1980.

McConnell, J. V. "Confessions of a Textbook Writer." *American Psychologist*, 1978, *33*, 159–169.

McGee, R. *Teaching the Mass Class*. Washington, D.C.: American Sociological Association, 1986.

McGovern, T. V., and Hogshead, D. L. "Learning About Writing, Thinking About Teaching." *Teaching of Psychology*, 1990, *17*, 5–10.

McGraw-Hill Primus. *101 Success Stories of Information Technology in Higher Education*. Hightstown, N.J.: McGraw-Hill, 1993.

Machlin, E. *Speech for the Stage*. New York: Theater Arts Books, 1966.

McKeachie, W. J. *Teaching Tips: A Guidebook for the Beginning College Teacher*. (8th ed.) Lexington, Mass.: Heath, 1986.

McKeachie, W. J., Pintrich, P. R., Lin., Y-G., and Smith, D.A.F. *Teaching and Learning in the College Classroom: A Review of the Research Literature*. Ann Arbor: National Center for Research to Improve Postsecondary Teaching and Learning, University of Michigan, 1986.

McKeachie, W. J., and others. "Using Student Ratings and Consultation to Improve Instruction." *British Journal of Educational Psychology*, 1980, *50*, 168–174.

McPeck, J. E. *Critical Thinking and Education*. New York: St. Martin's Press, 1981.

Madigan, R., and Brosamer, J. "Improving the Writing Skills of Students in Introductory Psychology." *Teaching of Psychology*, 1990, *17*, 27–30.

Madigan, R., and Brosamer, J. "Holistic Grading of Written Work in Introductory Psychology: Reliability, Validity, and Efficiency." *Teaching of Psychology*, 1991, *18*, 91–94.

Magolda, M.B.B. *Knowing and Reasoning in College: Gender-Related Patterns in Students' Intellectual Development*. San Francisco: Jossey-Bass, 1992.

Mann, R. D., and others. *The College Classroom: Conflict, Change, and Learning*. New York: Wiley, 1970.

Mares, J. "Validity of Students' Ratings of Instruction." *Ceskoslovenska-Psychologie*, 1988, *32*, 392–406.

Marques, T. E., Lane, D. M., and Dorfman, P. W. "Toward the Development of a System for Instructional Evaluation: Is There Consensus Regarding What Constitutes Effective Teaching?" *Journal of Educational Psychology*, 1979, *71*, 840–849.

Marsh, H. W. "The Influence of Student, Course, and Instructor Characteristics in Evaluations of University Teaching." *American Educational Research Journal*, 1980, *17*, 219–237.

Marsh, H. W. "Students' Evaluations of University Teaching: Dimensionality, Reliability, Validity, Potential Biases, and Utility." *Journal of Educational Psychology*, 1984, *76*, 707–754.

Marsh, H. W. "Applicability Paradigm: Students' Evaluations of Teaching Effectiveness in Different Countries." *Journal of Educational Psychology*, 1986, *78*, 465–473.

Marsh, H. W. "Multidimensional Students' Evaluations of Teaching Effectiveness: A Test of Alternative Higher-Order Structures." *Journal of Educational Psychology*, 1991, *83*, 285–296.

Marsh, H. W., and Hocevar, D. "Students' Evaluations of Teaching Effectiveness: The Stability of Mean Ratings of the Same Teachers over a 13-Year Period." *Teaching and Teacher Education*, 1991, *7*, 303–314.

Marsh, H. W., and Overall, J. U. "Long-Term Stability of Students' Evaluations: A Note on Feldman's 'Consistency and Variability Among College Students in Rating Their Teachers and Courses.'" *Research in Higher Education*, 1979, *10*, 139–147.

Marsh, H. W., and Overall, J. U. "The Relative Influence of Course Level, Course Type, and Instructor on Students' Evaluations of College Teaching." *American Educational Research Journal*, 1981, *18*, 103–112.

Marsh, H. W., Overall, J. U., and Kesler, S. P. "Validity of Student Evaluations of Instructional Effectiveness: A Comparison of Faculty Self-Evaluations and Evaluations by Their Students." *Journal of Educational Psychology*, 1979, *71*, 149–160.

Martin, B. "Parent-Child Relations." In F. D. Horowitz (ed.), *Review of Developmental Research*. Vol. 4. Chicago: University of Chicago Press, 1975.

Meredith, G. M. "Impact of Lecture Size on Student-Based Ratings of Instruction." *Psychological Reports*, 1980, *46*, 21–22

Meredith, G. M. "Intimacy as a Variable in Lecture-Format Courses." *Psychological Reports*, 1985, *57*, 484–486.

Meredith, G. M. "Dossier Evaluation in Screening Candidates for Excellence in Teaching Awards." *Psychological Reports*, 1990, *67*, 879–882.

Meyers, C. *Teaching Students to Think Critically: A Guide for Faculty in All Disciplines*. San Francisco: Jossey-Bass, 1986.

Meyers, C., and Jones, T. B. *Promoting Active Learning Strategies for the College Classroom.* San Francisco: Jossey-Bass, 1993.

Miller, R. I. *Evaluating Faculty for Promotion and Tenure.* San Francisco: Jossey-Bass, 1987.

Milton, O. "Classroom Testing." In O. Milton and others, *On College Teaching: A Guide to Contemporary Practices.* San Francisco: Jossey-Bass, 1978.

Milton, O., Pollio, H. R., and Eison, J. A. *Making Sense of College Grades: Why the Grading System Does Not Work and What Can Be Done About It.* San Francisco: Jossey-Bass, 1986.

Neff, R. A., and Weimer, M. *Classroom Communication: Collected Readings for Effective Discussion and Questioning.* Madison, Wis.: Magna Publications, 1989.

Newstead, S. E., and Arnold, J. "The Effect of Response Format on Ratings of Teaching." *Educational and Psychological Measurement,* 1989, *49,* 33–43.

Nield, A. F., and Wintre, M. "Multiple Choice Questions with an Option to Comment: Students' Attitude and Use." *Teaching of Psychology,* 1986, *13,* 196–199.

Nisbet, R. "Teggard of Berkeley." In J. Epstein (ed.), *Masters: Portraits of Great Teachers.* New York: Basic Books, 1981.

Overall, J. U., and Marsh, H. W. "Students' Evaluations of Instruction: A Longitudinal Study of Their Stability." *Journal of Educational Psychology,* 1980, *72,* 321–325.

Perez, J. "The Evaluation of Teaching by Students: What-How-When-by Whom-for Whom-and for What Purpose." *Revista de Psiquiatria de la Facultad de Medicina de Barcelona,* 1990, *17,* 3–11.

Perry, R. P., Abrami, P. C., and Leventhal, L. "Educational Seduction: The Effect of Instructor Expressiveness and Lecture Content on Student Ratings of Achievement." *Journal of Educational Psychology,* 1979, *71,* 107–116.

Perry, W. G., Jr. *Forms of Intellectual and Ethical Development in the College Years: A Scheme.* Troy, Mo.: Holt, Rinehart, & Winston, 1970.

Poonyakanok, P., Thisayakorn, N., and Digby, P. W. "Student Evaluation of Teacher Performance: Some Initial Research Findings From Thailand." *Teaching and Teacher Education,* 1986, *2,* 145–154.

Pratkanis, A. R., Breckler, S. H., and Greenwald, A. G. *Attitude Structure and Function.* Hillsdale, N.J.: Erlbaum, 1989.

Raskin, B. L., and Plante, P. R. "The Student Devaluation of Teachers." *Academe,* 1979, *65,* 381–383.

Reardon, M., and Waters, L. K. "Leniency and Halo in Student Ratings of College Instructors: A Comparison of Three Ratings Procedures with

Implications for Scale Validity." *Educational and Psychological Measurement*, 1979, *39*, 159–162.

Reemers, H. H., and Brandenburg, G. C. "Experimental Data on the Purdue Rating Scale for Instructors." *Educational Administration and Supervision*, 1927, *13*, 519–527.

Romero, J., Bonilla, M. P., Truhillo, D. A., and Rodriguez, M. "An Alternative in the Evaluation of Teaching." *Revista Intercontinental de Psicologia y Educacion*, 1989, *2*, 293–307.

Runco, M. A., Okuda, S. M., and Thurston, B. J. "A Social Validation of College Examinations." *Educational and Psychological Measurement*, 1991, *51*, 463–472.

Ruston, J. P., and Murray, H. G. "On the Assessment of Teaching Effectiveness in British Universities." *Bulletin of the British Psychological Society*, 1985, *38*, 361–365.

Ryan, J., and others. "Student Evaluation: The Faculty Responds." *Research in Higher Education*, 1980, *12*, 317–333.

Sale, K. *Human Scale*. New York: Coward, McCann and Geoghegan, 1980.

Satterfield, J. "Lecturing." In O. Milton and others, *On College Teaching: A Guide to Contemporary Practices*. San Francisco: Jossey-Bass, 1978.

Scarr, S. *Race, Social Class, and Individual Differences in I.Q.* Hillsdale, N.J.: Erlbaum, 1981.

Scott, A. M. *Castellon*. San Diego: Harcourt Brace Jovanovich College Division, 1987.

Seldin, P. *The Teaching Portfolio: A Practical Guide to Improved Performance and Promotion/Tenure Decisions*. Boston: Anker, 1991.

Seldin, P. *Changing Practices in Faculty Evaluation*. San Francisco: Jossey-Bass, 1984.

Shaffer, J. B., and Galinsky, D. *Models of Group Therapy and Sensitivity Training*. (2nd ed.) Englewood Cliffs, N.J.: Prentice-Hall, 1989.

Shea, C. "'Professor of the Year': A Soft-Spoken Engineer." *Chronicle of Higher Education*. May 26, 1993, p. A7.

Sherman, J. G., Ruskin, R. S., and Semb, G. B. (eds.) *The Personalized System of Instruction: 48 Seminal Papers*. Lawrence, Kans.: TRI Publications, 1983.

Sidanius, J., and Crane, M. "Job Evaluation and Gender: The Case of University Faculty." *Journal of Applied and Social Psychology*, 1989, *19*, 174–197.

Siegel, M, and Carey, R. F. *Critical Thinking: A Semiotic Perspective*. Bloomington, Ind.: ERIC Clearinghouse on Reading and Communication Skills, 1989.

Skinner, B. F. *The Technology of Teaching*. New York: Appleton-Century-Crofts, 1968.

Skinner, B. F. "The Evolution of Verbal Behavior." *Journal of the Experimental Analysis of Behavior*, 1986, *45*, 115–122.

Smith, B. L., and MacGregor, J. T. "What is Collaborative Learning?" In A. S. Goodsell, M. R. Maher, and V. Tinto (eds.), *Collaborative Learning: A Sourcebook for Higher Education*. University Park, Pa.: National Center on Postsecondary Teaching, Learning, and Assessment, 1992.

Smith, F. *To Think*. New York: Teachers College Press, 1990.

Smith, R. A. "Are Peer Ratings of Student Debates Valid?" *Teaching of Psychology*, 1990, *17*, 188–189.

Sprague, J., and Stuart, D. *The Speaker's Handbook*. (3rd. ed.) San Diego, Calif.: Harcourt Brace Jovanovich College Division, 1992.

Steele, C. M. "Race and the Schooling of Black Americans." *Atlantic Monthly*, April 1992, pp. 68–78.

Steele, S. *The Content of Our Character: A New Vision of Race in America*. New York: St. Martin's Press, 1990.

Stevens, L. A. *The Ill-Spoken Word: The Decline of Speech in America*. New York: McGraw-Hill, 1966.

Strupp, H. H. "Success and Failure in Time-Limited Psychotherapy: With Special Reference to the Performance of a Lay Counselor." *Archives of General Psychiatry*, 1980, *37*, 831–841.

Sykes, C. J. *ProfScam: Professors and the Demise of Higher Education*. Washington, D.C.: Regnery Gateway, 1988.

Thompson, R. "Legitimate Lecturing." *Improving College and University Teaching*, 1974, *22*, 163–164.

Thorne, G. L. "Student Ratings of Instructors: From Scores to Administrative Decisions." *Journal of Higher Education*, 1980, *51*, 207–214.

Tiberius, R. G. *Small Group Teaching: A Trouble-Shooting Guide*. Toronto, Canada: Ontario Institute for Studies in Education Press, 1990.

Uranowitz, S. W., and Doyle, K. O. "Being Liked and Teaching: The Effects and Bases of Personality Likability in College Instruction." *Research in Higher Education*, 1978, *9*, 15–41.

Vance, C. M. *Mastering Management Education: Innovations in Teaching Effectiveness*. Newbury Park, Calif.: Sage, 1993.

Wales, C. E., and Stager, R. A. *Guided Design, Part I*. Morgantown: West Virginia University Press, 1976.

Walsh, D., and Maffei, M. J. "Student-Professor Relationship Survey: Summary of Results." Unpublished manuscript, Miami University, Department of Management, Oxford, Ohio, 1994.

Waters, M., Kemp, E., and Pucci, A. "High and Low Faculty Evaluations: Descriptions by Students." *Teaching of Psychology*, 1988, *15*, 203–204.

Watzlawick, P., Beavin, J. H., and Jackson, D. D. *Pragmatics of Human Communication: A Study of Interactional Patterns, Pathologies, and Paradoxes*. New York: W.W.Norton, 1967.

Weimer, M. G. (ed.). *Teaching Large Classes Well*. New Directions for Teaching and Learning, no. 32. San Francisco: Jossey-Bass, 1987.

Weimer, M. G. "The Disciplinary Journals on Pedagogy." *Change*, November/December 1993, pp. 44–51.

Wheeler, D. L. "Championing the Philosophy and Beauty of Mathematics." *Chronicle of Higher Education*, July 29, 1992, pp. A6–A7.

White, R. W. "Sense of Interpersonal Competence." In R. W. White (ed.), *The Study of Lives*. New York: Atherton, 1963.

Wilhite, S. C. "Prepassage Questions: The Influence of Structural Importance." *Journal of Educational Psychology*, 1983, *75*, 234–244.

Williams, R. G., and Ware, J. E. "An Extended Visit with Dr. Fox: Validity of Student Satisfaction with Instruction Ratings After Repeated Exposures to a Lecturer." *American Educational Research Journal*, 1977, *14*, 449–457.

Wilson, R. C. "Improving Faculty Teaching: Effective Use of Student Evaluations and Consultants." *Journal of Higher Education*, 1986, *57*, 196–211.

Woditsch, G. A., and Schmittroth, J. *The Thoughtful Teacher's Guide to Thinking Skills*. Hillsdale, N.J.: Erlbaum, 1991.

Woods, D. "How Might I Teach Problem Solving?" In J. E. Stice (ed.), *Developing Critical Thinking and Problem-Solving Skills*. San Francisco: Jossey-Bass, 1987.

Wright, R. *The Moral Animal: Evolutionary Psychology and Everyday Life*. New York: Pantheon Books, 1994.

Zechmeister, E. B., and Reich, J. N. "Teaching Undergraduates About Teaching Undergraduates. A Capstone Experience." *Teaching of Psychology*, 1994, *21*, 24–28.

Zinsser, W. *Writing to Learn*. New York: HarperCollins, 1988.

Name Index

A

Abbott, R. D., 16, 297
Abrami, P. C., 5, 15, 26, 257
Ace, M. E., 229
Alcock, J., 39
Aleamoni, L. M., 17
Altman, I., 41
Angelo, T. A., 73, 132, 144, 163, 194, 198, 204–205, 242, 297
Applebee, A. N., 227
Aristotle, 312
Arnold, J., 303
Astin, A. M., 65, 275
Astleitner, H., 11
Austin, J., 308
Axelrod, J., 162, 287

B

Baba, V. V., 229
Baird, J. S., 15, 17, 228
Bales, R. F., 20, 59–60
Ballard, M., 17
Balthrop, V. W., 101, 111, 116, 139, 142, 153
Bandler, R., 75
Bandura, A., 53
Barnes-McConnell, P. W., 72, 88, 178, 179, 187
Barry, R., 197, 198
Basow, S. A., 18
Beavin, J. H., 50

Benassi, V. A., 45
Benjamin, L. T., 211, 212
Benton, S. E., 303
Bloom, B. S., 5, 22, 195–198
Boehrer, J., 170, 206
Bonham, L. A., 36
Bonilla, M. P., 11
Bonwell, C. C., 204
Boud, D., 260
Bowman, J. S., 133
Boyer, E. L., 292–293, 294, 299
Brandenburg, G. C., 11
Braskamp, L. A., 299, 302, 308
Bray, J. H., 301
Breckler, S. H., 41
Brinko, K., 301, 302, 306
Bronowski, J., 139
Brosamer, J., 244, 246
Browne, M. N., 139, 197, 235
Brownfield, C., 160
Buchtel, F. S., 17
Bugelski, B. R., 135
Bumstead, J., 146
Burns, K., 125
Burrough, W. J., 298

C

Cahn, S. M., 194, 251, 254
Carey, R. F., 197
Carpenter, C. B., 198
Carroll, J. G., 306

Cartwright, D., 27, 53, 59, 214
Cartwright, L. J., 143
Center for Teaching and Learning, 307, 308
Centra, J. A., 16, 298, 302, 306
Champion, C. H., 303
Chandler, T. A., 11
Chase, C. I., 245, 261
Christensen, C. R., 160, 170, 173, 185, 206
Christian, V. K., 15, 17
Cohen, P. A., 5, 257, 302
Coleman, J., 258, 299
Connolly, P., 242
Cottell, P. G., 208, 209–210
Cousins, M., 75
Crane, M., 18
Cranton, P. A., 303
Cronbach, L. J., 245
Cross, K. P., 73, 132, 144, 163, 194, 198, 204–205, 242, 297
Crouse, R., 268
Cuddy, L., 241

D

Daloz, L. A., 89, 306
D'Apollonia, S., 5, 257
Davis, B. G., 88, 90, 91, 96
Digby, P. W., 11
Dodd, D. K., 271
Doig, J. C., 198
Dorfman, P. W., 31
Doyle, K. O., 31
Drews, D. R., 298
Duffy, D. K., 42, 66, 135, 142, 202, 204
Durkin, D. B., 242

E

Eble, K., 63, 66, 91, 96, 135, 136, 145, 154, 161, 184, 185, 225, 240, 278, 281, 306
Educational Testing Service, 303
Eison, J. A., 7, 52, 53, 204, 229, 230, 231, 255–256, 261, 278
Epstein, J., 1, 23, 36, 296–297

Erickson, B. L., 306
Erickson, G. R., 306

F

Falchikov, N., 260
Feldman, K. A., 15, 16, 17
Fernald, P. S., 304
Firth, M., 16
Fromm, E., 291–292

G

Galinsky, D., 27, 59
Gardner, L. E., 110
Gaynor, J., 261
Gibbard, G., 53
Gigliotti, R. J., 17
Giordano, P. J., 307
Goldsmid, C. A., 307
Goldstein, G. S., 45
Grasha, A. F., 36, 306
Graves, W. H., 149–150, 220, 248
Gray, P., 197, 199–200
Green, S. B., 303
Greenwald, A. G., 41
Grinder, J., 75
Gronlund, N. E., 267
Gross, R. B., 300
Guildord, J. P., 7

H

Haemmerlie, F. M., 18
Hansen, A. J., 166, 170, 206
Harris, M. B., 18
Harris, R. J., 117
Hartman, J., 53
Hastings, J. T., 5–6, 22
Herman, B., 149–150, 220, 248
Herrnstein, J. J., 7
Highet, G., 22, 97, 129, 137, 141, 142, 143, 144, 193, 268
Highfill, L. A., 18
Hocevar, D., 15
Hodges, M. E., 150, 220
Hoffman, C. D., 16
Hogshead, D. L., 244
Howard, G. S., 257, 301
Howe, M.J.A., 129, 146–147

I

Ikponmwosa-Owie, S. H., 11
Iuppa, N. V., 150

J

Jackson, D. D., 50
Jacobs, L. C., 245, 261
Jacobson, C., 268
Janick, J., 272
Janzow, F., 256
Johnson, D. W., 207, 208
Johnson, R. L., 15, 17
Johnson, R. T., 207, 208
Jones, E. E., 41
Jones, J. W., 42, 66, 135, 142, 202, 204
Jones, T. B., 204, 250
Jöreskog, K. G., 13

K

Kadel, S., 208
Keehner, J. A., 208
Keeley, S. M., 139, 197, 235
Keith-Spiegel, P., 95
Keller, F. S., 219, 220, 259
Kemp, E., 15
Kesler, S. P., 17
King, J., 227
King, P. M., 6, 163
Kinichi, A. J., 74
Kissinger, H., 104
Kitchener, K. S., 6, 163
Kolstoe, O. P., 221
Korth, B., 16
Kremer, J. F., 17, 296
Kyle, B., 130, 133

L

Lahr, J., 99
Lane, D. M., 31
Lattal, K. A., 306
Leak, G. K., 110
Leal, L., 271
Leventhal, L., 26
Levinson-Rose, J., 307
L'Hommedieu, R., 301, 302, 306

L (second column)

Lin, Y-G., 5
Linklater, K., 117
Linsky, M., 170, 206

M

Maas, J., 202
McConnell, J. V., 125
McCurdy, H., 309–310
McGee, R., 210–211
McGovern, T. V., 244
McGraw-Hill Primus, 149, 220, 248
MacGregor, J. T., 208
Machlin, E., 103, 104, 106, 122
McKeachie, W. J., 5, 91, 136, 142, 145, 161, 167, 175–176, 211, 213, 227, 230, 232–233, 234, 245, 246, 258, 265, 270, 276, 284, 299, 302
McPeck, J. E., 197
Madaus, G. F., 5–6, 22
Madigan, R., 244, 246
Maffei, M. J., 89
Magolda, M.B.B., 6, 86–88, 195
Mann, R. D., 27, 39, 48–49, 53, 58–59, 60–61, 62, 76, 77–86, 87
Mares, J., 11
Marques, T. E., 31
Marsh, H. W., 13, 14, 15–16, 17, 31, 303
Martin, B., 53
Mathie, V. A., 214, 306
Maxwell, S. E., 257
Menges, R., 301, 302, 307
Meredith, G. M., 16, 159, 213, 295
Meyers, C., 204, 242, 250
Miller, R. I., 299
Millham, J., 261
Millis, B. J., 208, 209–210
Milton, O., 7, 52, 53, 229, 230, 231, 253, 255–256, 261, 267, 268, 270, 276, 278
Murray, C., 7
Murray, H. G., 11

N

Neff, R. A., 171
Nelson, L., 17

Newstead, S. E., 303
Nield, A. F., 271
Nisbet, R., 311
Nokovitch, D., 298
Nyquist, J. D., 297

O

Okuda, S. M., 252
Ory, J. C., 299, 302, 308
Overall, J. U., 16, 17
Overholt, C., 308

P

Perez, J., 11
Perkins, D., 16
Perry, R. P., 26
Perry, W. G., Jr., 86
Pintrich, P. R., 5
Plante, P. R., 11
Pollio, H. R., 7, 52, 53, 229, 230, 231,
   255–256, 261, 278
Poonyakanok, P., 11
Pratkanis, A. R., 41
Pucci, A., 15

R

Raskin, B. L., 11
Rearden, J., 17
Reardon, M., 16
Reemers, H. H., 11
Reich, J. N., 299
Rodriguez, M., 11
Romero, J., 11
Ropp, V. A., 297
Runco, M. A., 252
Ruskin, R. S., 219
Ruston, J. P., 11
Rutherford, E., 22
Ryan, J., 11

S

Sale, K., 54
Sansalone, M., 66–67
Sasnett, R. M., 150, 220
Satterfield, J., 103, 131, 139
Sauser, W. I., 303
Scarr, S., 7

Schmittroth, J., 140, 195
Schriesheim, C. A., 74
Scott, A. M., 220
Seldin, P., 11, 298, 306
Semb, G. B., 219
Shaffer, J. B., 27, 59
Shea, C., 67
Sherman, J. G., 219
Sidanius, J., 18
Siegel, M., 197
Silberg, N. T., 18
Skinner, B. F., 50, 205, 219
Slater, P. E., 20, 60
Small, A. C., 300
Smith, B. L., 208
Smith, D.A.F., 5
Smith, F., 135, 162, 195, 196
Smith, K. A., 207, 208
Smith, R. A., 204, 303
Socrates, 28
Sörbom, D., 13
Sprague, J., 104, 106, 120
Stager, R. A., 170
Steele, C. M., 88
Steele, S., 88
Stevens, L. A., 100
Strupp, H. H., 94
Stuart, D., 104, 106, 120
Sweet, A., 308
Sykes, C. J., 291

T

Taylor, D. A., 41
Teggart, F., 311
Thisayakorn, N., 11
Thompson, R., 133
Thorne, G. L., 301
Thurston, B. J., 252
Tiberius, R. G., 171, 177, 215
Truhillo, D. A., 11

U

Uranowitz, S. W., 31

V

Vance, C. M., 170
Vilardi, T., 242

W

Wales, C. E., 170
Walsh, D., 89
Ware, J. E., 26
Waters, L. K., 16
Waters, M., 15
Watzlawick, P., 50, 75
Weimer, M. G., 171, 210–211, 306
Wheeler, D. L., 227
White, R. W., 53
Wilhite, S. C., 233
Williams, R. G., 26

Wilson, E. K., 307
Wilson, R. C., 302, 306
Wintre, M., 271
Woditsch, G. A., 140, 195
Woods, D., 230–231, 236, 237
Wright, R., 39
Wulff, D. H., 297

Z

Zander, A., 27, 53, 59, 214
Zechmeister, E. B., 299
Zinsser, W., 244, 245

Subject Index

A

Ability, academic, 6–8, 135
Accessibility, instructor, 71, 212–213; and student conferences, 91–95. *See also* Interpersonal rapport
Achievement needs, 311
Achievement standards, 197–198
Acoustics, 112, 118–119
Active learning, 135, 139–140; and cooperative learning, 206–207; in course format, 203–204; and discussion, 164–165; in large classes, 211. *See also* Independence, student
Active Learning: Cooperation in the College Classroom (Johnson, Johnson, Smith), 207
"Adequate" style, 33, 34, 35
Administration, class: as discussion topic, 167; of large classes, 213
Affection needs, 27, 53–54
Affective messages: instructor, 50–51; student, 58–59. *See also* Emotions
American Psychological Association (APA), 95
Analogue studies, 13, 14, 18
Analysis skills, 196
Anger control: with anxious-dependent students, 79; with hostile students, 83–84
Anxiety: and examinations, 252, 264, 266; and frustration, 238; and learning, 136; and quizzes, 230; reduction of, for discussion, 175–177; and written assignments, 244
"Anxious-dependent" students, 78–79, 93, 252, 258
Applicability paradigm, 14–15, 303–304
Application skills, 196
Apprentice teaching, 307
Approval needs, 53–54, 56
Articulation, 113–114
As-if thinking 163, 173, 220. *See also* Thinking skills
"Ascent of Man, The," 139
Assessment, defined, 308. *See also* Classroom assessment techniques; Evaluation, instructor; Evaluation, student; Feedback, student; Student ratings
Assignment-giving: affective messages in, 50–51; indirect-control methods for, 75–76; for written assignments, 243–244
Assignments: and course objectives, 226–228; hands-on, 247–250; integration of, with classroom, 225–250; motivation strategies for, 228–232; observational, 247–250;

problem-solving, 230–231, 236–239; reading, 232–236; writing, 239–247

Attention-getter, for lecture, 138

"Attention-seeking" students, 84–85

Attitudes: and class morale, 42–43; as class progresses, 60–63; and examinations, 253–254; reciprocity in, 41–42; student, 41–42, 163–164; teacher, 42

Audiovisual aids, 147–151. *See also* Videotaping; Visual aids

Awards, teaching, 295–296

B

Blackboards, 146–147, 151

Body movements/gestures: analyzing and improving, 106–110; developing sensitivity to, 105–106; during discussions, 177; importance of, 102; improvement exercises for, 113–118

Books: prepared text versus original source, 233–234; as props, 119–120. *See also* Textbooks

Breathing, 104, 112, 114–115

C

Card technique, 72–73

Case method, 205–206, 220

Castellon, 220

Cheating, 213, 252, 281–283

Chronicle of Higher Education, 227

Clarity, 21, 22–23, 289

Class meetings: initial, 66–70, 201; last, 59, 62–63, 201; versus outside assignments, 226–228; planning for individual, 221–222; scheduling of, 200–201

Class progression: and emotional dynamics, 60–63; and student independence, 76

Classes: computer-assisted, 219–221; course design for, 202–210; course design for large, 202, 210–214; course design for small, 214–216; discussion in, 174–175, 202

Classroom assessment techniques: in course format, 204–205; for evaluating teaching, 297; versus grading, 261; minute papers, 73, 144, 205, 242–243. *See also* Feedback, student

Classrooms: acoustics in, 112, 118–119; attitudes and interpersonal phenomena in, 40–43; changes in, over time, 59–63; dividing of, into discussion groups, 167–168; as dramatic arenas, 99–101; emotional dimension in, 26–31, 40–63; entrance to, 119; exercising indirect control in, 74–76; instructors' psychology and, 44–51; integrating outside assignments with, 225–250; morale of, 42–43; physical features of, 118–120, 175; props in, 119–120; size of, 54, 118, 174–175, 202, 210–216; students' psychology and, 52–59

Cognitive learning, 134–136; and critical thinking, 139–140; educational objectives for, 195–197. *See also* Learning; Thinking skills

Collaborative learning, 206, 207–208. *See also* Cooperative learning

College Classroom, The: Conflict, Change, and Learning (Mann et al.), 48

Comments, evaluative: on examinations, 253, 265–266, 277; on written assignments, 246–247

Commitment, instructor, 32, 33, 309–312. *See also* Motivation, instructor

Communication: affective, 48–51, 58–59; and classroom features, 118–119; classroom, techniques for improving, 102–117; and discussion, 171–190; and eye contact, 120–123; two-way, 72–74. *See also* Discussion; Performance; Presentation

Communication Assessment Rating Form, 108, 125–128

"Competent" style, 34

Competition, student, 53, 177, 178

"Complete exemplar" style, 34, 36

"Compliant" students, 77–78, 263

Comprehension, 196

Computer-assisted classes, 219–221, 248

Computers: for case simulation, 206, 220; for classroom lecture aids, 149–151, 153–154; for hands-on assignments, 248; for instruction, 219–221; for scoring examinations, 272

Conferences, student: issues in, 91–95; providing opportunities for, 71

Confirmatory factor analysis, 13–14

Consultation programs, 306–307

Content, course: classes versus outside assignments for covering, 226–228; and examinations, 262; planning of, 193–195, 199–200

Content, lecture: feedback on, 144; presentation of, 140–145; quantity of, 136; selection of, 136–138; using discussion to understand, 161–162, 172–173. See also Lecture

Control: as class progresses, 60–62; during discussions, 183, 184–185; indirect, in classroom, 74–76; and group behavior, 59; instructor, 46–47, 48–51, 74–76, 183; student, 53, 55. See also Leadership

Cooperative learning, 28, 31; versus collaborative learning, 206, 207–208; in course format, 206–210; and discussion length, 167; pairing technique in, 168–169, 179, 209–210; techniques of, 208–210

Counseling, 94–95

Course design: for computer-assisted classes, 219–221; constraints in, 200–202; forming skill objectives in, 200; forming topic objectives in, 199–200; modifying, 223–224; and planning individual class meetings,

221–222; selecting formats in, 202–210; selecting topics and skills in, 199; time elements in, 200–201; for tutorials, 216–219; for very large classes, 210–214; for very small classes, 214–216

Course objectives: consensus on, with students, 198; constraints on, 200–202; determining, 195–199; and discussion, 161–162; and grading, 246–247; influence of, on learning, 5, 9; and integrating outside assignments, 226–228; levels of, 195–197; sharing of, with students, 75–76, 144, 202, 243, 262; and skill objectives, 200; specifying, in advance, 197–199; and topic objectives, 199–200; for tutorials, 219; using computers to meet, 220–221; and writing assignments, 240–242, 243–244

Course organization: influence of, on learning, 5, 9; and planning, 193–224

Course requirements, 223–224. See also Assignments

Craft of Teaching, The (Eble), 66, 154

Crib sheets, 272

Critical thinking: demonstrating, in presentation, 139–140; and discussion, 160, 162–163; teaching of, 195, 196, 197. See also Thinking skills

Criticism, 55–58, 217, 218

Culture, institutional, 291–296

D

Demonstration-lecture, 132

Dependence, student, 77–79. See also Independence, student

Development, faculty, 305–309

Development, student, 86–88; gender subthemes in, 86–87; and success, 259–260

Disabled students, 88

"Discouraged workers," 79–80

Discussion: on administrative matters,

167; advantages and disadvantages of, 159–161; calling on individuals for, 183–184; and class size, 167, 174–175, 211, 215; dominance of, 189–190; drifting of, 188; educational objectives for, 161–166, 171–174, 175; eliciting of, 179–181; encouraging participation in, 175–178, 181–184; ending of, 187–188; guiding of, 184–186; lecture combined with, 132, 171, 175; length of, 166–167; personalized, 174; for teacher training, 307–308; time used for, 166–167, 175; types of, 166–170; uncontrolled emotion in, 188–189; withdrawn students in, 190. *See also* Cooperative learning

Discussion-leading, 2, 3; difficulties of, 161; and discussion forms, 166–170; general considerations in, 171–178; special problems of, 188–190, 215; techniques of, 179–188; in tutorials, 217

Distraction: in communication habits, 102–104, 106; in visual aids, 152

"Drain then explain," technique, 153

Drama, 99, 100–101, 124–125, 139. *See also* Performance, classroom

E

Educational objectives, 22; affective, 227, 238–239; approach of, 197–199; determining, for course planning, 195–199; discipline, 227–228; for discussion, 161–166, 171–175; as ethical criterion, 95; and evaluation, 258, 261; intellectual, 226–227; taxonomy of cognitive, 195–197; and writing assignments, 240–243

Emotional impact dimension, 21, 22, 23. *See also* Intellectual excitement

Emotions, 39; and adolescence, 97–98; and affective objectives, 227, 238–239; and attitudes, 41–43; in body movement, 116–117; changing needs of, as class progresses, 60–63; and class size, 214; as classroom influences, 26–27, 40–63; and cognitive learning, 135–136; in discussion, 174, 179–180, 188–189; around grading, 252–253, 266; in individual student conferences, 93–94; and instructor behaviors, 48–51; messages of, 50–51, 58–59; and preparing for examinations, 262–263; and preparing for performance, 123–124; and psychology of instructors, 44–51; and psychology of students, 52–59, 76–90; in speaking, 101–102, 110

Engagement: at beginning of lecture, 139; in discussion, 164–165, 175–178, 179–180; in lecture, 134; in performance, 120–124; recognizing lapses of, 143–144; and variety, 142–143. *See also* Discussion; Lecture

Entrance to classroom, 119

Environment, effects of, on teaching, 291–296

Essay examinations, 275–277

Ethics of teaching, 95–97

Evaluation, instructor, 296–305; administration of, 304–305; forms for, 303–304, 305; to support excellent teaching, 293–294; and technique for self-assessment, 108, 125–128. *See also* Classroom assessment techniques; Student ratings

Evaluation, student: comprehensive, 254–255; for discussion participation, 177; emotional factors in, 55–58, 252–253; examination strategies for, 260–267; flexibility versus planning of, 223–224; in large classes, 213; myths about, 256–258; negative examples of, 283–285; purposes of, 253–255; social functions of, 258–260; and student motivation, 253–254, 255–256; of written assignments, 244–247. *See also* Examinations; Grading

Evaluation skills, 196

Examinations: administering of, 264; cheating on, 281–282, 283; content of, 261–262; of content versus thinking skills, 268–269; essay, 275–277; evaluating, 265–266; versus grading, 253–254; identification/short-answer, 273–275; multiple-choice, 267, 268–273; negative examples of, 283–285; oral, 277–278; pacing of, 260–261; practice, 262; preparing for, 260–263; returning of, 266–267; review sessions for, 263; scoring of, 271, 272–273, 274–275, 277; selection of, 278; selection versus supply, 267–268; and student motivation, 253–254, 255–256, 258; types of, 267–278

"Exemplary facilitator" style, 34, 35

"Exemplary lecturer" style, 34, 35

Expectations: at beginning, 61–62; communication of, 50–51; and instructor satisfaction, 46; and morale, 41–43; and motivating students, 232

Exploratory factor analysis, 13

Expository lecture, 131

Expressiveness, 18–19, 20

Eye contact, 105, 120–123

F

Factor analysis, 13–14, 19

Faculty. *See* Instructors

Failing, 252–253

Fairness: in grading, 95, 245–246, 258, 265, 276, 280; in testing, 261–262

Feedback, student: in discussion, 163, 167; about examinations, 267; soliciting, during class, 143–144; soliciting, techniques for, 72–74;

for teaching evaluation, 297. *See also* Classroom assessment techniques; Student ratings

Flip-charts, 146–147, 151

Formats: computer-assisted, 219–221; course, 202–210; discussion, 166–170; lecture, 130–133; tutorial, 216–219

Freshmen, special pressures of, 89

Frustration, 238–239

G

Gatekeeping, 45

Gender: instructor, 18–19; student, 86–87, 88–89

Gestures. *See* Body movements/gestures

Grade point average (GPA), 257

Grading: attitudes towards, 251, 252, 278–279; concerns/complaints about, dealing with, 93–94, 281; for discussion participation, 177, 280; ethics of, 95; of examinations, 265–266, 275–276, 277; versus examining, 253–254; fairness in, 245–246; final, 279–281; negative examples of, 283–285; of problem-solving assignments, 230–231, 239; providing comparative data on, 266; reliable, 246, 275–276; and student motivation, 253–254, 255–256, 258; and student quality, 257; and student ratings/satisfaction, 17–18, 257–258; tough versus easy, 256–257; valid, 246; of written assignments, 244–247. *See also* Evaluation, student; Scoring

Grading orientation, 7, 53, 76, 93, 177; and abuse of grading, 278; and anxiety about grades, 252; and examinations, 255–256, 264, 266; and motivation strategies, 231–232, 280

Group behavior, 27, 53, 59–62

Groups: cooperative base, 210; cooperative learning, 206–210; discus-

sion, 167–169, 179; formal,
208–209; informal, 209–210

H
Handouts, 146, 213
Hand-raising, 183, 184
Hands-on assignments, 247–250
"Heroes," 81–83
Holistic scoring, 246
Hostility, student, 83–84
Human Scale (Sale), 54

I
Identification examinations, 273–275
Imagery, 101–102, 135
Immediacy, 141–142
"Inadequate" style, 34
Inconsistency, 53
Independence, student: development
of, over time, 86–88; and discussion, 160, 166, 172; lecturing to
promote, 139–140; and indirect
classroom control, 74–76; and outside assignments, 228–229; in student types, 80–82; and tutorials,
216–219
"Independent" students, 80–81, 252
Inflection, 104
Informalism, 65–66
Information-gathering skills, 240–241
Instructors: achievement needs of,
311; affective messages of, 50–51;
attitudes of, 42; attitudes of,
towards discussion, 160–161; attitudes of, towards students, 295; as
authority/parental figures, 96;
behavior types of, 48–49; behaviors
of, and eliciting discussion,
180–181; behaviors of, in student
conferences, 91–95; emotions of,
26–27; environmental influences
on, 291–296; exemplary, and clear
exposition, 22–23; exemplary,
descriptors of, 31–33; exemplary,
images/memories of, 1–2, 10; exemplary, supportive environments for,
291–296; exemplary, talent versus

effort in, 288–290; exemplary, variations among, 287–288; gender of,
18; influences of, on learning, 5, 6,
8–9; influences of, on student
development, 87–88; objections of,
to student rating, 299–301; pressures on, 291; psychology of, 44–51;
research on, 20–21; responsibilities
of, 9–10; scholarship opportunities
of, 292–293, 294; sources of dissatisfaction of, 46–48; sources of satisfaction of, 44–46; training of,
305–309. *See also* Evaluation,
instructor; Motivation, instructor;
Teaching
Instrumental traits, 19, 20
"Intellectual authority" style, 34, 35
Intellectual excitement, 20, 21–26;
combined with interpersonal rapport dimension, 33–37; descriptors
of, 32; versus entertainment, 26;
impact of, on students, 24–25; and
lectures, 134, 154; levels of, 24–25;
objective descriptions of, 24–26;
student response to, 24–25. *See also*
Lecture; Presentation
Internet, 248
Interpersonal rapport, 20, 26–31; and
administering examinations, 264;
attitudes and, 40–43; with challenged students, 90; changes in,
over time, 59–63; and class size,
212–213, 214–215; combined with
intellectual excitement dimension,
33–37; descriptors of, 32; and discussion, 159, 165–166; fostering
personal relationships for, 66–72;
with gifted students, 89–90; impact
of, on students, 29–30; and indirect
classroom control, 74–76; and individual meetings with students,
91–95; levels of, 29–30; objective
descriptions of, 29–30; and psychology of instructors, 44–51; and psychology of students, 52–59, 76–90;
soliciting student feedback for,
72–74; and student development,

86–88; and student types, 76–86; with students under special pressure, 88–89; techniques for developing, 65–98; and tolerance for adolescent behavior, 97–98; in tutorials, 217–219. *See also* Personal relationships, student-teacher
Item analysis, 272–273

J
Jigsaw technique, 208

K
Knowledge, 22

L
Laboratory, 133, 247, 250
Language: for assignment-giving, 50–51, 232; for eliciting discussion, 180; used for indirect control, 74–76. *See also* Speech
Leadership: and group dynamics, 27, 53, 59, 60; indirect, in classroom, 74–76; and motivation strategies, 228–232; social-emotional, 85; structured versus unstructured, 229–231. *See also* Control; Discussion-leading
Learning: categories of, 5–6; cognitive, principles of, 134–136; and grading, 253–254, 256–258; influences on, 4–10; model of, 3, 4–10; with outside assignments, 228–232; programmed, 219–220; and student evaluation, 259–260; and teaching styles, 33–37, 229. *See also* Active learning; Cognitive learning; Cooperative learning; Educational objectives
Learning orientation, 7, 80–81, 177, 252; and examinations, 255, 256, 266; and motivation strategies, 231–232, 280
Lecture, 2, 3; choosing material for, 136–139; and cognitive learning effectiveness, 135–136; communication skills for, 102–117; eliciting

feedback during, 143–144; engaging students in, 120–124; formal, 130–131; forms of, 130–133; guidelines for, 155–157; linear versus nonlinear, 139; notes, 142; objectives of, 133–134; organization of, 138–139, 144–145; presentation style of, 140–145; storytelling in, 124–125; survival of, 129–130; using emotion in, 101–102, 110; using visual aids with, 145–154; variety in, 142–143. *See also* Body movements; Performance, classroom; Presentation; Speech
Lecture-demonstration, 132
Lecture-discussion, 132, 171, 175, 247. *See also* Discussion
Lecture-laboratory, 133
Lecture-recitation, 132–133
Linear/nonlinear organization, 139
LISREL statistical package, 13
LOGO questionnaire, 256

M
Maintenance needs, 20, 59–60
Making Sense of College Grades (Milton, Pollio, Eison), 255–256
"Marginal" style, 34, 35
Mastery, student need for, 52, 55–56
Memory, 136, 196
Mentoring, 89, 306
Minority students, 88–89
Minute papers, 73, 144, 205, 243–244
Model of effective teaching, two-dimensional, 4, 288; background research for, 20–21; descriptors in, 31–33; intellectual excitement dimension of, 21–26, 32; interpersonal rapport dimension of, 26–31, 32; nine teaching styles in, 33–37; use of, for evaluating teaching, 303–304, 305. *See also* Intellectual excitement; Interpersonal rapport; Teaching
Morale, 42–43, 61–62; and discussion, 165–166, 183
Motion pictures, 149

Motivation, instructor, 4, 8–9, 31, 32, 33, 291–292; for classroom excellence, 309–312; and effectiveness, 37; and sources of satisfaction, 44–48

Motivation, student: and classroom emotional atmosphere, 28; and classroom leadership, 74–76; for completing assignments, 228–232, 235–236, 239; for different student types, 76–86; and discussion, 165; and grading, 253–254, 258; influence of, on learning, 7–8; influence of examinations on, 253–254, 255–256; influence of lectures on, 134; influence of presentation style on, 140; and instructor quality, 32–33; and learning versus grading orientation, 7; strategies for eliciting, 228–232, 235–236, 239. *See also* Grading orientation; Learning orientation

Multimedia: for classroom lecture aids, 149–151, 153; and computer-assisted classes, 219–221

Multiple-choice examinations, 267, 268–273; construction of, 270–271; scoring of, 271, 272–273; variations on, 271–272

N

Names: learning and using students', 66–70, 183; using instructors' first, 65–66

Nasality, 115

Notes: instructors' lecture, 142; students', 145, 146, 148

O

Objectives. *See* Course objectives; Educational objectives

Observational assignments, 247–250

Observers, 308

Office hours: of instructors, 71, 91–92; of teaching assistants, 213

Older students, 80, 89

Oral essay, 130–131

Oral examinations, 277–278

Outlines, 146

Overhead transparencies, 148, 153

P

Pacing: and class attendance, 227; of examinations, 260–261; of outside assignments, 227–228; of visual aids, 153

Pairing, 168–169, 179, 209–210, 212, 243

Peer ratings, 16–17

Performance, classroom, 45; and classroom physical features, 118–120; communication skills for, 102–117; and drama, 99–101; eye contact in, 122–123; and lecture style, 140–145; preparing emotionally for, 123–124; and storytelling, 124–125; training novices in, 308–309; using emotion in, 101–102, 110. *See also* Body movements; Lecture; Speech

Personal concerns, students', 94–95, 217–218

Personal relationships, student-teacher, 45–46, 54–55, 63; ethics in, 95–97; and individual student conferences, 91–95; in large classes, 212–213; in small classes, 214–215; with silent students, 85–86; techniques for fostering, 66–72. *See also* Interpersonal rapport

Personalized System of Instruction (PSI), 219, 259

Photography, 69–70

Pitch, voice, 104

Plagiarism, 282–283

Planning: for computer-assisted classes, 219–221; and course design, 199–210; and course objectives, 195–199; general guidelines for, 193–195; for individual class meetings, 221–222; for large classes, 210–214; modification of, 223–224;

for small classes, 214–216; for tutorials, 216–219. *See also* Course design; Course objectives

Portfolios, teaching, 298, 306

Posture, 105–106, 115. *See also* Body movements

Power, 44–45, 51; minimizing discrepancy of, in discussions, 177–178; and motivating students, 231–232; and personal relationships, 96; and student conferences, 92–93. *See also* Control; Leadership

Predictability, 53

Preparation: of content, 136–138; emotional, 123–124; for examinations, 260–263; versus spontaneity, 141–142; of visual aids, 151. *See also* Planning

Presentation: choosing material for, 136–138; clarity in, 21, 22–23; computer, 149–150; demonstrating critical thinking in, 139–140; emotional impact in, 22, 23; and lecturing, 130–136; organization of, 138–139, 144–145; and student ratings, 19, 20; style of, 140–145; visual aids to, 145–154. *See also* Intellectual excitement; Lecture; Performance, classroom

Previews, 144

Problem sets, 230–231

Problem-solving: assignments, 230–231, 236–239; discussion, 170; emotional dimension of, 238–239

Projection, voice, 111–113

Props, 119–120, 132. *See also* Visual aids

Provocative lecture, 131–132

Punctuated lecture, 132

Q

Quizzes, 230

R

Readings: accessibility of, 234–235; assigned, for students, 232–236; integration of, into classroom, 235–236; oral, in lecture, 122, 133

Recall, 196

Recapitulation, 144–145

Reciprocation, 41–42

Recitation lecture, 132–133

Rejection, 56

Relaxation, and energy, 105, 108, 116, 117

Requirements. *See* Course requirements

Review sessions, 263

Role-playing, 169–170

Romantic relationships, 95–97

S

SADTIE technique, 139

SAT scores, and student types, 78, 82

Satisfaction: and grading, 257–258; sources of instructor, 44–48, 309–312; sources of student, 52–58. *See also* Student ratings

Scheduling, 200–201

Scholarship, and teaching, 292–293, 294

Scholarship Reconsidered (Boyer), 292–293

Scoring: by computer, 272; difficulty versus discrimination, 272–273; of essay exams, 275–276, 277; by hand, 271; of identification/short-answer exams, 274–275; of multiple-choice exams, 271, 272–273. *See also* Grading

Seating, 118, 175

Selection examinations, 267–268. *See also* Multiple-choice examinations

Self-discipline, 228–229

Self-disclosure, 45, 67

Seminars, teaching, 307–308

Sexual relationships, 95–97

Short-answer examinations, 273–275

"Silent" students, 85–86

Simulations, 205–206, 220

Size, class, 54, 118; and course design, 202, 210–216; and discussion,

174–175, 211; influence of, on achievement/satisfaction, 211; quantified definition of, 211

Slides, 148–149, 153

"Snipers," 83–84

Social-emotional leaders, 85

Social events, 65–66

"Socratic" style, 34, 35

Sore throats, 115

Speaking, 100–101. *See also* Lecture; Speech

Speech: analyzing and improving, 106–110; articulation in, 113–114; developing sensitivity to, 103–105; expressive, 101–102; importance of, 102; and voice improvement exercises, 110–115; and voice quality, 104, 114–115

Spontaneity: in discussion, 170; in lecturing, 108, 116–117, 141–142

Storytelling, 124–125

Stridency, 114–115

Student ratings: administration of, 304–305; consulting on, 301–302; dimensions underlying, 19–20; and equal treatment, 89; faculty objections to, 299–301; forms for, 303–304, 305; and instructor gender, 18–19; on interpersonal rapport, 31; at last class session, 63; measurement bias in, 15–19; methods of, 11–15; prevalence of, 11; versus peer ratings, 16–17; purposes of, 298–300; scales for, 303; of teaching effectiveness versus course value, 15; types of, 298; using, 301–305; voluntary participation in, 301. *See also* Evaluation, instructor

Student-teacher relationship: and interpersonal rapport, 20, 26–31; and student ratings, 16, 19, 20. *See also* Interpersonal rapport

Student types: anxious-dependent, 78–79; attention-seeking, 84–85;

compliant, 77–78; discouraged workers, 79–80; independent, 80–81; heroes, 81–83; silent, 85–86; snipers, 83–84

Students: adolescent behavior of, 97–98; attitudes of, 41–42, 163–164; attitudes of, towards grading, 251, 252; challenged, 90; classroom behaviors of, 58–59, 76–86, 194–195; developmental patterns of, 86–88, 259–260; domineering, 189–190; emotional messages of, 58–59; emotions of, 26, 27–28, 52–59; gifted, 89–90; grade point averages of, 257; influences of, on instructor dissatisfaction, 46–48; influences of, on learning, 5, 6–8; older, 80, 89; with personal concerns, 94–95; psychology of, 52–59, 76–90; showing interest in, 72; soliciting feedback from, 72–74, 143–144; sources of dissatisfaction of, 54–58; sources of satisfaction of, 52–54; typology of, 76–86; under special pressure, 88–89; withdrawn, 190. *See also* Evaluation, student; Motivation, student

Success, and evaluation, 258–260

Summarizing: of discussion comments, 182, 185; of lecture, 144–145

SuperShrink, 206

Supply examinations, 267, 268

Support groups, 210

Suspense, dramatic, 124–125

Synthesis, 196

T

Talent, in teaching, 288–290

Task needs, 20, 59–60

Teachers. *See* Instructors

Teaching: awards and recognition for, 295–296; effective, evaluation of, 296–301; effective, two-dimensional model of, 20–37; empirical research on, 11–20; ethics of, 95–97; exemplary, characteristics of, 3–4, 11–37; exemplary, descriptors of, 31–33; exemplary, talent versus effort in, 288–290; exemplary, versus techniques, 202–203; institutional respect for, 294; masculine and feminine qualities in, 18–19; observation of, 308; relationship of, to learning, 4–10; and scholarship, 292–293; supportive environments for, 291–296; student ratings of, 11–20; training in, 305–309. *See also* Model of effective teaching, two-dimensional

Teaching assistants (TAs): versus apprentices, 307; for grading assistance, 246, 265; institutional respect for, 294; for large classes, 213–214

Teaching skills, traditional, 2–3. *See also* Discussion-leading; Intellectual excitement; Interpersonal rapport; Lecture; Performance, classroom; Planning; Presentation

Teaching styles: and behavior towards students, 48–49; categories of, 33–37

Teaching Tips (McKeachie), 91

Teaching Within the Rhythms of the Semester (Duffy, Jones), 42

Technology. *See* Audiovisual aides; Computers; Videotaping

Tenure, 293–294, 310

Testing. *See* Examinations

Textbooks, 233–235, 270

Thinking skills: as-if, 163, 173, 220; critical, 139–140, 160, 162–163, 195, 196, 197; and discussion, 160, 162–163, 172, 173; and examinations, 269, 275; and lecturing, 139–140; outside assignments for, 230–231. *See also* Cognitive learning; Independence; Problem-solving

Time: class-meeting versus outside-assignment, 226; for completing examinations, 264; and determining course objectives, 200–202; for discussion, 166–167, 175; pressures of, on instructors, 291

Tools for Teaching (Davis), 91

Training, instructor, 305–309

True-false examinations, 268

Tutorials, 216–219

U

University of North Carolina at Chapel Hill (UNC), 21

V

Values: and discussion, 160, 163–164, 173–174; and independent thinking, 140; and observational assignments, 248

Variety, 142–143

Videocassettes, 149

Videotaping: to analyze speech and movement, 106–110; for hands-on assignments, 248–249; to improve teaching, 308–309; to recognize students, 70

Visual aids: availability of, 151; and body movement, 106–110, 113–118; and classroom props, 119–120, 132; disruptive, 152; electronic audiovisual, 147–151; and eye contact, 120–123; as lecture aids, 145–154; preparation needed for, 151; principles of using, 152–154. *See also* Videotaping

Voice: improvement exercises for, 110–115; projection of, 111–113; quality of, 104, 114–115. *See also* Speech

W

Workshops, teacher, 306–307

Writing: assignments, 239–247; for-

mal, 240–242; evaluation of,
244–247; informal, 242–243; integrated, 244; objectives for,
240–243; teaching of, 9. *See also*
Minute papers

"Writing across the curriculum" programs, 244
Writing in the Disciplines (Durkin), 242
*Writing to Learn Mathematics and Sci-
ence* (Connolly, Vilardi), 242